PRAISE FOR *Ameri...*

"Audacious. . . . Classically Feiler."

"Intriguing."

—*Washington Post*

"This is one of the most original, intelligent, and endlessly fascinating books I have read in years: it should become a set book for anyone wanting to know what truly makes America tick." —Simon Winchester, author of *The Man Who Loved China* and *The Professor and the Madman*

"In clear, engaging prose, Feiler demonstrates how the figure of Moses appealed to Americans across political and religious spectrums. . . . Feiler is a cheerful and earnest guide. . . . Most original." —*Forward*

"Feiler has a knack for asking perceptive, thoughtful questions."

—*St. Louis Post-Dispatch*

"A page-turner. . . . Compellingly interesting and sometime wonderfully gossipy. . . . The force of these pages from Feiler are so powerful." —*The Christian Century*

"Feiler gives us the American struggle—from the Pilgrims escaping religious persecution and slaves seeking human dignity to European Jews fleeing anti-Semitism and African Americans demanding equal rights—and in the same straightforward, readable style as his previous works. Yet the book possesses a depth and a gravitas that belie the accessible text, attributable to the numerous authorities—religious and civic, historians, and others—interviewed for the book."

—*Library Journal*

"A superb book . . . well-written, enlightening. . . . Wow."

—*Washington Jewish Week*

"What a smart, original, and deeply intriguing reflection on the role Moses played—yes, Moses—in U.S. history. *America's Prophet* is Bruce Feiler at his innovative best: compelling, sweeping, and engaging. Highly recommended!"

—Douglas Brinkley, author of *The Wilderness Warrior* and *Parish Priest*

AMERICA'S PROPHET

HARPER ⬤ PERENNIAL

NEW YORK • LONDON • TORONTO • SYDNEY • NEW DELHI • AUCKLAND

AMERICA'S PROPHET

HOW THE STORY OF MOSES SHAPED AMERICA

BRUCE FEILER

HARPER ● PERENNIAL

A hardcover edition of this book was published in 2009 by William Morrow, an imprint of HarperCollins Publishers.

P.S.™ is a trademark of HarperCollins Publishers.

HarperCollins books may be purchased for educational, business, or sales promotional use. For information please write: Special Markets Department, HarperCollins Publishers, 10 East 53rd Street, New York, NY 10022.

FIRST HARPER PERENNIAL EDITION PUBLISHED 2010.

Photograph on title page spread © by Andrew Geiger/Glasshouse Images.

Designed by Cassandra J. Pappas

The Library of Congress has catalogued the hardcover edition as follows:
    Feiler, Bruce S.
        America's prophet : Moses and the American story / Bruce Feiler.
—1st ed.
            352 p. : ill., ports.. ; 24 cm.
        ISBN 978-0-06-057488-8
    1. Moses (Biblical leader)—influence. 2. Religion and politics—United States—History. 3. United States—History. I. Title.
978 22
306.0973   22   2010277160

ISBN 978-0-06-172627-9 (pbk.)

10 11 12 13 14   OV/RRD   10 9 8 7 6 5 4 3 2 1

For Debbie and Alan Rottenberg

Next year with you

Contents

AMERICA'S
PROPHET

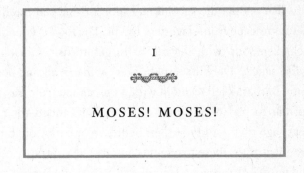

I

MOSES! MOSES!

THANKSGIVING IS THE mandatory holiday in my family. It's the one time of year when we clear our calendars, pack up gifts, and travel across the country for a ritual that is one part Americana, one part Hanukkah, one part nostalgia. The event begins when my mother polishes dozens of apples, pears, pomegranates, and kumquats and arranges them with a pumpkin, some Indian corn, and cranberries to create a cornucopian centerpiece. It continues with Thanksgiving dinner, a mix of trendy roasted this and that along with some embarrassing 1950s classics we love, notably a hot fruit compote made with five different kinds of canned fruit baked with macaroons and sherry. During the meal, in a custom that makes me cringe yet always seems to work, my sister insists that we go around the table and say why we are thankful. The weekend concludes with an early celebration of Hanukkah, the Jewish festival of lights. It's a classic American event, a mix of church, state, shopping, and turkey.

Passover is the equivalent holiday for my in-laws. Every spring, my mother-in-law hosts thirty-five people on one night and a different thirty-five people the second night for a ritualized retelling of the Israelites' escape from slavery in Egypt. The food is equally ritualized: chicken soup with matzoh balls; gefilte fish with hot pink horseradish sauce; "Debbie's tasty brisket" with carrots and potatoes; and Auntie Barbara's Jell-O mold with, yup, canned fruit. Passover is so important to my in-laws that when they expanded their home some years ago they redid not their bedroom or bathroom but their dining room, just for these two nights a year. The centrality of these two holidays to our respective families is such that when my mother met my future mother-in-law for the first time they retreated into a corner and came out a few minutes later with smiles on their faces: The Feilers would get Thanksgiving; the Rottenbergs would get Passover.

Though it took me a while to realize it, discovering the unexpected bridge that links these two holidays would occupy the coming years of my life.

Before attending my first Passover with my in-laws, I warned them that I would make the world's most insufferable seder guest. I had just returned from a yearlong journey through the Middle East, in which I actually crossed the likely Red Sea, tasted manna, and climbed the supposed Mount Sinai. In the liturgical list of Four Sons included in the seder service, I would surely be the Pedantic One. In ensuing years, I continued my biblical wanderings, traveling through Israel, Iraq, and, with my bride, Iran. "A honeymoon in the Axis of Evil," she called it. A year later she gave birth to identical twin girls: Eden, for the Garden of Eden; and Tybee, for the beach near Savannah where I grew up and where we celebrated our wedding. They seemed like emblems of our lives: ten toes in the Middle East, ten toes at home.

One theme of these travels was exploring the explosive mix of religion and politics. But I realized upon returning that the front line of that battle had migrated back home. The United States was involved in its own internal war over God that in many ways mirrored—and in some cases fed—the wars being waged in the Middle East. The buzzwords only hinted at the battle lines: left/right, red/blue, believer/nonbeliever, extremist/moderate.

These tensions were reflected in all the usual places of modern discourse—the ballot box, the call-in show, the Bible study, the book group. Yet they were most acute at home. So many of the laments I heard about religion were variations on a theme: "I can't talk to my brother about it without getting into a fight." "My father is a Neanderthal." "My daughter is making a big mistake." "He doesn't understand what made this country great." With greater mobility and more choices, we no longer passed down religion seamlessly from one generation to the next. Nearly half of Americans change religious affiliations in their lives, a Pew study concluded. Stuck with our parents' genes, we seemed less interested in being burdened with their God as well. And we certainly didn't want to talk to them about it.

Thanksgiving, the symbol of American blessing, the one holiday that marked the union of God, the people, and the land, had, for many families, become a minefield of fraught conversation.

Around this time I began noticing something else. On a trip to visit my in-laws on Cape Cod, we stopped off in Plymouth and I took a tour of the *Mayflower II*. A reenactor was reading from the Bible. "Exodus fourteen," he explained. "The Israelites are trapped in front of the Red Sea, and the Egyptians are about to catch them. The people complain, and Moses declares, 'Hold your peace! The Lord shall fight for you.' Our leader read us that passage during our crossing." *Moses, on board the* Mayflower.

On a trip to visit my parents in Savannah, I stopped off at my childhood synagogue. A letter from George Washington hangs in the lobby, sent after his election to the presidency: "May the same wonder-working Deity, who long since delivered the Hebrews from their Egyptian oppressors, planted them in the promised land, whose providential agency has lately been conspicuous in establishing these United States as an independent nation, still continue to water them with the dews of Heaven." *Exodus, on Washington's pen in the first weeks of the presidency.*

On a trip to visit my sister in Philadelphia, we went to see the Liberty Bell. The quotation on its face is from Leviticus 25, which God gave to Moses on Mount Sinai: PROCLAIM LIBERTY THROUGH-OUT ALL THE LAND UNTO ALL THE INHABITANTS THEREOF. *The law of Sinai, in the bell tower where the Declaration of Independence was signed.*

In coming weeks, I found a similar story over and over again. Columbus comparing himself to Moses when he sailed in 1492. George Whitefield quoting Moses as he traveled the colonies in the 1730s forging the Great Awakening. Thomas Paine, in *Common Sense,* comparing King George to the pharaoh. Benjamin Franklin, Thomas Jefferson, and John Adams, in the summer of 1776, proposing that Moses be on the seal of the United States. And the references didn't stop. Harriet Tubman adopting Moses' name on the Underground Railroad. Abraham Lincoln being eulogized as Moses' incarnation. The Statue of Liberty being molded in Moses' honor. Woodrow Wilson, Franklin Roosevelt, and Lyndon Johnson tapping into Moses during wartime. Cecil B. DeMille recasting Moses as a hero for the Cold War. Martin Luther King, Jr., likening himself to Moses on the night before he was killed. The sheer ubiquity was staggering and, for me, had been completely unknown.

For four hundred years, one figure stands out as the surprising symbol of America. One person has inspired more Americans than any other. One man is America's true founding father. His name is Moses.

For two years, I traveled to touchstones in American history and explored the role of the Bible, the Exodus, and Moses in inspiring generation after generation of Americans. I examined how American icons of different eras—from the slave girl Eliza carrying her son to freedom across the Ohio River in *Uncle Tom's Cabin* to an orphaned Superman being drawn out of a spaceship from Krypton— were etched in the image of Moses. And I probed the ongoing role of Moses today, from the Ten Commandments in public places to the role of the United States as a beacon for immigrants. Even a cursory review of American history indicates that Moses has emboldened leaders of all stripes—patriot and loyalist, slave and master, Jew and Christian, fat cat and communist. Could the persistence of his story serve as a reminder of our shared national values? Could he serve as a unifying force in a disunifying time? If Moses could split the Red Sea, could he unsplit America?

Just as I was completing my journey, the 2008 presidential election was reaching its historic climax. Once again, Moses played a prominent role. Hillary Clinton compared herself to the Hebrew prophet. With "every bit of progress you try to make," she said, "there's always gonna be somebody to say, 'You know, I think we should go back to Egypt.'" She asked, "Do we really need to move forward on transformative social change?" before answering: "Yes, we do." Barack Obama also placed himself in the Mosaic tradition, though he claimed the role of Moses' successor. "We are in the presence of a lot of Moseses," he said in Selma, Alabama, in 2007. "I thank the Moses generation; but we've got to remember that Joshua still had a job to do. As great as Moses was . . . he didn't cross over the river to see the Promised Land." He concluded: "Today we're called to be the Joshuas of our time, to be the generation that finds our way across this river."

Obama's use of the Exodus story became so prominent that his rival, John McCain, issued a video in which he mocked Obama for anointing himself "The One." The video concluded with a clip of Charlton Heston splitting the Red Sea in *The Ten Commandments*. But the echoes of the Exodus only continued. On the day before the election, the African Methodist Episcopal Church bishop for Ohio stood up before 60,000 people in Columbus and thanked God for "having given us a Moses and a Martin called Barack Obama." As civil rights pioneer Andrew Young said to me days later, "We are living in biblical time. The amount of time that passed between Martin's assassination and Obama's election—forty years—is the same amount of time the Israelites spent in the desert."

Four centuries after the earliest colonists in North America likened themselves to their Israelite forebears, Americans once again found meaning by drawing parallels between their ongoing struggles and those of the central figures of the Hebrew Bible. The analogy took on added poignance as Americans again confronted challenging times, with economic turmoil at home and a shifting role in the world. As with every hard time in American life—from the frozen cliffs of early New England to the snowy camps of Valley Forge; from the fractured fields of the Civil War to the bloody streets of the civil rights era—Americans turned to the Exodus for direction, inspiration, and hope. And so they did in another moment of national anxiety, when the country was asking, What is the meaning of America? What are our values? Will we rise again? As he had for generations, one figure held the answers and pointed the way. And I couldn't help wondering if our ability to repair our damaged sense of purpose and reclaim our national unity might depend on our ability to recall the centuries-old interplay between the Thanksgiving and Passover narratives and remember the central figure in both stories and why he had proven so inspirational all along.

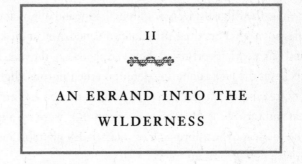

II

AN ERRAND INTO THE
WILDERNESS

THANKSGIVING BEGINS EARLY in America's Hometown. It doesn't start on the last Thursday in November, the day Abraham Lincoln first invited Americans to observe a festival of praise to honor the country's "fruitful fields and healthful skies." It doesn't begin on the second Saturday in October, the day the re-created Pilgrim village outside Plymouth, Massachusetts, hosts the first of its seventeenth-century Harvest Dinners with turkey, mussels, corn pudding, and psalms. It kicks off, instead, on a Friday in mid-June, the day the members of the Old Colony Club, the "oldest gentlemen's club in America," board rickety vessels on Plymouth's clam-covered shore and set out toward the mysterious Clark's Island. For these Keepers of Thanksgiving, this excursion is their annual pilgrimage to the accidental spot of America's First Sabbath.

Clark's Island is the forgotten front door of America's founding story. On a stormy Friday evening in 1620, a band of nine beleaguered

Pilgrims, half a day's sail from their families on the *Mayflower*, were scouting the Massachusetts coastline in an open boat for a suitable place to settle. Having barely escaped from a skirmish with Indians that morning, the Pilgrims were frightened, lost, and out of food. But as the afternoon wore on, their situation worsened. And at dusk, fierce winds and rain nearly overturned their vessel, forcing the men ashore. The wreck was the latest deflating detour on the Pilgrims' flight from slavery to freedom. For these men had crossed the sea and arrived in this great and terrible wilderness, convinced they were on a mission from God to escape the oppression of a latter-day pharaoh and build in America a new Promised Land.

Everything the Pilgrims had done for two decades was designed to fulfill their dream of creating God's New Israel. When they first left England for Holland in 1608, they described themselves as the chosen people, casting off the yoke of their pharaoh, King James. A dozen years later when they embarked on a grander exodus, to America, their leader, William Bradford, proclaimed their mission to be as vital as that of "Moses and the Israelites when they went out of Egypt." And when, after sixty-six days on the Atlantic, they finally arrived at Cape Cod, they were brought to their knees in gratitude for safe passage through their own Red Sea. "May our children rightly say," Bradford wrote, echoing a famous passage in Deuteronomy, the fifth book of Moses, "Our fathers were Englishmen which came over this great ocean, and were ready to perish in the wilderness; but they cried unto the Lord, and he heard their voice."

And the Pilgrims weren't alone in applying the Exodus story to their lives in the New World. The settlers at Jamestown had likened themselves to Moses when they arrived in Virginia in 1607. John Winthrop, gliding into Boston Harbor aboard the *Arbella* in 1630, quoted Deuteronomy three times in his sermon, "Model of Christian Charity," and ended by quoting Moses' farewell speech to the Israelites on Mount Nebo. Cotton Mather, writing in 1702, said these pioneers had no choice. "The leader of a people in a wilderness had need be a Moses," he said. "And if a Moses had not led the people of Plymouth Colony," he wrote of Bradford, then the colony would not have survived.

Yet these leaders did have a choice. For centuries, European explorers had set out for new lands without using expressions like *pharaoh* and *promised land, New Covenant* and *New Israel, Exodus* and *Moses.* By choosing these evocative lyrics, the founders of America introduced the themes of oppression and redemption, anticipation and disenchantment, freedom and law, that would carry through four hundred years of American history. Because of them, the story of Moses became the story of America.

But why? Why did these leaders choose this three-thousand-year-old story? Why did they take an ancient tale, unproven and unprovable, and transform it into a revolutionary ideal that would sacrifice lives, launch wars, unmoor millions of families from their lives and propel them through uncertain waters into an unknown wilderness based only on an untested notion of freedom? In short: Why did this story have such power?

ON BOARD THE small fleet of boats heading toward Clark's Island this afternoon, the men of the Old Colony Club were ebullient. This annual excursion was one of the highlights of their year, along with the August clambake, Past Presidents Night in the fall, and Forefathers Day, held every December since 1769, when the members dress in top hats, bear arms, and celebrate the landing on Plymouth Rock with "a breakfast that can't be beat." The men, ranging in age from old to older, were more casual today, drinking beer and waving at other boaters on the water.

"Plymouth Harbor is naturally shallow," explained Roger Randall, a lifelong resident. When I first pitched up in town, I quickly learned that the Pilgrims' legacy is nursed by a tight-knit gentry of descendants and devotees who protect the *Mayflower* like Beefeaters guarding the crown jewels. Roger was kind enough to invite me along on their expedition.

"It's very difficult to get in and out of this harbor," he continued, "but it's well channeled. There's conjecture that if Plymouth had been a deepwater harbor, this could have been Boston today."

"So why did the Pilgrims settle here?"

He smiled. "The wreck."

Almost everything about the Pilgrims' mission was spectacularly poorly planned. Like the Israelites, the Pilgrims were so convinced they were chosen by God that they didn't prepare themselves for the harsh conditions they would face in the wilderness. From their outpost in Holland, they had secured a charter to settle near the Hudson River. A small group left Holland on the *Speedwell* over the summer, and more joined in England on the *Mayflower*. The two vessels departed Southampton on August 5 but were diverted to land when the *Speedwell* began taking on water. The ships sailed a few weeks later but again turned back when the *Speedwell* proved unseaworthy and had to be abandoned. On September 6, 1620, the *Mayflower* successfully set sail with 102 passengers.

For all the poetry it later inspired, the *Mayflower* was hardly a beautiful craft. A merchant ship that mostly shuttled wine across the English Channel, the one-hundred-foot vessel was said to have a sweet hull, which meant the spillage of French Bordeaux had seeped into the planks, tempering the noxious fumes from the bilge. In 1957 a replica of the *Mayflower* was built using the exact dimensions of the earlier craft. Roger Randall worked as a rigger on the ship. "It was like a big old tub," he remembered. "Part of the problem was it had such a high freeboard. A low-sheer vessel you can control a lot better, but the *Mayflower* had a lot of flat surfaces that present themselves to the wind. It must have been very harrowing crossing the ocean at that time of year."

Blown off course, the *Mayflower* arrived off Cape Cod on November 9. The crew proceeded along the back side of the peninsula toward the Hudson but were soon whiplashed by wicked shoals off Nantucket. Half the shipwrecks on the Atlantic Coast are said to occur in this area. With the ship on the brink of disaster, Master Christopher Jones made the historic decision to sail northward around Cape Cod. The Pilgrims would settle in New England.

The Mayflower Compact, 1620. William Bradford leads the Pilgrims in signing the Mayflower Compact aboard the *Mayflower,* November 11, 1620. Engraving, 1859, after Tompkins Harrison Matteson. *(Courtesy of The Granger Collection, New York)*

In his memoir, William Bradford described the next few weeks in language drawn directly from Moses. Searching the cape for a suitable place to settle, some Pilgrims encountered a band of Indians, who summarily fled, and a stash of dried corn, which they promptly stole. Bradford justified the thievery by citing the spies Moses sent into the Promised Land, noting that in both cases the purloined goods made their brethren "marvelously glad." A crew member who had visited the area before recalled a "good harbor" across the bay, and on Wednesday, December 6, a small expedition set out in an open boat with a pilot, nine Pilgrims, and a servant.

Camping out the following night, the settlers were awakened by a hail of arrows. "Be of good courage," the Pilgrims shouted to one another, echoing Moses' farewell speech to the Israelites. "Woach! Woach! Ha! Ha! Hach! Woach!" the Indians responded (echoing no known biblical passage). As the boat sailed north in the freezing air that Friday afternoon, its rudder came loose and the vessel careened out of control. Moments later, the mast splintered, bringing down the sails and any hope of reaching the mainland. The men took up oars but had no idea where they were.

"That *still* happens," said Roger Randall. "Even if you've lived here forever, you can get lost in bad weather."

The Pilgrims steered into what they later learned was the lee of a small island, where they slept for the night. The following morning proved to be a "fair, sunshining day," and the men discovered they were on an island, safe from the Indians. They dried their sails and tried to calm their nerves. The next day, their first Sunday on American soil, they observed a day of rest and gave God thanks for his "deliverances," yet another reference to what the Bible calls the Israelites' "deliverance" from Egypt. For the Pilgrims, twenty miles from the *Mayflower*, more than three thousand miles from their homeland, this simple act of thanksgiving introduced into American life one of the central themes of the Bible: God hears his children when they suffer and helps deliver them to safety. As Bradford memorialized the occasion, in words taken from the Ten Commandments, "And this being the last day of the week, they prepared there to keep the Sabbath."

THE STORY OF Moses begins in the second book of the Hebrew Bible—Exodus—known with Genesis, Leviticus, Numbers, and Deuteronomy as the Five Books of Moses. These books are also called the Pentateuch, from the Greek for "five books," or the Torah, from the Hebrew for "teaching." Genesis tells a multitude of stories—Creation, the Flood, the patriarchs, Joseph—and covers almost two thousand years of history, but the Moses story slows considerably, covering only forty years in four books. This ratio suggests that Moses dominates these books, but that's not quite true, as the Pentateuch devotes no more than 14 of the 167 chapters in the last four books to Moses' life. Instead of a domineering and heroic character, Moses is presented as a largely passive, even reactive figure who is clearly subservient to the primary actor in the story, God.

Exodus opens around the beginning of the thirteenth century B.C.E. with the Israelites living under forced labor in Egypt, the dominant power in the ancient Near East. The pharaoh, fearing the expansion of an alien force within his borders, orders the slaughter of all newborn Hebrew males. A woman of the Levite tribe hides her boy for three months, then sets him afloat on the Nile in a wicker basket. The daughter of the pharaoh is bathing by the Nile and draws the boy out of the basket. "This must be a Hebrew child," she says. The boy's sister, who has been watching, offers to get a Hebrew wet nurse, and summons the boy's mother to suckle her son. When the boy gets older, the mother returns him to the pharaoh's daughter, who raises him as her son. She names him Moses, explaining, "I drew him out of the water." Since it's unlikely that the daughter of the pharaoh spoke Hebrew, Moses' name probably comes from the common Egyptian suffix meaning "born of," as in Rameses, son of Ra. Moses is the Hebrew boy who carries an Egyptian name. He's the child of hardship who's raised in the greatest palace on earth. He's the "son of" nobody, a hole not filled until he finds his true calling and becomes what Deuteronomy calls "God's man."

Commentators have observed that Moses' life is defined by four choices. Each moment is a test of character in which Moses' behavior shapes not only his own fate but the nature of the people he is destined to lead. The first choice occurs early in his adulthood. A gap of decades has passed since his rescue, and a grown Moses witnesses an Egyptian beating a Hebrew, which the text identifies as "one of his kinsmen." No clue is given as to how Moses discerns his ancestry. His dilemma is whether to cling to the life of opulence he has enjoyed or cast his lot with the suffering people he barely knows. In a flash, Moses aligns himself with the powerless against the powerful. He murders the overseer, then bolts to the desert after the pharaoh issues a death warrant against him. For the child of privilege, Moses' move is a life-defining act of rebellion. The prince of Egypt rejects the loftiest house on earth and aligns himself with the lowest members of society.

In the desert land of Midian, Moses marries a shepherdess, Zipporah, and they have a son, Gershom. The Bible explains the boy's name as meaning "I have been a stranger in a foreign land," a Hebrew wordplay suggesting that Moses still feels alienated from his homeland. One day while tending his new family's flocks, Moses catches sight of a bush aflame. He says, "I must turn aside to look at this marvelous sight; why doesn't the bush burn up?" God then calls out, "Moses! Moses!" "Here I am," the shepherd answers, echoing the words of Abraham when he first heard God's voice eight hundred years earlier. God enjoins Moses to remove his sandals, for he is standing "on holy ground," then announces, "I have marked well the plight of my people in Egypt." God asks Moses to help rescue the Israelites from Egypt and deliver them to a "good and spacious land, a land flowing with milk and honey."

This challenge represents Moses' second choice. Will he stay in Midian and enjoy the pleasant life he has built, or will he follow the call of this mysterious voice and attempt to free a people enslaved for centuries? This time Moses hesitates. "Who am I that I should go to Pharaoh and free the Israelites?" he asks God. "What if they do not believe me?" In a plea long taken to mean that Moses was a stutterer, he adds, "I have never been a man of words" and "I am slow of speech and slow of tongue." Finally Moses wails, "Please, O Lord, make someone else your agent." God is unmoved. He unleashes a series of miracles, and finally Moses relents. More than just a husband and a father, Moses elects to become a savior. The man of choices chooses to lead the chosen people.

Back in Egypt, Moses confronts the pharaoh, his surrogate grandfather: "Thus says the Lord, the God of Israel: Let my people go." The pharaoh resists and redoubles the workload of the Hebrews, crying, "You are shirkers, shirkers!" God unfolds a series of ten plagues designed to impress upon the pharaoh the power of the Lord. The early four are nuisances—blood, frogs, lice, and insects. The next four are more serious—pestilence, inflammation, hail, and locusts. The ninth is an act of terror, covering the country in darkness. And the tenth is the ultimate retribution for the pharaoh's decision to kill the newborn Israelite males. "Toward midnight," God says, "I will go forth among the Egyptians, and every first-born in the land of Egypt shall die, from the first-born of Pharaoh who sits on his throne to the first-born of the slave girl who is behind the millstone."

To prevent the Israelite firstborns from being killed, God instructs the Hebrews to slaughter a lamb and spread the blood on the doorposts and lintels of their houses. They shall eat the roasted flesh that night, God says, "with unleavened bread and with bitter herbs." It is a "passover offering to the Lord," the text says. "When I see the blood I will pass over you." This final plague works. Faced with the carnage and the loss of his firstborn child, the pharaoh relents. "Begone!" he tells Moses. "Go, worship the Lord as you said."

Freed from bondage, more than six hundred thousand Israelite men, along with women and children, flee toward the Promised Land, being led by a pillar of cloud by day and a pillar of fire by night. But the pharaoh changes his mind and pursues them with his army, including six hundred chariots. The Egyptians soon trap the Israelites before the Yam Suf, or Sea of Reeds, a name mistranslated for centuries as Red Sea. The frightened Israelites turn on Moses. "Was it for want of graves in Egypt that you brought us to die in the wilderness?" At the final hour, God moves the pillar of cloud so that it shields them from the Egyptians, then instructs Moses to stretch out his arms over the water. The Lord drives back the sea with a strong east wind, turning it into dry ground. "The waters were split," the text says, forming a wall on their left and another on their right. The Israelites cross to safety, then God sends the waters plunging back on the Egyptians, who have charged into the path between the waters. Moses leads the Israelites in a song of praise.

For the first months in the desert, the "stiff-necked" Israelites complain to Moses about the lack of food and water. If only we had died "in the land of Egypt," they cry, "when we sat by the fleshpots." God converts salt water into sweet and rains down quail and manna from the sky, but still the Israelites grumble. "Before long they will be stoning me!" Moses complains. After two months the Israelites arrive at Mount Sinai, and God summons Moses to the top, saying,

"I bore you on eagles' wings" so you could become a "holy nation." God utters 10 commandments and 613 additional laws, then gives Moses two stone tablets containing their pact. The first five commandments cover humans' relation with God, the second their relationship with one another.

But as soon as Moses descends the mountain, he discovers that the Israelites have grown anxious over his absence and molded an Egyptian god, a golden calf, as a surrogate deity. God is furious and offers to destroy the people and create a new one from Moses' seed. I will "make of you a great nation," God says. Here Moses faces his third choice. Will he accept this tempting offer to choose a people made in *his* image, or will he continue to struggle with the one made in God's? In his greatest act of leadership, Moses opts for selflessness over self. He talks God out of his impulse. Then, turning to the orgying masses, Moses hurls the tablets to the ground and compels the Israelites to sign the covenant, though not before thousands are killed for apostasy. God provides replacement tablets, and the Israelites continue on toward the Promised Land.

But no sooner do they leave the mountain than the rebellions begin anew. Moses sends twelve spies to scout the land of Canaan. After forty days the spies return and report that the land "does indeed flow with milk and honey." But the cities are fortified, and the men appear like giants. Only two of the dozen spies—Caleb and Joshua—believe the land can be captured. The Israelites once again lose hope, crying, "Let us head back for Egypt!" God is furious. He wipes out the apostate spies and punishes the entire population by announcing that they will be forbidden to enter the Promised Land. "Your carcasses shall drop in this wilderness, while your children roam the wilderness for forty years." The duration of forty years is chosen, the text says, with one year corresponding to every day the spies were gone.

Moses is soon denied entry to the Promised Land, too. In a cryptic incident described in Numbers 20, God instructs Moses to assemble the community, who are grumbling over the lack of water, and "order the rock to yield its water." Moses instead raises his hand and strikes the rock twice with his rod. "Out came copious water." But in what appears to be God's final attempt to undermine Moses, the Lord says, "Because you did not trust me enough to affirm my sanctity in the sight of the Israelite people, therefore you shall not lead this congregation into the land that I have given them." Here Moses faces his final choice: Will he stand up to God and fight for his just reward, or will he accept God's decision and prepare the Israelites for their future? Will he think of himself, or his people? Moses' final choice is in keeping with his others. The leader chooses his followers. He will spend the remainder of his days teaching the people what they must know. As he guides his people toward Mount Nebo, Moses knows that the peak from which he will see the Promised Land will be his final spot on earth. What will the man of few words choose as his final words? What will his farewell message be?

CLARK'S ISLAND TODAY is more wooded than it was in 1620, nearly overgrown, and privately controlled by a few families who have been feuding for centuries. One of the founders of the Old Colony Club, John Watson, was a loyalist during the Revolution and took refuge here to avoid being tarred and feathered. In 1873, Henry David Thoreau stayed in the Watson family home. Our boats landed on the same narrow beach, covered in scallop shells and horseshoe crabs, and from there we stepped onto a grassy lawn.

A cookout was set up, with a large pot of chili, corn bread, and half as many plastic bowls as men. The members made drinks and enjoyed the breeze, a tailgate party in the antechamber of America.

I was struck by the seriousness of their purpose; they were a self-appointed Thanksgiving Protection Society.

When the Pilgrims settled in Plymouth, explained Jim Baker, a local historian, they had little for which to give thanks. They lost half their population in the first year and were forced to survive on scrod, flounder, and salted cod. A year later they celebrated their initial harvest, and while this occasion is often referred to as the first Thanksgiving, Jim explained, it was not a traditional day of prayers. The first official Day of Thanksgiving and Praise was not held until 1623, and it was a solemn occasion of worship to mark the end of a drought and the arrival of fresh colonists. There was no feasting, as the impoverished settlers could offer their guests only "a lobster or a piece of fish without bread or anything else but a cup of fair water."

In time, harvest festivals would be celebrated across the colonies, and President Washington called for a onetime day of Thanksgiving in 1789, but these had nothing to do with the Pilgrims, as Bradford's *Of Plymouth Plantation* and other accounts were lost until the nineteenth century. The only people who seemed to care about the zealots from England were the men of the Old Colony Club, who invented Forefathers Day in 1769. Even Lincoln's 1863 proclamation that declared Thanksgiving an annual holiday does not mention the Pilgrims or a mythical "first Thanksgiving." That connection did not occur until the late nineteenth century with a retroactive romanticization of the small band from Plymouth. As poet James Russell Lowell wrote in 1870, "Next to the fugitives whom Moses led out of Egypt, the little ship-load of outcasts who landed at Plymouth . . . are destined to influence the rest of the world."

But even then, Jim Baker lamented, Plymouth Rock got all the glory, and Clark's Island was forgotten. Baker is a dry, studious man with an accent as pure Boston as the Red Sox. A winner of the Distinguished Mayflower Scholarship Prize, he had just completed a book on Thanksgiving. After dinner, he led me to the island's center and a giant boulder known as Pulpit Rock, the reputed spot where the Pilgrims worshiped in 1620.

The idea of linking the founding of America with the birth of Israel was not inevitable. If anything, it was a historical anomaly. For all the importance of the Moses narrative in the Bible, Moses himself played an ambivalent role in the religions that revered his story. Early Jews considered Moses a great prophet and an inspired teacher, but they repeatedly stressed that God was the real founder of the nation. Moses did not liberate the Israelites from slavery, God did. Moses was not the true lawgiver, God was.

Early Christians downplayed Moses even more. Moses is mentioned more than eighty times in the New Testament, more than any other figure in the Hebrew Bible. Yet the Gospel according to Matthew presents Jesus as the new Moses, sent to supplant the first one. Just as the pharaoh kills baby Israelite males and only Moses is saved, so Herod kills the children around Bethlehem and only Jesus escapes. Just as Moses was born in Egypt and leads Israel to freedom, so Jesus goes to Egypt and leads humanity to freedom. "I have come not to abolish" the law, Jesus says, "but to fulfill."

Islam performed a similar diminution. The Koran calls Moses the "confidant of God" and mentions him in thirty-four chapters, more than a quarter of the total. "We showed favor to Moses and Aaron," God says in the Koran. "We gave them the glorious book." But elsewhere Moses is used to undermine the role of the Jews, "those to whom a portion of the Scripture was given."

Jewish leaders often objected to these characterizations, but their ghettoized voices rarely penetrated. At the close of the Middle Ages, Moses was a marginalized figure, confined largely to superseded Scripture, with few prospects for influencing world events. The idea that the founders of any nation would attempt to legitimize their actions by likening themselves to Moses would have been preposterous.

So why did this happen in the United States?

The American elevation of Moses grew out of an extraordinary collusion of trends—geographic, religious, and technological. For waves of believers who left the civilized world, crossed a forbidding sea, and arrived in untamed territory, the New World could plausibly be considered a wilderness. As early as 1492, Christopher Columbus likened himself to the Hebrew prophet. On September 23, seven weeks after departing Spain, Columbus experienced an uncommon swelling of the ocean. "The rising of the sea was very favorable to me," he recorded in his journal, "as it happened formerly to Moses when he led the Jews from Egypt." On a later voyage Columbus claimed that God had treated him like Moses and David, adding, "What more did he do for the people of Israel when he brought them out of Egypt?"

What makes Columbus's evoking of Moses so notable is that the Bible was not widely read in Europe at the time. Throughout the Middle Ages, the Roman Catholic Church, eager to monopolize its power, insisted that the Bible was so sacred it must be read only in Latin, could be interpreted only by its clergy, and had to be kept only in church. The penalty for violating these edicts could be death. Also, since the Bible contains around 774,000 words, creating a new volume by hand was prohibitively time-consuming. Two monks working full-time would take at least four years to transcribe an entire Bible. Very few churches had one. Simply put, there were few people of the book because there were few books.

Within decades, though, Martin Luther began agitating against the Church, accelerating a process that, along with the invention of the printing press, would open the Bible to millions of lay readers and convert the epic narrative of the Israelites from a little-read relic into a living inspiration. Protestants believed civilization should be based on *sola scriptura*, Scripture alone, as opposed to Scripture interpreted exclusively by the Church. Soon vernacular Bibles popped up across Europe—especially in Britain. One scholar estimates that 1,342,500 Bibles were printed in England between 1520 and 1649, enough for every household. "Consider the great historical fact," wrote Thomas Huxley, that the Bible "has become the national epic of Britain."

If the Bible was the national epic of Britain, it was the national birthright of America. What the Reformers realized when they read the text—particularly the narrative books of the Hebrew Bible, which the Catholic liturgy downplayed—was that the Bible argues against the divine right of kings. It constitutes a veritable call to revolution. The Hebrew Bible has always been a radical political document, wrote Jonathan Sacks, the chief rabbi of Britain, "testifying to the right of prophets to criticize kings, the inalienable dignity of the human person . . . and a clear sense of the moral limits of power." Though these ideals appear throughout the Bible, they are introduced with Moses: the prophet who stands up to the mightiest king ever known; the individual to whom God entrusts the Ten Commandments; and the figure stopped short of his ultimate destination when he disobeys God's word.

Among Protestants, Moses was arguably the preeminent figure of the Hebrew Bible. Luther himself was frequently compared to him. As the centenary of Luther's posting the Ninety-five Theses approached in 1617, an occasion for which Protestants invented the century as a landmark of historical measurement, the German monk was hailed as Europe's Moses, the man who led the chosen people out from papal bondage. The Pilgrims took the Protestants' interest in Hebrew Scripture to its ultimate extreme by reenacting Moses' journey. By foisting themselves across the sea on an "errand into the

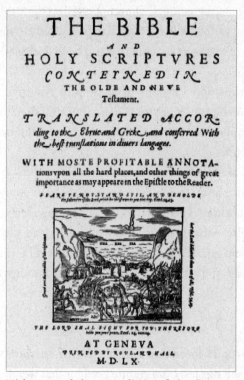

Title page of the 1560 edition of the Geneva Bible, which depicts the Israelites camped before the Red Sea. *(Courtesy of The Library of Congress)*

wilderness" of America, ordinary citizens could now cast themselves as actors in the greatest drama ever conceived. In effect, everyone could now be Moses. As John Milton wrote in 1644, "The time seems come, wherein Moses the great Prophet may sit in heaven rejoicing to see that . . . all the Lord's people are become prophets."

"Protestants viewed themselves as living in biblical time," Jim Baker explained as we walked toward Pulpit Rock. "To them, the

Bible represents the original church, and they want to be a part of it. In coming to God's New Israel, they viewed themselves as re-creating God's original kingdom that had been occluded by the man-made church."

For Pilgrims and Puritans who came to America, the Exodus story took on an even deeper resonance because they were breaking away not simply from the Catholic Church but from the Church of England as well.

"There's very little precedent for what they did," Jim said, "and they realized that their actions were not going to go over very well with the authorities. Therefore you've got to convince yourself—and everybody else—that breaking away from England was a good idea. To do that, you go back to the source, like a lawyer citing precedent. The Bible was the ultimate source, and the Exodus the ultimate example."

PULPIT ROCK IS located in a small clearing, surrounded by clover, dandelions, and daisies. It's a granite boulder that weighs about thirty tons and was deposited here during the last glacier period, when retreating ice ferried down chunks of granite from New Hampshire. Plymouth Rock arrived in the same way. Neither boulder appears in contemporaneous accounts; they were added to the story more than a century after the Pilgrims landed.

Once the men of the Old Colony Club had assembled, a member climbed to the top of Pulpit Rock and began tapping out a tune on a snare drum. He later told me he had played a similar song upon the arrival of the *Mayflower II* in 1957 when the captain sidled up to him and said, "Laddie, could you pick up the pace. We haven't had a bath in sixty days."

Then Harold Boyer, at ninety-seven, the senior member of the club, was hoisted to the summit. "Friends of the Old Colony Club," he said. "When I first became a member, I was attracted by the fellowship, but also the responsibility to perpetuate the memory of the Pilgrims."

He carefully recapitulated the Pilgrims' story, from their departure from Holland to their landing on Cape Cod to the dawning of their first day on Clark's Island. "They were ready to set out the next day, Sunday," he said, "and seek a permanent place for landing. But Sunday was the Sabbath, so they set aside every other thing and worshiped. The first service in the New World." He pointed out a carving on Pulpit Rock that said ON THE SABBOTH DAY WEE RESTED.

"Today, my friends, Americans have lost connection with the Pilgrims. We have forgotten the biblical faith that they had. We desecrate the Sabbath. We no longer see ourselves as exiles searching for the Promised Land." He paused.

"My brothers, I may not be here next year with you," he continued. "So on my last visit to this sacred place, I beg of you to remember the words the great prophet said on Mount Nebo. God has promised us this land. He will make the land flow with milk and honey. But we must remember to give him thanks."

In the background, the drum began to sound. A bluebird settled on the grass. I could hear waves splashing on the shore. And on Pulpit Rock, Harold Boyer closed his eyes and continued reciting what are among the most oft-cited lines in the Bible, from Deuteronomy 30. They are the words from Moses' farewell address on Mount Nebo in which the man of choices offers his people the ultimate choice. John Winthrop quoted these words on the *Arbella* in 1630, Martin Luther King, Jr., invoked them the night before he was killed in 1968, and Ronald Reagan repeated them at the base of the Statue of Liberty on its centennial birthday in 1986:

> See, I have set before you this day life and good, death and adversity. For I command you this day to love the Lord your God, to walk in his ways, and to keep his commandments. But if you turn away, you shall certainly perish; you shall not long endure on the soil that you are crossing the Jordan to enter. I have put before you life and death, blessing and curse. Choose life—that you and your offspring shall live.

IN MANY WAYS, Plymouth was an unfortunate choice for the Pilgrims. While the soil and water were good, the shipping would have been better in Boston, the fishing superior on Cape Cod. Today the town is still stranded between these more attractive neighbors. It has many signatures of New England—white clapboard churches, green copper cupolas, American flags—as well as its share of wry tributes, like Bradford's Package Store on Route 3A. An eighty-one-foot-tall statue of Faith, known as Forefathers Monument, stands on a hill. A slightly squat cousin of the Statue of Liberty, the female figure rests her foot on Plymouth Rock and holds a Bible.

A few miles away is Plimoth Plantation, a re-creation of the town circa 1627. (The facility uses the original spelling of the name.) The village includes thatched cottages, herb gardens, and dozens of re-enactors in buckled shoes, bonnets, and white lacy collars. Visiting the plantation is like walking into an elementary school Thanksgiving play, except the actors have Ph.D.'s in their pockets instead of peanut butter and jelly sandwiches. Jim Baker had suggested I meet the park's premier historian, John Kemp, the author of a book about 1620, who that day was playing the role of William Brewster, the preacher on the *Mayflower*. He had a gray Vandyke and was tending a fire on his hearth. He offered to show me his Bible.

"Our leader has a phrase he often mutters—Scrutinized Scriptures," Kemp, er, Elder Brewster, said. "He speaks of the need for each family to make studying Scripture a daily duty." The Pilgrims even named their children after biblical virtues, he explained. Brewster had daughters named Fear and Patience. He had a son named Love and another named Wrestling, after the Hebrew word *Israel*, which means "wrestling with God."

But the Pilgrims' attachment to the Bible goes even deeper, to another idea at the heart of the Moses story: covenant. The Moses narrative is built on two pillars. The first is freedom. In times of oppression, slavery, or pain, the story suggests, humans can cry out and God will liberate them from their distress. "I have marked well the plight of my people," God tells Moses at the burning bush. "I am mindful of their suffering."

But freedom alone is not God's desire for humans. Freedom must be accompanied by the second pillar of the story: responsibility. In the Bible, this notion is captured in the word *brit*, or covenant, an agreement between two parties to perform and/or refrain from certain activities. In Genesis, God makes quasi covenants with Adam, Noah, and Abraham. But the climactic covenant comes at Mount Sinai, when the agreement finally takes written form. Having freed the Israelites from slavery, God now demands that they follow his laws, namely, the Ten Commandments and 613 other mandates. The Bible's message: There is no freedom without obligation. True freedom depends on *giving up* some freedoms in return for a civil and just society.

One reason the Puritans proved so influential in American history is that they were the first to sear these twin pillars into American life—freedom and law, Exodus and Sinai. A century and a half later, these parallel ideas would be entrenched in the defining events of American history, the liberation of the Revolution followed by the constriction of the Constitution. In both cases, the language was heavily influenced by Moses.

I was struck during my visit to Plimoth Plantation by how profoundly strict the Pilgrim covenant was. Sinners were whipped in public or placed in stocks. In those early, brutal months, one of the few healthy residents had his hands and feet bound. Later, adulterers were forced to wear an AD on their outer garments and a sodomizer was put to death. Bradford justified the punishment by citing verses of Mosaic law. Considering the Pilgrims had traveled halfway across the world, had virtually no food, were surrounded by Indians, and steadily lost family and friends, you'd think they might have relaxed their religious convictions. Instead, they tried to out-Moses Moses. Having just crossed their version of the Red Sea, they quickly implemented their own Sinai.

The Pilgrims' commitment to covenant began with the Mayflower Compact, signed immediately before they came ashore on Cape Cod, in which they agreed to "covenant and combine ourselves" into a civil body. In 1636, John Cotton presented the commonwealth of Massachusetts with an elaborate legal code based on the books of Moses that included forty-six separate laws drawn from the Hebrew Bible. Though Cotton's plan was watered down, the commonwealth still adopted laws taken directly from Deuteronomy, including punishing crimes associated with the "first table" of the Decalogue, the first five of the Ten Commandments. These offenses included incest, bearing false witness, even cursing one's parents. A cage was set up for people who did not honor the Sabbath. Over time, the idea of covenant became part of the fabric of America. The word *federal,* for instance, comes from the Latin *foedus,* or "covenant."

I asked John Kemp in his role as Elder Brewster why a group of Christians would rely so heavily on Old Testament notions of freedom and law.

"For us, freedom is not as important as you might think," he said. "We wanted freedom from oppression, and freedom from the bondage of the Church. But what we really wanted was freedom to go back to the Bible."

"So you didn't come here to be free?" I asked.

"We wanted to be free from the tyranny of England, absolutely. But we really came to obey God. In reading the Bible, we learn that the true church of God is all his elected leaders of the past, and that includes the Hebrew prophets. Of those, Moses was the greatest. We know that God chose to give the law to him, and through him it comes down to all of us."

MY LAST STOP in Plymouth was an exquisite white Victorian house on the grassy shore of the harbor overlooking Clark's Island. Squint your eyes and double the acreage, and the lawn would be the perfect setting for a game of Kennedy touch football. Only this home belongs to the least likely member of the Old Colony Club and the most unexpected tender of the *Mayflower* flame.

The Reverend Peter Gomes has as much stature as Forefathers Monument and an even firmer grip on the Bible. He's the preacher at Memorial Church of Harvard University and the Plummer Professor of Christian Morals. A former president of the nearly two-hundred-year-old Pilgrim Society, he was named Clergy of the Year in 1998 by the magazine *Religion and American Life*. He's also black, Republican, and gay. (He later changed his registration to Democrat to help elect the state's first black governor.) Unable to attend the pilgrimage to Clark's Island, he invited me to his home the following day to discuss the Pilgrims and their role in introducing Moses to American life. I arrived to find him wearing slippers and watering gardenias on his porch. He offered me a glass of lemonade, and we settled into rocking chairs.

"It's one of the great spots in the world, to sit here and look out at this landscape and realize that most of it was quite accidental," he said in an accent that suggested he could teach the king a few things about the King's English. "They never would have gotten here had they not wrecked on Clark's Island."

"Is there any significance that they took a day off to pray?" I asked.

"I like the notion that 'On the Sabbath day we rested,'" he said. "They had church. That I can understand. I view Clark's Island as an anticipation, the point from which a great adventure begins afoot."

I asked him why this group of radical Christians was so openly motivated by Moses.

"By the early 1600s, English translations of the Bible had been around for almost seventy-five years," he said. "Biblical metaphors were already ripe and rich. The Puritans saw themselves as a chosen people being oppressed by a great imperial force. Also, Jews had been kicked out of Britain by then, so in the absence of real Jews, it's possible for everyone to be Jewish. You can hijack their ideology lock, stock, and barrel, which is essentially what they did. I would suspect the Pilgrims didn't like Jews as persons, but the Exodus is the greatest narrative there is, so you take it and make it your own."

"Did they see themselves as continuing the biblical narrative, or re-creating it?"

"Oh, *fulfilling* the biblical narrative," he said. "There's a big difference. They're not just a group of people in succession. They want everybody to see that they really are biblical truth come to light. All the mutuality, the bearing of one another's burdens, the rich taking care of the poor, was to build a society that was so ideal that everybody would want to duplicate it."

"And did they succeed?"

"They viewed landfall as a success," he said. "They weren't killed at sea! The Indians didn't kill them! They didn't all starve! I think they saw those as special providences. Only later did they sense that they were losing the dream."

When I set out looking at Moses in America, I assumed the Hebrew prophet was the ultimate model of success. The Pilgrims crossed the Atlantic as the Israelites crossed the Red Sea; the colonists confronted King George as the Israelites confronted the pharaoh; the slaves escaped on the Underground Railroad as the Israelites escaped Egypt. But I quickly realized that I had overlooked one of the central reasons for Moses' appeal: He fails. He does not reach the Promised Land. Moses is as much a model of disappointment as he is of achievement.

Which is another reason he became so appealing to the Pilgrims. Like the Israelites freed from slavery, the Pilgrims saw their excitement at their emancipation from England turn quickly to despair once they arrived in Massachusetts. In Plymouth, they were isolated from trade, surrounded by Indians, and hamstrung by debt. It took them two years to replace the settlers they lost in their first year; a decade later they still had only three hundred people; twenty-five years later only twenty-five hundred. Worse, their faith waned. By the 1660s, Puritanism was under assault in England and in decline in America. Clergy bewailed the "degeneracy of the rising generation." America had not become a New Israel. It was the Old Israel all over again. "What should I do with such a stiff-nekt race?" God complained in a 1662 poem.

William Bradford was particularly overcome with despondence. A passionate man, with a prophet's fire and a psalmist's

soul, Bradford had been elected governor every year but five between 1621 and 1656. Toward the end of his life he withdrew from
day-to-day running of the colony and retreated into the Old Testament. He even began studying Hebrew. The original manuscript
of *Of Plymouth Plantation* included eight pages of Hebrew vocabulary notes and a remarkable hymn to God's sacred tongue, for
having brought Bradford closer to his hero of heroes.

> Though I am growne aged, yet I have had a longing
> desire to see with my own eyes, something of that most
> ancient language, and holy tongue, in which the law
> and Oracles of God were write; and in which God
> and angels spake to the holy patriarchs of old
> time; and what names were given to things
> from the creation. And though I can not
> attaine to much herein, yet I am refresh-
> ed to have seen some glimpse hereof
> (as Moyses saw the land of
> Canan a farr of).

I asked Peter Gomes if he was surprised by the level of disappointment in the Pilgrims' tale.

"Oh, it's always there," he said. "Success is a very dubious enterprise. In a way, the children of God are always meant to be in
opposition. They're outsiders. When they become successful, that's
when the problems begin. It seems to me Bradford captures the
ambiguity of ambition and success. He's very American in that way.
Plymouth was as well off as any English village; they established the
longest peace treaty with the Indians ever observed in the region. Yet
Plymouth wasn't what Bradford had in mind. It wasn't a biblical fellowship. So in the end, he was melancholy."

"And that may be the thing he shared most with Moses," Gomes continued. "I think Moses, too, can be described as clinically depressed at the end. *I've done all this, God, and you do this to me!* There's a similar sense of not being rewarded. And yet, you bargain for that. You don't know God's will. You really don't. If there is any lesson to be learned, it is a certain modesty in the face of great opportunity. The biblical mandate is not success, it's humility. You're not God. You're not supposed to be too fat and happy."

"But that's not the lesson most Americans take from the Bible."

"No, they take American exceptionalism. But it seems to me that an exceptional people has to be willing to subordinate their own ambitions to God's ultimate design. And no one's ever accused Americans of doing that!" He chuckled. "What we've done is take God's design and make it conform to our ambition. But it often doesn't work out. We have the Revolution, but then slavery. We have the Civil War, but then Jim Crow. It's similar to the pattern described in the Hebrew Bible. First they're faithful, then they become successful. Then they become unfaithful, God destroys them, and they become unsuccessful again. Then they repent and the cycle starts over."

"I'm beginning to think that cycle of failure is one reason Moses endures through so many generations in America," I said. "If any one of these Moseses succeeded—Bradford, Washington, Lincoln, King—there would be no need for another one."

"Indeed! As the Bible suggests, there is never going to be a moment of extended success. The very roots of destruction are in the achievement of success itself."

"That leads me to a question I wanted to ask you," I said. "Why are you so connected to the Pilgrims?"

"Yes, I know," he said drolly. "My ancestors weren't on the *Mayflower.*"

"Yet there's something powerful about your sitting here, in your rocking chair, overlooking Plymouth Harbor," I said. "Somehow the sadness has cycled around and become success."

"I've been connected to the Pilgrims for more than forty years," Gomes said. "It's the most important narrative, outside my own family, that I have. In Plymouth, you grow up either loathing the Pilgrims or finding them fascinating. As a little boy, I decided to find out everything that I possibly could about them. And I remember my father saying, 'Now, that's not for you.' And I didn't understand. The Pilgrims are for everybody, I thought. But he didn't want me to get hurt. His view of the Pilgrims was exclusive, white, Yankee." He paused. "But I showed him!"

"So what do you like about them?"

"I found in their story my story. They were aliens in a strange land, just as I was. They seized an opportunity to escape discrimination, just as I did. And they had the privilege to watch their dream develop, pass it on to a new generation, and know that the same thing might happen to other people. The Pilgrim story is the most inclusive narrative that I know. And I never dreamed I would someday have the chance to stand before the Pilgrim Society on Forefathers Day and make a toast."

"And what was your message?"

"That the story is true. I've lived it—and so have you. In America, unlike any other culture that I know, we choose our heroes. And we choose the Pilgrims, I think, because of their struggles. It's dealing with adversity that is character-making. The cycle of failure, recovery, struggle, success. It's very American, and it's very Mosaic. And it ceases to work if the cycle is interrupted for any prolonged period—too much adversity, too much success. There has to be a moderating balance. That was my message to the Pilgrim Society, and it still rings true today."

III

PROCLAIM LIBERTY
THROUGHOUT
THE LAND

THEY WERE TRAPPED. They had broken away from the greatest power on earth but were still far short of independence. They
were determined to escape oppression but were deeply afraid they
would die for their beliefs. They had declared themselves God's
chosen people but were being pursued by the fiercest army in the
world. As the Continental Congress gathered in Philadelphia in 1776,
comparisons with the Exodus filled the air. From politicians to
preachers, pamphlets to pulpits, many of the rhetorical high points
of the year likened the colonists to the Israelites fleeing Egypt.
Thomas Paine invoked the analogy in *Common Sense,* the best-selling
book of the year; Samuel Sherwood made it the centerpiece of the
year's second best-selling publication, *The Church's Flight into the Wilderness.* And on the afternoon of July 4, after passing the Declaration
of Independence, the Continental Congress asked John Adams,

Thomas Jefferson, and Benjamin Franklin to come up with a public face of the new United States. They chose Moses.

Decades later, when Americans went looking for a symbol of 1776, they didn't select the Declaration of Independence, the building where it was signed, or a myriad of other relics from Philadelphia. They chose the 2,080-pound bell that once hung in the belfry of the State House of Pennsylvania. And they did so not because of its shape, its sound, or even its crack. They made the Liberty Bell the icon of America because of the eleven words molded near its crown that were taken from the story of Moses and linked the aspirations of the United States to the ideals formed on the shores of the Red Sea and sung from the mountaintops of Sinai.

But how did this happen exactly? How did a quote from one of the most frustrating books of the Bible end up as the beloved watchword of American freedom? How did the reluctant leader of Israelite slaves end up as the favorite son of the Founding Fathers? In short, how did Moses become the hero of the Revolution? These questions were on my mind as I stood in front of Independence Hall on a balmy summer morning with nearly impossible-to-get permission and prepared to climb the six flights of stairs and two ladders that lead from the room where the Declaration was signed to the top of the cupola where the bell once hung.

"To me, the story about the bell's accidental rise to fame is really its most interesting aspect," said Karie Diethorn, a historian and chief curator of Independence Hall, who agreed to take me to the top. "We can explain it academically, but you really have to feel it to understand it. Shall we go?"

BEFORE SETTING OUT on this expedition, I had discovered that nearly everything I thought I knew about the Liberty Bell was wrong.

For starters, it wasn't called the Liberty Bell in 1776. The building where it hung was not called Independence Hall. It was not rung on the Fourth of July. The gap in its side did not come from a crack. And the most famous word inscribed on its face, LIBERTY, is a mistranslation.

Oh, and it sounded horrible: tinny and meek.

But it was connected to the intimate relationship among the colonies, the Bible, and freedom. Though it sounds counterintuitive today, colonial life in the early eighteenth century was actually becoming more English, not less. What historians refer to as an Anglicization was under way, the result of greater economic ties among the colonies, tighter political control, and increased prosperity. Religion shared in this English influence. In the early 1700s, churches were largely top-down, hierarchical institutions: God chose whom to bless, ministers enforced ecclesiastical law, and individuals had little role to play in their own salvation.

But Americans were beginning to chafe under this system and were casting around for new ways of relating to power. The Puritan lament about the loss of piety, so powerful in the late seventeenth century, only accelerated in the early decades of the eighteenth century with the rise of commercialism, the migration of young people into godless frontiers, and the advent of Newtonian science. Cotton Mather said the faithful needed to "bring religion into the marketplace." The religious revivals that blossomed in the 1730s, known as the Great Awakening, responded by introducing a new form of worship, one that became the foundation of an emerging American way of God. A new breed of charismatic preachers offered believers the opportunity to read the Bible themselves, hear the good news of salvation in a language that was inviting, and experience a "new birth."

Time and again, revivalists used the language of Exodus to

encourage individuals to stand up to oppressive institutions, specifically the Anglican Church. Jonathan Edwards, the most intellectually potent of the Great Awakening preachers, preached that finding redemption in God meant coming out of "spiritual bondage" into a "new Canaan of liberty." George Whitefield, the firebrand populist and cofounder of Methodism, said that Moses experienced a "new birth" at the burning bush and was a Methodist himself. Whitefield was an unlikely messenger for his message. He was short, mousy, histrionic, and cross-eyed. His nickname was "Dr. Squintum." Beginning in 1739, he made more than a dozen trips up and down the eastern seaboard, speaking in parks, squares, and empty fields to the largest public gatherings North America had ever seen. In New England in 1740, he spoke to eight thousand people a day, every day for a month. In Philadelphia he attracted a crowd of thirty thousand. Historian Mark Noll called him "the single best-known religious leader in America of that century, and the most widely recognized figure of any sort in North America before George Washington." Fans praised him as "another Moses."

Together, these Great Awakening preachers created the first intercolonial movement and a vital precursor to the Revolution. At a time when newspapers were rare and books expensive, the pulpit was still the dominant source of information. As one historian put it, "Ordinary people knew their Whitefield and Edwards better than they knew their Locke and Montesquieu." The Great Awakening's chief contribution was to introduce a language of dissent that emboldened people to challenge conventional truths and distant authorities. And what happened first in churches happened next in government. The Revolutionary period, preacher Horace Bushnell said, was marked by "Protestantism in religion producing republicanism in government."

This democratic notion of faith especially took hold in Philadelphia, where Benjamin Franklin was Whitefield's biggest booster as well as his publisher. Between 1739 and 1741, more than half the books Franklin printed were by Whitefield. Pennsylvania had been a refuge for religious outsiders since its founding by William Penn in 1681. Penn nominally gave preferential treatment to Anglicans, but his guarantee of religious freedom attracted Germans, Swedes, Dutch, Mennonites, Amish, and Jews. His original frame of government failed and was replaced in 1701 with the Charter of Privileges, which provided for a resident governor, a small elective council, and a large assembly with limited powers. But the new formulation only made his life worse. "I am a crucified man between Injustice and Ingratitude [in America]," Penn said, "and Extortion and Oppression [in England]."

By 1729, Pennsylvania had fallen into depression and the assembly voted to print its own paper currency. When the influx of money arrived, the assembly siphoned off a large chunk to erect a new assembly house, which they termed a "State-house" to emphasize their independence from the governor. Their plan called for a massive, Palladian-style building, 107 feet long and 45 feet deep, twice the size of the next-biggest building in Pennsylvania.

"The colony was showing off with this building," explained Diethorn, a bob-haired expert in colonial daily life. With encyclopedic knowledge of every molding, paint chip, and metallic compound, she could have taught the famously polymath Franklin a few things about being multifaceted. "They didn't build this building to house the Continental Congress. They built it to rule an English colony. But the mix of grandeur and intimacy ended up aiding the American cause."

Inside, a large foyer is flanked by two gray rooms, forty feet square with twenty-foot ceilings, which were originally used for the Pennsylvania Assembly and Supreme Court. The Assembly Room is where the Declaration of Independence was debated and signed, and today the space is decorated with period Windsor chairs gathered around tables covered in green baize. Upstairs is a long, open room that runs the length of the building. When the British captured Philadelphia in 1777, the American officers imprisoned here grew so hungry that they threw down buckets to passing citizens and begged for food. Just off this hall is a locked wooden door that leads to the bell tower.

In 1751, the Pennsylvania Assembly voted to procure a bell for the State House. With no suitable craftsmen in the colonies, Speaker Isaac Norris wrote the assembly's representative in London to "get us a good Bell."

> Let the Bell be cast by the best Workmen and examined carefully before it is Shipped with the following words well shaped in large letters round it *viz:*
> By order of the Assembly of the Province of Pensylvania for the Statehouse in the City of Philadelphia 1752.
>   and Underneath
> Proclaim Liberty thro' all the Land to all the Inhabitants Thereof Levit. XXV. 10.

Little is known about Norris, except that he was a Quaker merchant who had studied in England and is said to have known Hebrew, Latin, and French. Even less is known about why he chose this specific inscription, especially considering that the bell would be heard by almost everyone but seen by virtually no one.

Leviticus is the third of the Five Books of Moses. It is the least read and least loved of the Pentateuch and one of the most maligned of the Hebrew Bible. The English name Leviticus comes from the Latin "of the Levites," the tribe of Moses' mother. Levites are priests and much of the book is taken up with regulations that cover priestly habits, many of which haven't been practiced for two thousand years. My daughters were born on April 15, during the time of the year when Leviticus is read in synagogues. I feared that in thirteen years they would have to read one of its more boring passages at their Bat Mitzvahs. I asked a friend to find out which Torah portion they were born under, and he reported back, Leviticus 14:1 through 15:33. It features regulations on how to handle leprosy, mildew, nocturnal emissions, and menstruation. Now, there's a way to get a teenager interested in the Bible! But my friend also came with a message: Even the rabbis agreed this was a tedious portion and advised giving sermons based on the imminent arrival of Passover.

In fairness, Leviticus also includes some of the loftiest values of the Hebrew Bible—specifically the Holiness Code, which outlines the moral responsibilities of the chosen people. These laws forbid harvesting all your fields or picking your vineyard bare, steps intended to leave food for the poor. They mandate against insulting the deaf or putting objects in front of the blind. They insist that people show deference to the aged and tend the infirm. Leviticus 18 contains one of the moral high points of Scripture, the golden rule, "Love your neighbor as yourself." And Leviticus 19 includes one of the core themes of the Moses narrative: "You shall love the stranger as yourself, for you were strangers in the land of Egypt."

Leviticus 25 occurs in the middle of the Holiness Code. It discusses how the Israelites should tend their fields. The land, like the people, deserves a Sabbath, God says. Every seventh year the Israelites should let their land lie fallow. After seven sets of seven years, or forty-nine years, the Israelites should mark an additional year of celebration. During that year, called the jubilee, all debts are to be forgiven, all debtors freed, all workers are to return to their ancestral land, and all families split by economic hardship reunited. The message is that the land belongs to God, not humans, and nobody should benefit too greatly or suffer too mightily for their work with God's bounty.

The King James Bible, which most Pennsylvanians would have been using, describes the central moment as an act of economic liberation: "Ye shall hallow the fiftieth year, and proclaim liberty throughout all the land unto all the inhabitants thereof: it shall be a jubilee unto you; and ye shall return every man unto his possession, and ye shall return every man unto his family." But there's a problem with this translation. The Hebrew word *deror*, which the King James renders as *liberty*, is more precisely translated as *release*. Modern Bibles usually translate Leviticus 25:10 as "You shall proclaim release throughout the land," stressing that the liberation is a freeing from economic duress, not political servitude. Considering all that would befall Isaac Norris's bell, the one misfortune that proved most beneficial was preventing America's treasured icon from being called . . . the Release Bell.

What made Norris choose this line? He left no clue. The prevailing theory has been that the inscription marks the fiftieth anniversary of Penn's 1701 Charter of Privileges, its jubilee year. By adopting Leviticus 25:10, Norris was declaring to the Crown that free men of God should be included in the determination of their economic future. But if that's the case, why inscribe 1752 on the bell and not 1751? A rival view suggests that Benjamin Franklin proposed the line to Norris. By 1751, Franklin was advocating a union of the colonies and honorable transactions between nations, mirroring a line in Leviticus 25. A third theory suggests that the misspelling of Pennsylvania on the bell (there's only one *n* in Penn) was the assembly taking a shot at the founding family, who weren't paying taxes. Freedom meant independence from them.

Karie Diethorn dismissed the novel theories, saying that no mention of the bell appears in Franklin's voluminous correspondence and misspellings were common in the eighteenth century when universal rules for spelling had yet to be adopted. "My sense is that Norris, as a Quaker, thought about the applicability of biblical verse to everyday life. And the significance of the jubilee year would not have been lost on him. Having spent so much time on the architecture of the building, he probably wanted to follow that to the nth detail and make the statement that the Charter of Privileges was a meaningful experience."

I asked if the quotation suggested Norris and his colleagues viewed themselves as a continuation of the Israelites.

"I doubt they considered themselves chosen like the Israelites," she said. "I think they looked on themselves as Englishmen, first and foremost, and that they were entitled to the rights of Englishmen. Winthrop, Bradford, and others in the seventeenth century viewed themselves more as exceptional. By the eighteenth century, people were more practical. The idea that the Bible portrays oppression, and everybody knows the text, made it easy for them to quote the Bible."

AS SOON AS we stepped through the door and into the bell tower I began to sweat. The first two floors are air-conditioned, the others are not. A worn wooden staircase leads to the third floor, an unfinished space that reminded me of the attic in my childhood home. In

the building's early years, Diethorn explained, the State House employed a doorkeeper, who cleaned the fireplaces, lugged wood, and
replaced the candles. This floor was his living quarters. "In the late
eighteenth century, the doorkeeper's wife had a baby in this room,"
she said. The next level up, the fourth, is where the bell ringer would
have stood—Philadelphia's Quasimodo. This floor is where Isaac
Norris's ill-fated bell spent much of its life, inactive and trapped.

Norris's request for a bell arrived in London in the spring of 1752
and was quickly relayed to Whitechapel Bell Foundry. The foundry
cast the bell using the customary method of an inner mold, called
the core, and an outer mold, called the cope, into which the founders
poured molten bell metal, an alloy of 77 percent copper and 23 percent tin, mixed with traces of arsenic and gold. "Basically, it's like a
fruitcake," Diethorn said. A bell has five parts: the lip; the sound bow,
where the clapper strikes; the waist, the concave part in the middle;
the shoulder, which is where the Leviticus quote is located; and the
crown, which connects the bell to the wooden yoke. The note Norris's bell sounded was an E-flat.

The bell arrived in Pennsylvania that September, and eager workers made a critical misstep: They hurriedly unpacked the bell,
mounted it on a temporary rigging, and bolted in the clapper. They
pulled back the metal clapper, dropped it toward the lip, and listened
intently as a deadly thud reverberated through history. The bell
cracked. A horrified Norris blamed Whitechapel for using metal that
was "too high and brittle." Whitechapel, in turn, blamed "amateur
bell-ringers." Wars have been launched over less. Norris tried to send
the bell back, but the ship's captain refused to transport it, so Norris
dispatched the bell to "two Ingenious Work-Men" in Pennsylvania,
Charles Stow and John Pass, who melted it down and recast it. Tin-
kering with the alloy, they added an ounce and a half of copper for

each pound of bell, yet another miscalculation. The following April they lugged the recast bell to the top of the tower for a ceremonial chime. Instead of a sonorous peal, the bell issued an atonal *bonk,* which one witness described as the sound of two coal scuttles being banged together. Far from proclaiming liberty throughout the land, the bell couldn't be heard on the ground floor.

Stow and Pass were so humiliated by the "witticisms" hurled at them that they hurriedly prepared for a second recasting. "If this should fail," Norris wrote, "we will ... send the unfortunate Bell" back to Whitechapel for remolding. A frantic six weeks later, the recast bell was ready to be toted to the belfry. This version at least rang, but its sound pleased few. "I Own I do not like it," Norris wrote, and ordered a replacement from Whitechapel. He planned to return the original bell for credit, but the assembly ultimately kept both. The "Old Bell" hung in the tower, while the "Sister Bell" hung in a secondary cupola on the fourth-floor roof where it tolled the hours. The Old Bell was still hanging in the State House steeple in July 1776, though the tower was so rotted it was dangerous to enter.

The drama of that summer was marked by four key dates: July 2, when the Congress voted for independence; July 4, when it adopted Jefferson's document; July 8, when the Declaration was read aloud for the first time; and August 2, when most members signed. The only date for which evidence exists of bells being rung in the city is July 8. "There were bonfires, ringing bells, with other great demonstrations of joy," wrote a witness. But no one specified that the State House Bell was among those sounded, and there's reason to at least be skeptical, considering the poor state of the belfry. Five years later the tower was considered so rickety it was removed entirely and the bell retired to the fourth floor, where it remained mute for the next forty years and was rung only on ceremonial occasions. Twice officials actually sold the bell, but both times they balked before handing it over. For all practical purposes, Pennsylvania's E-flat bell was impounded, a forgotten slave to its own misfortune, unable to peal even for its own release. (The Sister Bell was also removed, in 1828, when the new bell tower was finished. It was given to a Catholic church, which was burned in 1844 in a wave of anti-Catholic riots. The bell crashed to the floor and broke into smithereens. Workers collected all the pieces they could find and recast them into a 150-pound bell, down from the original 2,080 pounds. The recast version now hangs at Villanova University.)

During one of the original bell's ringings, likely in the 1820s or 1830s, it cracked again. Some witnesses claimed the cracking occurred on the visit of Marquis de Lafayette in 1824; others said it followed the passage of the Catholic Emancipation Act in Britain in 1829; still others suggested it was at the funeral of Chief Justice John Marshall in 1835. The truth, Diethorn explained, is that the bell was probably cracking all along, just not visibly. On Washington's Birthday 1843, the crack had become so substantial that it rendered the bell unusable. Officials performed a repair technique called stop drilling, in which they actually removed chunks of metal to prevent the jagged edges from scraping, thereby creating the inch-wide gap that became the bell's most distinctive feature. The rounded edges from this procedure are still visible. At the time, officials actually took the metal fragments and made them into trinkets, which they sold. "It was like buying a piece of Noah's ark jewelry," Diethorn said.

So why such misfortune?

"In effect, the bell was doomed from the start," she stressed. "They were taking the same metal, subjecting it to heat, breaking it down, and reconstituting it. Plus, their casting techniques were highly flawed. Today, they use sterile environments and humans don't get anywhere near the bells when they're being cast."

I asked her why the bell came to have such meaning.

"It's hard to get your heart around a building," she said. "But the bell is timeless, in its shape, its function. It's easier to understand on an emotional level."

And so much of that emotion, she added, comes from the inscription. "You have to remember, the cultural identity of these people is so vividly informed by the Bible," Diethorn said. "It's not the same as saying they were religious, but it was the common language of all members of that society. What I think is fascinating about this era is how the idea of reason, science, and objectivity, which inform the Enlightenment so completely, can coexist in their minds with the idea that there is a divine presence in the world.

"I think a lot of laypeople in America today feel that the Enlightenment was somehow antireligious," she continued. "That people like Thomas Paine, Benjamin Franklin, and others were deists and didn't believe in God. That couldn't be further from the truth. The language of religion is so ingrained in their culture in the form of the stories, the aphorisms, the proverbs, and the characters, and this religious language is readily adopted as the language of liberty, whether you're talking about the Israelites, their captivity, and their freedom, or leaders like Moses, David, or Solomon. The eighteenth century is big on parallels. They're searching for historical precedent for their own actions, and they're finding it in religious rhetoric because everyone understood and could relate to that."

"And it seems that specifically what they were looking for is authority," I suggested. "An authority higher than the king. God gives you that authority."

"The heart and the head need to be equally stimulated to make something worth doing," Diethorn said. "The Enlightenment may give you intellectual credibility, but the Bible gives you emotional credibility."

THE STAIRCASES IN the tower get wobblier the higher you climb. Above level five, you enter the new tower, installed during the building renovation in 1828. When the nation's capital moved to Washington and the state capital to Harrisburg, the State House was slated to be torn down, but a wave of nostalgia accompanied the visit of Lafayette and the fiftieth anniversary of the Declaration of Independence. Ceremonies inspired by the French hero's arrival introduced the name Independence Hall into popular use.

The sixth flight of stairs is by far the most narrow, and the steps are placed at uneven intervals. About halfway up, they are interrupted by jutting steel girders that now buttress the structure. I had to lift my hands above my head and squeeze between the railing and the beam, like climbing through the pistons in a car engine. And then the stairs stop. The only way to reach the cupola is via a wooden ship's ladder. This seventh level is dark and much smaller than those below it. The air is stale and dusty, more like descending into a dungeon than ascending to a summit. I grasped the rungs and began to climb.

In the mid-nineteenth century, the fractured, largely forgotten, nearly century-old State House bell suddenly experienced a remarkable renaissance resulting from a newfound fascination with the Mosaic phrase on its face. In 1839 a Boston abolitionist group called Friends of Freedom circulated a pamphlet that featured on its cover an idealized drawing of the bell, including the inscription PROCLAIM LIBERTY TO ALL THE INHABITANTS. The drawing was captioned "Liberty Bell," and inside was a poem "inspired by the inscription on the Philadelphia Liberty Bell." Six years later another abolitionist group adopted the same image in a poem by Bernard Barton.

Liberty's Bell hath sounded its bold peal
Where Man holds Man in Slavery! At the sound—
Ye who are faithful 'mid the faithless found,
Answer its summons with unfaltering zeal.

The emphasis on the newly coined Liberty Bell was part of the abolitionists' desire to deflect attention away from the Constitution that had enshrined slavery into law and to return attention to the Declaration and its ideal of liberty for all.

The notion soon took hold among Americans. Benson Lossing's popular *Pictorial Field-Book of the Revolution*, published in 1850, featured a brief history of the Liberty Bell. The account included the fictitious story of a blue-eyed boy who waited outside the Assembly Room on July 4, 1776, heard the passage of the Declaration of Independence, and scurried up the bell tower to the "gray-bearded" guard crying, "Ring! Ring!" The story had been circulating for a decade and quickly became accepted fact. To capitalize on the new popularity, officials in 1852 carted down the bell from the rafters and placed it on display along with a portion of George Washington's pew from Christ Church, a Bible from 1776, and Ben Franklin's desk. As Mayor Robert Conrad said at the dedication, "We acknowledge even a profounder feeling of exultation over the contacts and deeds that have made this the holiest spot—save one—of all the earth; the Sinai of the world, upon which the Ark of Liberty rested."

Completing its resurrection, the Liberty Bell began traveling around the United States. It made seven journeys by rail between 1885 and 1915, for a total of 376 stops in thirty states, including world's fairs in Chicago, New Orleans, and Atlanta. Three of the four first trips were in the South, where Northerners tried to use the bell as an instructional tool to enlighten former Confederates. Stereopticons

"The Bellman informed
of the passage of the
Declaration of
Independence," depicting
the mythical story of the
ringing of the Liberty Bell.
From the cover of *Graham's
Magazine,* June 1854. *(Courtesy
of The Library Company of
Philadelphia)*

Transferring the Liberty Bell from truck to train at St. Louis after
the Exposition, 1905. *(Courtesy of The Library of Congress)*

showed former slaves bowing down to the bell. John Philip Sousa wrote "The Liberty Bell" march. Along with renewed interest in the Stars and Stripes through Flag Day and the Pledge of Allegiance, the Liberty Bell became part of a wave of American exceptionalism, which held that God had chosen America to lead the world into a new Promised Land. As another Philadelphia mayor, Charles Warwick, put it in 1895, "No religious ceremony in the bearing of relics could have produced more reverence than this old bell."

And by rallying so intently around the words of Leviticus 25, Americans were reaffirming their commitment to the country's moral foundations and its roots in the Hebrew Bible. During the years when the Liberty Bell was assuming its stature, Americans had near-universal biblical literacy, which means that most people would have recognized the context of the inscription. They would have seen it as part of God's larger call to free the enslaved, salve the sick, uplift the poor. That recognition didn't mean Americans went rushing to change their public policy, but it did mean they wanted their greatest symbols to be associated with their highest aspirations.

And sure enough, successive waves of ostracized Americans attempted to commandeer the Liberty Bell to support their own liberations. Suffragettes molded a replica of the Liberty Bell, dubbed "the Justice Bell," to promote women's rights, chaining the clapper until women could vote. Civil rights leaders made pilgrimages to the bell, and in 1963 Martin Luther King, Jr., invoked its symbolism in his jubilant phrase "Let freedom ring" at the March on Washington. During the Cold War, Jewish groups laid a wreath at what they deemed the "Bell for Captive Nations" to promote the plight of Soviet Jewry. And as early as 1965, gay-rights groups marched at the bell calling themselves "our last oppressed minority." The process was like a form of Liberty Bell midrash, with each minority group proclaiming liberty unto itself. More than any other emblem of 1776, the Liberty Bell had become the embodiment of America.

AT THE TOP of the ship's ladder is a small trapdoor. I pushed it open, hoisted myself through the narrow opening, and suddenly found my head in the mouth of a giant bell. The cupola is an octagon, with narrow arches open to the air. Some wasps had built a nest inside the bell. The Centennial Bell, dating from 1876, is considerably larger than its ancestor, weighing thirteen thousand pounds in honor of the thirteen colonies. Its metal is a mixture of American and British cannonballs from Saratoga and Union and Confederate cannonballs from Gettysburg. Around its lip is the inscription PROCLAIM LIBERTY THROUGHOUT ALL THE LAND UNTO ALL THE INHABITANTS THEREOF.

After the oven of the tower, the open air of the cupola felt freeing. The ground floor of this building may have given birth to the prose of America, but this was a place of song. I could see all the way down the expanse of Independence Mall, a beautification begun in the 1950s, and up the Delaware River, where, thirty-nine miles upstream, Washington crossed on Christmas night in 1776. For the first time on my climb, I felt proud. I rested my hand on the lip of the bell, which felt cool and vibrated with the slightest touch. I was so accustomed to thinking of the Liberty Bell in its climate-controlled museum across the street, I was jolted to remember that the bell had lived for decades on top of this building.

Karie Diethorn joined me in the cupola. For a second her academic mien melted away. She smiled ruefully. I asked her if she had ever experienced a personal moment with the bell.

"I'm always awestruck with how people react to it," she said. "Once we did a military swear-in. The navy brought sailors and they took their oaths in front of the Liberty Bell. It was extremely moving. They committed themselves to serving their country in front of one of its greatest icons. To them, the Liberty Bell embodied all the sacrifices that came before them. I didn't expect to be as overwhelmed as I was."

"So why do you think people need that object?"

"I think it symbolizes hope. In the 1950s a lot of people looked at the Liberty Bell and thought about America as the greatest country in the world. Now, we still see the patriotic story, but we also see the incredible tragic events of our history. The irony of slavery and liberty coexisting in our nation. The Liberty Bell embodies all of those ideas. It's a very flexible symbol. I think that's why people relate to it.

"Also, the message is very poignant," she continued. "That inherent in our history is tragedy and victory simultaneously. From slavery comes freedom. But freedom is easily lost and can become slavery again. To me, it's like looking down a long hallway, and the Leviticus verse resounds throughout that hallway for whatever period you're in."

"I love how it comes back to sound."

"Hearing is our most fundamental sense," Diethorn said. "Even a deaf person can feel vibration. And it's the same with this place. The bell is the most important part of this otherwise public building. It's the universal part. It sings the Declaration of Independence. The smallest part of the building turns out to have the biggest voice."

IF THE CUPOLA atop Independence Hall is one of Philadelphia's most glamorous spots, the basement of the Christ Church parish house is surely one of its dingiest. It's cramped, poorly lit, and overflowing with books, the kind of room where some Dickensian waif would be locked away during his childhood. The rector of the church took me into that morass and showed me one of the least known artifacts of July 4, 1776, and one of the most stirring relics I'd ever held.

Christ Church was always something of a twin of Independence Hall. The two were built within months of each other, in the same formal Georgian style. When its own bell tower was completed in 1754, Christ Church was the tallest building in the colonies, a distinction it held until 1810, the longest any structure has enjoyed that honor in American history. The front door was lorded over by a three-foot-high relief of Charles II, with garlands and a toga in the manner of Julius Caesar, yet George Whitefield was invited to preach here. Christ Church was a royal building but open to change. And with bells, it superseded its crosstown twin: The State House had one; the church had eight.

"The reason this church was the largest building in the colonies was to send a message," explained Tim Safford, the nineteenth rector. With his WASPy good looks and staunch commitment to social justice, he could be the poster preacher for the contemporary Anglican Church. He is also a voracious student of the Revolution. "And the king was the ruler of the church. What happened in the State House was fine, but not until it happened in the church did independence hit home. That's why Jacob Duché was such a hero."

Jacob Duché was the rector of the most important church in America at a time when the most important Americans sat in his pews every Sunday. His father had been a mayor of Philadelphia, and the Duchés were descended from Huguenots, antiestablishment French Protestants. "He's steeped in the intense cauldron of Philadelphia," Safford said, "where blacksmith is living next to banker, banker next to seamstress, and they all meet in Christ Church. Only in Philadel-

Stained-glass window at Philadelphia's Christ Church depicting the Reverend Jacob Duché's reading of Psalm 35 at the first Continental Congress, Carpenter's Hall, 1774. *(Courtesy of Christ Church, Philadelphia; photograph by Will Brown)*

phia could Betsy Ross sit next to the president of the United States in church, even though she could afford only a cheap pew."

That diversity threatened many of the delegates who gathered in Philadelphia on September 6, 1774, for the first Continental Congress. The meeting was held at Carpenter's Hall, around the corner from the State House. A lawyer from Boston motioned that the assembly open with a prayer, but delegates from New York and Charleston objected. The members were simply too divided by religious sentiments, with Episcopalians, Quakers, Congregationalists, and Presbyterians among them. Samuel Adams suggested they invite Duché, who he had heard was a "Friend to his Country." The next morning Duché, dressed in clerical garb and white wig, read that day's appointed psalm from the Book of Common Prayer, the thirty-fifth. "Plead my cause, O Lord, with them that strive with me: fight against them that fight against me."

"I never saw a greater Effect upon an Audience," John Adams wrote his wife, Abigail. "It seemed as if Heaven had ordained that Psalm to be read on that Morning." But then Duché did something even more extraordinary. He deviated from the prescribed Anglican readings and, in homage to the revivalist spirit of the time, offered what Adams called "an extemporary Prayer, which filled the Bosom of every Man present. I must confess I never heard a better Prayer or one so well pronounced. . . . It has had an excellent Effect upon every Body here."

"This was the ultimate Great Awakening moment," Tim Safford said. "Many of the delegates just fell to their knees and began to cry. The antiauthoritarian spirit of the Awakening had suddenly been transported into the command center of the Revolution."

But Duché's revolutionary fervor reached its climax, along with that of the rest of the city, on July 4, 1776. That Thursday afternoon, after the Congress had approved the Declaration of Independence but before the text had been printed, signed, or read aloud, Jacob Duché strode to Christ Church and convened a special meeting of the vestry. The members unanimously agreed that Duché could strike out all homages to the king from the Book of Common Prayer. The minutes of that meeting are stored in this basement room and were the first book Safford pulled from the shelves to show me: "Whereas the honourable Congress have resolved to declare the American Colonies to be free and independent States, in consequence of which it will be proper to omit those petitions in liturgy wherein the King of Great Britain is prayed for as inconsistent with the said declaration."

Safford then reached to the uppermost bookcase and pulled out a particularly clean cardboard box, tied with a ribbon. He laid it on the table, opened it, and removed a maroon leather book, about sixteen inches tall and ten inches wide. Considering its age and the poor conditions in the room, the book was in remarkably good condition. He opened to the title page. *The Book of Common Prayer, and administration of the Sacraments and other rites and ceremonies of the Church according to the use of the Church of England.* It was printed by Mark Baskett in 1716. "I get goose bumps every time I hold it," Safford said. "This was the physical manifestation of the king. And to Duché, the king was God."

Safford slowly turned the pages of the mammoth book and pointed out the half dozen passages where Duché had crossed out references to the Crown and replaced them with tributes to the new country. Duché scratched through words that asked God to bless "thy servant George, our most gracious king and governor," and wrote in by hand, "the Congress of these United States." He excised parts of a prayer beseeching God on behalf of "this kingdom in general, so especially for the high court of Parliament under our most religious and gracious King," and inked in "these United States in General, so especially for the delegates in Congress." He drew a line through entreaties for the "prosperity and advancement of our Sovereign and his kingdoms," and inserted the "honour and welfare of thy people." In half a lifetime of reading American history, I had never seen an artifact that more vividly captured the epic transformation that day represented. And this gesture would not have taken months to sink in. Worshipers at the most powerful church in the land would have heard it that Sunday, July 7, the day *before* the Declaration of Independence was read aloud for the first time. Christ Church rang the true bell of liberty.

"I think this book represents Christ Church's way of blessing what happened over at the State House," Safford said. "The Congress has gone and done this. What could be more helpful than to have Christ Church say, 'We agree.' Almost every other church was loyalist or refused to participate in the Declaration. And speaking as a priest, I can say that it was Duché who had to live with the consequences of what he did."

"So what was he thinking at that moment?"

"I think he's probably scared to death. I think he's excited. I think he's worried he might be hanged. I think he believes he's doing God's work." Safford lifted his head as if toward some invisible authority and clenched his hands as if to build up courage himself. He wasn't really speaking to me now. "And I've always thought this was the real Mosaic moment of the Revolution. Duché must have felt like Moses, going before the pharaoh. How could you do anything but quake? Every molecule in your being had trained you to believe that the king was the king because God had put him there. Duché was denying everything in his heart. And the only way you can do that is if you believe that God has called you to do it."

Safford turned back to look at me. "And I'm sure his agony is the agony of all Moseses in American history. He had all the anguish that Dr. King had in 1968. He had all the doubt that Abraham Lincoln had. He had all the concerns of George Washington. *Is this the right thing?*"

Duché's torment only increased in the next year as the American cause suffered a series of debilitating blows. Finally, in September 1777, when the British conquered Philadelphia, one of their first acts was to arrest Jacob Duché. A night in jail shook the preacher, as did Washington's bloody defeat the following week at nearby Germantown. On October 8, Duché wrote Washington an eight-page private letter begging him to call off the war. "He is saying, 'George, I know you. Put an end to this before it becomes a travesty,'" Safford said. "'The British are going to destroy you and slaughter these young men. Congress is leading you astray.'" But Washington found the letter a "ridiculous, illiberal performance" and released it to Congress. Duché, the hero of 1776, was finished, forced to seek exile in England. Years later he returned to Philadelphia a broken and forgotten man, buried in an unmarked grave.

How quickly a Moses can fall.

I asked Tim Safford if he thought Duché failed the leadership moment.

"I don't. I'm his successor, and I think the life of a pastor is trying to hold very distant poles in some sort of tension with each other. Loyalty to the Crown, loyalty to the freedom movement of Washington. Granted, in that moment, he's more like the Israelites complaining in the desert. It's a greater Moses moment for Washington. But like a lot of preachers, Duché never gives up hope that justice can be served without killing people. He inspires me."

BACK UPSTAIRS WE settled in the stark white sanctuary with the worn stone floor. I wanted to press Safford on why he thought the Moses narrative was so prevalent during the Revolution. Duché was hardly the only person to invoke the biblical hero. If anything, the Exodus became the lingua franca of the casus belli.

As early as 1760, Ezra Stiles, the president of Yale, stressed that God "is now giving this land to us who in virtue of the ancient covenant are the Seed of Abraham." He urged all Americans to read the story of their past in Deuteronomy 26:6–9. "The Lord freed us from Egypt by a mighty hand, by an outstretched arm and awesome power, and by signs and portents. He brought us to this place and gave us this land, a land flowing with milk and honey." In 1765, John Adams wrote that he always considered the settlement of America "the opening of a grand scene and design in Providence for the illumination of the ignorant, and the emancipation of the slavish part of mankind all over the earth."

The themes these orators drew from the Exodus were similar to the ones the Puritans and Great Awakening preachers had emphasized: Freedom is a God-given right; God promises liberation to the oppressed; God freed the Israelites from Egypt, and he can free the colonists. But the new generation of Exodus-lovers went further, insisting that the Bible expressly rejects the British form of government, the divine right of kings, and endorses the kinds of freedom the patriots were proposing. In 1775, Samuel Langdon, the president of Harvard, said Americans should adopt the form of government that God handed down to Moses on Sinai. "The Jewish government," he wrote, "was a perfect republic."

Thomas Paine's *Common Sense* and Samuel Sherwood's *The Church's Flight into the Wilderness,* both published in 1776, invoked the Moses story to make similar attacks on the English political system. Paine was the antireligious zealot who continually cited religious examples. He hated Scripture but quoted it relentlessly, showing the enduring power of the Bible even for deists. In *Common Sense* he cites Gideon, Samuel, and David, to show how the Bible argues against kingship. And he calls King George III a pharaoh. "No man was a warmer wisher for reconciliation than myself, before the fatal nineteenth of April 1775, but the moment the event of that day was made known, I rejected the hardened, sullen tempered Pharaoh of England for ever."

Sherwood, a Connecticut pastor, calls on the same biblical passages that John Cotton quotes on the *Arbella* to argue that America's revolutionary leaders are finally fulfilling the promise of the Puritans. He quotes God's message to the Israelites in the Sinai: "Ye have seen what I did unto the Egyptians, and how I bore you on eagles' wings, and brought you unto myself."

> [God] was not conducting them from a land of liberty, peace, and tranquility, into a state of bondage, persecution and distress; but on the contrary, had wrought out a very glorious deliverance for them . . . and was now, by his kind providence, leading them to the good land of Canaan, which he gave them by promise.

By contrast, these two popular treatises never quote Locke, Voltaire, Rousseau, or Bacon, the pantheon of Enlightenment thinkers.

The pace of Mosaic references seemed to escalate as independence drew closer. On May 17, 1776, the Reverend George Duffield, speaking to a Philadelphia audience that included John Adams, also compared George III to Egypt's pharaoh. The Reverend Jonathan Mayhew, preaching a week later in Boston, declared monarchy "unbiblical" and said: "If any miserable people" in Europe seek refuge from their slavery, "O let them find one in America." The Reverend Samuel West, addressing the Massachusetts legislature a few days later, praised Jethro's advice to Moses that he lead Israel by appointing a council of leaders. The seeds of promise first hinted at by Columbus in 1492 and planted by William Bradford in 1620 finally appeared to be reaching full flower in 1776. Like Moses, the country was prepared to stand up to the most powerful force in the world and declare, "Let my people go."

"I think what's important about all this language," Safford said, "is that these leaders were using the Bible to convince themselves they were free. They're not that biblically pure; often they're not that religious. But they're using these stories to build the case that they're justified in standing up to the Crown. You're individuals, they're say-ing to the colonists. You're children of God. You're no longer subject to the king."

"So you don't think this reliance on the Exodus is unusual, or over-the-top?"

"The founders were otherworldly to a great degree," he said, "but generally they were hugely influenced by rationalism and pragma-tism. For them, this whole notion of deliverance was a practical mat-ter. They weren't looking for the freedom of Christ in the next world, they were looking for the freedom of Moses in this world."

"So they wanted the story to be true."

"It certainly seems that way. John Adams sailed multiple times to Europe. Benjamin Franklin did the same. They were willing to risk everything because they believed in something. And what they be-lieved is that you should sacrifice your own fat and happiness for something far greater than yourselves. That is an Old Testament narrative. You risk. You don't look back, or you'll end up a pillar of salt like Lot's wife."

"Do you believe," I said, "that Bradford could have gotten on that ship, or Duché could have crossed out the name of that king—"

He cut me off. "The only reason they could have done that is because they had a narrative larger than their own lives. A narrative of God delivers me through the Red Sea. A narrative that if you're lost in exile, you can remain holy. A narrative of life is stronger than death, love is more powerful than hate. If you do not have a narrative larger than the world gives you, you're just going to get sucked up by the world.

"Whether or not the Bible is true," he continued, "is insignificant, compared to *Are you going to live by the narrative you find there?* The Pilgrims, George Whitefield, even Benjamin Franklin I would say, trusted the narrative. They believed God would deliver them. They never sank into the pure limitations of rationalism, that the world was only what they could perceive. They always seem to be fueled by a reality they couldn't see. And because of them, that narrative became America's narrative."

PHILADELPHIA'S HISTORIC DISTRICT has grown since I first visited in high school and now covers one square mile around Independence Hall. There's a sign marking the spot where the first edition of *Common Sense* was printed. The house where Jefferson wrote the Declaration has been rebuilt. Franklin's home has been memorialized by a two-story "Ghost House" consisting of an empty gray frame in the shape of a town house. A major excavation was under way on the mall of the house where Washington and John Adams lived as president. Found by accident when the Liberty Bell was relocated, the house contains quarters where Washington housed slaves, even though this was illegal in Philadelphia. An archaeologist pointed out the circular bay of the parlor, where the presidents met visitors, and which is believed to have inspired the Oval Office in the White House.

Three of these men were involved in another little-known chapter of American independence, one that more than any other shows the intimate connection between Moses and the young nation.

The next-to-last order of business of the Continental Congress on July 4, 1776, was to form a committee to design a new seal for the United States. Pendant seals were widely used in the eighteenth century, and the new Congress must have craved one desperately to form a committee just minutes after they had adopted the Declaration. As further proof of the seal's importance, the committee

John Adams, Benjamin Franklin, and Thomas Jefferson's proposal for the Great Seal of the United States, as drawn by Benson J. Lossing for *Harper's New Monthly Magazine*, July 1856. *(Courtesy of The Library of Congress)*

consisted of three members, "Dr. Franklin, Mr. J. Adams, and Mr. Jefferson." No records of their deliberations remain, but correspondence indicates that each member submitted a proposal to the others. Franklin's proposal reads as follows (the words in brackets appear on his original description but were struck out):

> Moses [in the Dress of High Priest] standing on the Shore, and extending his Hand over the Sea, thereby causing the same to overwhelm Pharaoh who is sitting in an open Chariot, a Crown on his Head and Sword in his Hand. Rays from a Pillar of Fire in the Clouds reaching to Moses, to express that he acts by [the] Command of the Deity.

Franklin also included a motto: "Rebellion to Tyrants is Obedience to God."

An intriguing feature of Franklin's suggestion is that he doesn't focus on the moment of triumph for the Israelites, when they cross through the Red Sea on dry ground. Instead, he homes in on the moment of defeat for the pharaoh, when the waters come crashing down on him. But that moment does not actually appear in the Bible. The pivotal scene in which the Israelites escape Egypt begins in Exodus 13. God, fearing that the Israelites will lose the stomach for their escape if they encounter resistance, leads them away from the obvious route, along the Mediterranean, where the main trading route of the region passed. He leads them instead on what the Bible calls the "roundabout" way, via the Sea of Reeds.

The pharaoh, meanwhile, having recently approved the Israelites' departure, suddenly changes his mind and decides to pursue them with the full vigor of his armed forces. Fearing certain death, the Israelites panic, and God responds by shifting the pillar of cloud from in front of them to behind him. "Then Moses held out his arm over the sea and the Lord drove back the sea with a strong east wind all that night, and turned the sea into dry ground. The waters were split." Israel's moment of birth bears striking similarities to the opening sentence in Genesis in which a strong wind also sweeps over an expanse of seas and land emerges from a watery chaos.

But what happens next is more confusing. The Egyptians come plunging into the sea after the Israelites, including "all of the pharaoh's horses, chariots, and horsemen." But God locks the wheels of their chariots so that they can't move. "Then the Lord said to Moses, 'Hold out your arm over the sea, that the waters may come back upon the Egyptians and upon their chariots and upon their horsemen.'" The sea returns to its normal state and "Pharaoh's entire army that had followed after them into the sea; not one of them remained."

But the Bible offers not a word about what happens to the pharaoh. Did he lead his army into the sea, or let them proceed alone?

Jewish commentators have suggested various interpretations over the years. Some say the pharaoh was spared so he could repent to God; others suggest he was tortured underwater; still more propose that he was sent to the portal of hell so he could mock other kings when they arrived. Franklin's design seems to suggest a slightly different interpretation: The tyrant, sword in hand, goes down fighting, while Moses, the obedient rebel, is bathed in God's embrace.

Jefferson, meanwhile, proposed another scene from the Exodus story. The Israelites, having passed through the waters, are marching across the desert. As Adams describes it: "Mr. Jefferson proposed, The children of Israel in the wilderness, led by a cloud by day, and a pillar of fire by night." Jefferson also suggested an image for the back of the seal, the semilegendary Saxon rulers Hengist and Horsa, "whose political principles and form of government we have assumed." Adams proposed Hercules as depicted in an allegorical painting from the time but dismissed his own idea as "too complicated" and "not original."

Clearly close to a compromise, the committee sought out Pierre Eugène du Simitière, an expert in heraldry who had designed the seals of Delaware and Virginia. In keeping with the needs of wax pendant seals, which were hung from ribbons and thus double-faced, the final version had two sides. One side was an original shield divided into six quarters for the countries that had populated the United States, surrounded by the initials of the thirteen states, flanked by the goddesses of liberty and peace. Above the crest is the eye of Providence in a pyramid, and below is the slogan E PLURIBUS UNUM, meaning "Out of many, one," which had been taken from a magazine company that used the phrase to advertise a year-end compendium of four issues. The other side (for which no depiction remains) was Jefferson's edited version of Franklin's proposal:

> Pharaoh sitting in an open Chariot, a Crown on his head and a Sword in his hand, passing through the divided Waters of the Red Sea in Pursuit of the Israelites: Rays from a Pillar of Fire in the Cloud, expressive of the divine Presence and Command, beaming on Moses who stands on the shore and extending his hand over the Sea causes it to overwhelm Pharaoh.

The echo of the Exodus language widely used in America at the time is haunting. The committee's report, submitted to Congress on August 20, 1776, offers vivid, behind-the-scenes evidence that the founders of the United States viewed themselves as acting in the image of Moses. Three of the five drafters of the Declaration of Independence and three of the defining faces of the Revolution—Franklin, Jefferson, and Adams—proposed that Moses be the face of the United States of America. In their eyes, Moses was America's true founding father.

This news stunned me. Why hadn't I heard about this before? Is it widely known? I sought out an expert. John MacArthur is a sixty-year-old historian from Oregon who grew interested in the seal as a teenager and has since collated every scrap of evidence and every representation. Faced with waves of conspiracies, he created a kind of Great Seal Anti-Defamation League at www.greatseal.com. I asked him if it was a coincidence that Franklin and Jefferson had both come up with Exodus imagery.

"We don't know if they discussed it," he told me, "but if they had, why did they come up with such different ideas? I get the impression it was independent."

"Then why Moses?"

"He's like an action hero," MacArthur said. "He's a role model. And they're saying, 'We're doing the same thing he did. And God wants us to do it.' That's the key message: It's God's will. The motto 'Rebellion to tyrants is obedience to God' evolves into the final motto, *'Annuit Coeptis,'* 'Providence has favored our undertakings.'"

But Franklin and Jefferson are widely regarded as among the least religious of the Founding Fathers, and here they are proposing for the seal an act that shows God's involvement in human history. "Jefferson later publishes a New Testament where he excises all the miracles," I said, "yet this is the greatest miracle in the Hebrew Bible."

"For them, slavery violates the rights of man," he said. "So they view the Exodus as part of natural law, not religious. The Creator gave us life and liberty, so fighting for that freedom is a natural part of being human."

After the frenzied rush to design the seal, the Congress, faced with a British invasion of New York that August, tabled the idea and didn't take it up again until 1780. A second committee, made up of what MacArthur called "nobodies," proposed an entirely new seal, with a seated goddess of liberty on one side and a heraldic shield on the other. That design was also put aside for several more years. A third committee submitted the final design on June 20, 1782. It has the American bald eagle holding an olive branch in one talon and a bundle of arrows in the other, with E PLURIBUS UNUM flowing from its beak. The only hint of the first design is the image of light "breaking through a cloud" above the eagle's head. The reverse side depicts an Egyptian pyramid topped with the eye of Providence, also a legacy image.

"But why ditch Moses?" I asked. "If the later two committees were of nobodies, the first committee was made up of *three of the towering figures of the Revolution.*"

"I think those committees didn't believe it was proper to have a human being on the seal," he said. "Too much like the king. Seals are supposed to be more stylized."

"But it's worse," I said. "Not only did they scrap Moses, they replaced him with a *pyramid*. It doesn't take a Talmudic scholar to point out that we've gone from the Israelites being freed from slavery and the pharaoh dying in the Red Sea to the pyramid, which is the burial spot and tribute to the pharaoh, and which they probably (and wrongly) believed had been built by the Israelites when they were slaves. We've regressed."

"The two words they used to describe the symbolism of the pyramid were *strength* and *duration*," MacArthur said. "They chose it because it was thousands of years old and they wanted America to be strong and endure." Also, he noted, Exodus imagery may have been appropriate for the liberation of 1776, but by 1782 the country was more focused on rallying around Washington and building an infrastructure. As for claims that the eye and pyramid are Masonic symbols, MacArthur said he had found little evidence that this influenced the design. "You don't have to be a Mason to be fascinated by the pyramids."

"So you've been looking at these proposals for forty years," I said. "Do you wish they'd kept Moses?"

"I've actually written a screenplay in which Moses is the key to solving the puzzle."

"So you've become Dan Brown!"

He chuckled. "The truth is, when I think of the seal today, I don't see the dollar-bill version. I see the description. The true form of the seal is the written word that Congress adopted. Anybody can interpret that description. The seal is like the national anthem. It's really just a piece of sheet music, and every musician makes a slightly different song from the same piece of music."

BEFORE LEAVING PHILADELPHIA, I went to stand in front of Independence Hall. Night had fallen and the crowds had thinned, leaving the crisp formality of the seventeen multipaned windows in front and the elegant tower above. With its state-of-the-art lighting and grand presence at the head of the mall, the building may be more arresting today than it was in 1776, when it was surrounded by taverns and dirt alleyways. Time and adoration have elevated it to its position as headquarters of American democracy.

Yet across the street, the Liberty Bell hangs suspended in its exquisite glass chapel, arguably upstaging its former home. The word LIBERTY faces the tower. I learned during my visit that Independence Hall receives around 750,000 visitors a year. The Liberty Bell, 2 million. More than just a symbol of 1776, the Old State House bell has become the global icon of freedom. Replicas have been erected over the years in Hiroshima, Berlin, and, in a fitting coming-home, Jerusalem, facing Mount Zion, in 1976. Whenever oppressed peoples march for emancipation, in places like Tiananmen Square or Soweto, they stride behind a Liberty Bell.

And it seems only fitting that a phrase from the Five Books would help shape this mascot of liberty. If the Hebrew Bible makes anything clear, it is that Israel should remember that God freed them from ancient Egypt. More than fifty times the Pentateuch uses a variation of the statement "Remember that you were slaves in the land of Egypt and the Lord your God redeemed you" (Deut. 15:15). The first sentence of the Ten Commandments repeats the idea, as does Leviticus 25. A similar thought is expressed more than one hundred times in the rest of the Hebrew Bible. In part because of this repetition, the Exodus emerges as the central event in biblical history.

It also becomes a defining event in the history of freedom itself. As German poet Heinrich Heine wrote, "Since the Exodus, freedom has always spoken with a Hebrew accent." Since 1776, freedom has also spoken with an American accent in many places—and been visualized with the Liberty Bell. The union of the Exodus and 1776 in the form of the Old State House bell is a celebration of the idea that human beings can imagine a better life for themselves. As I was leaving Christ Church, Tim Safford told me a story that brought home this ideal and captured the unlikely path of Leviticus 25:10 from a forgotten verse in an unloved book of the Bible to the international expression of human dignity.

In July 1999 the archbishop of Cape Town paid a visit to Philadelphia and Safford volunteered to escort him around town. "Njongonkulu Ndungane had lived in the shadow of Desmond Tutu internationally," Safford said, "but in South Africa, he was highly regarded because he had served on Robben Island with Nelson Mandela." On his first night in town, as Safford was dropping the archbishop off at the hotel, Ndungane asked, "Is the Liberty Bell in Philadelphia?" Safford arranged a special tour, and the next day Ndungane arrived at the bell as a student was asking a Park Service ranger, "What is the meaning of the inscription?"

"Well, we don't know exactly," the ranger said. "It probably honors the fiftieth anniversary of the Charter of Privileges and has nothing to do with freedom—"

"All of a sudden, Ndungane interrupts him," Safford said. "'No, that's not right,' Ndungane says. 'Leviticus twenty-five means that God will always free his people. Humanity corrupts itself and people get enslaved. So God makes a provision that every fiftieth year, you stop the economic hardship, you stop the political oppression, and you set everyone free and start again on an equal level. Because no doubt in fifty years you will have messed everything up again. That's why the Liberty Bell proclaims freedom. Because we will always have oppression, but God will always deliver us from it. There's reason to hope.'"

The ranger stood flabbergasted, his mouth agape. The students were transfixed. After a minute, the ranger said, "Wow, you seem to know a lot about our bell. I'm not exactly sure if that's true . . ."

Archbishop Ndungane replied, "On Robben Island, we always dreamed it was true."

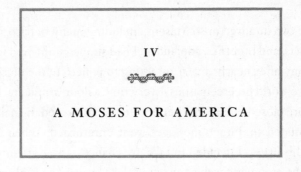

IV

A MOSES FOR AMERICA

THE VERY WORSHIPFUL Geoffrey Hoderath stepped to the pulpit of Saint Paul's Chapel in lower Manhattan. To his right was a painting commemorating the survival of the chapel on 9/11. Around him was the oldest public building in continual use in New York City, dedicated in 1766. Behind him rose a dazzling gilded altarpiece depicting Mount Sinai in clouds and lightning, the Hebrew name for God, Yahweh, in a medallion, and the two tablets of the Ten Commandments. And this was a church, not a synagogue. Hoderath was wearing a blue suit, a red tie, and a white lambskin apron.

"On behalf of the Grand Lodge of the State of New York, Free and Accepted Masons," he announced in a tone that suggested he was reading the Decalogue to the Israelites at Mount Sinai, "I welcome you to this reenactment of the inauguration of George Washington as the first president of the United States, on this the anniversary of that historic event. Our purpose is to honor the father of our country, to commemorate the founders of our great republic, many of whom were Freemasons, and to proclaim our living heritage as a free nation."

The two hundred or so Masons, including many in tricorne hats, blue coats, and breeches, applauded. I had slipped uninvited into this ceremony after nearly a year of trying to penetrate the elusive and secretive world of Freemasons. Every time a door would crack open, two more closed before me. Letters went unanswered. E-mails went unresponded to. Phone messages went unreturned. When I heard about this event, I decided to take my chances. I was attempting to probe the enigmatic web connecting the Masons, the Bible, and the building of America. More, I was hoping to get a closer look at a hidden treasure of the founding era, the Masonic Bible that Washington used to take the oath of office. The Bible lay at the heart of a centuries-old riddle about the passage where the president rested his hand.

I was also trying to unravel the deep-seated bond that connected the leading prophet of the Israelites with the first president of the United States. From the night he led the Continental Army across the Delaware in 1776 to his leadership of the Constitutional Convention in 1787 through his death in 1799, Washington was compared to Moses. In some ways the analogy was understandable. The War of Independence, with its vulnerable, ragtag population pitted against a much stronger, military superpower, had deep parallels with the Exodus. As the reluctant leader trying to hold together an anxious population and lead his people out of subjugation and into freedom, Washington was the natural heir to the Mosaic longings of Americans.

But in the years that followed the Revolution, the analogy would seem less appropriate. Moses, I expected, would have retreated into semiretirement in America, like Washington. Instead, the opposite happened. Having sounded the bell for Revolution, Moses became the clarion for the Constitution. Having offered the road map for freedom, he became the model for imposing strict federal law. Why? What is it about Moses that once more made him such a necessary presence in the volatile first decade of American life? And what does it say about the identity of early Americans that they viewed the founding leader of the Israelites and the patriarch of the United States as such analogous leaders?

"As we gather to reenact one of history's most momentous events," Hoderath continued, "let us begin as they did, by invoking the aid of the Great Creator of Heaven and Earth. On that day, Thursday, April 30, 1789, the rector of Trinity Church offered the invocation, which Washington himself had composed. 'Almighty God, we make our earnest prayer that thou will keep the United States in thy holy protection . . .'" Hoderath continued to the end of the short prayer, then uttered, "Amen." As he did, a fife-and-drum corps paraded down the nave.

"If ever history knew an indispensable man," Hoderath continued, "George Washington was that man. When the thirteen colonies needed leadership in the War of Independence, the Continental Congress chose Washington. When liberty seemed lost in the fall of 1777, Washington kept the soldiers in the field. When independence lapsed into sectional conflict after the war, the framers asked Washington to chair the Constitutional Convention. And when the new republic elected its first president, again the natural choice was Washington."

As Hoderath suggested, the period immediately following the Revolution proved to be one of disarray. The Articles of Confederation were ineffective; Congress was impotent; Europe jeered.

Washington complained that thirteen states all ruling independently would soon ruin the whole. "What astonishing changes a few years are capable of producing," he wrote. Distraught, Americans searched everywhere for answers—science, philosophy, the classics. But many viewed the crisis as a moral one and turned to the Bible for guidance. "This revolution," one delegate to Congress said, "has introduced so much anarchy that it will take half a century to eradicate the licentiousness of the people."

For many Bible lovers, the Exodus appeared to provide direction. As the story of the Israelites in the desert suggested, maybe the way to secure freedom was to give up some freedom. Maybe what was needed was a firm leader and firmer law. Maybe, one Boston preacher said, the United States needed a national charter that would leave a glow upon the nation like that "upon the face of Moses when he came down from the holy mountain with the tables of the Hebrew constitution in his hand!"

And so the narrative resumed. The Constitutional Convention would play the part of Mount Sinai—and Washington would be Moses.

"As a young man beginning his career of greatness," Hoderath continued, "Washington was made a Freemason in Virginia. His lodge still meets in Alexandria. Later, when serving as president, Washington was the worshipful master of that lodge. In that regard, he was like many of the nation's founders who were ardent Freemasons. Today, Freemasons around the world take pride in our early brothers' contributions to the new nation and to the cause of freedom."

Hoderath then set the stage for the inauguration. "More than two hundred years ago, everything we see around us in lower Manhattan was entirely different." Trinity Church had yet to be rebuilt following the fire that swept through the city in 1776. The Canyon of

Heroes, the section of Broadway later devoted to ticker-tape parades, was a street of fashionable houses. The meeting under a grove of buttonwood trees that led to the New York Stock Exchange was still several years away. Yet the city's population was 33,000, more than that of Philadelphia or Boston. Its size and centrality contributed to its being chosen the first capital.

Washington personally oversaw every detail of his installation. After learning of his election while in Mount Vernon on April 14, the general paid a final visit to his ailing mother, then proceeded by coach toward New York, switching to horseback in some towns to lead parades spontaneously organized in his honor. He recrossed the Delaware under a triumphal arch supported by thirteen pillars and surrounded by women and children dressed in white. From New Jersey, he traveled via water on a red, white, and blue barge, manned by thirteen pilots in white. As he entered New York Harbor, twenty singers rowed up alongside him and regaled him with a version of "God Save the Queen":

> *Joy to our native land!*
> *Let ev'ry heart expand*
> *For Washington's at hand*
> *With Glory crown'd!*

On the morning of April 30, thousands flocked to the old city hall on Wall Street, which had been renovated and rechristened Federal Hall. Washington proceeded to the second floor to meet with the House and Senate. Careful to leave his military uniform behind, he was clad "in a full suit of dark-brown cloth of American manufacture, with a steel-hilted dress sword, white-silk stockings, and silver shoe-buckles. His hair was dressed and powdered in the fashion of

George Washington being inaugurated with
his hand on Genesis 49-50 of a Masonic
Bible, Federal Hall, New York, April 30, 1789.
Colored engraving, 19th century. *(Courtesy of
The Granger Collection, New York)*

the day." As one observer wrote, the great man seemed agitated and
nervous "more than ever he was by the levelled cannon or pointed
musket." Outside, the roofs of the houses were crowded, and the
throngs were so dense "it seemed as if one might literally walk on
the heads of the people." All eyes were focused on the balcony.
"In the centre of it," one observer wrote, "was placed a table, with a
rich covering of red velvet; and upon this a crimson-velvet cushion."
The stage was set for the inaugural swearing-in of the president of
the United States.

But there was a problem. Washington had nothing to rest on that cushion. There was no Bible. The Constitution does not require taking the oath of office on a Bible. John Adams had not used a Bible when he was sworn in as vice president nine days earlier. But the Bible's role in oath taking goes back as far as Augustine, and incoming kings and queens in Britain had taken their coronation oaths on Bibles for centuries.

For the most part, Washington was not particularly religious. Historian Joseph Ellis called him a "lukewarm Episcopalian and a quasi-Deist." Even religious scholar Michael Novak and his daughter Jana, who argue in *Washington's God* that the president believed in the Hebrew notion of God, conclude that he wasn't exactly a Christian. He never took Communion; he rarely knelt during prayer; he did not use Christian names for God such as Redeemer or the Trinity; and in decades of private correspondence he referred to Jesus only once or twice.

But he did believe in Providence, a deity that acted in history to free the Americans from bondage under the British. As he stated in his Thanksgiving Proclamation of October 1789, all Americans must unite in rendering unto Almighty God "our sincere and humble thanks for His kind care and protection of the people of this country previous to their becoming a nation." Four years later, after Benedict Arnold's treason was uncovered hours before he did serious damage, Washington wrote that the providential train of circumstances "affords the most convincing proof that the Liberties of America are the object of divine Protection." And Washington clearly knew his Hebrew Bible. In a letter to the Jews of Newport, he acknowledged the shared roots of Jews and Christians: "May the Children of the Stock of Abraham who dwell in this land, continue to merit and enjoy the good will of the other inhabitants." His decision to be inaugurated with the Bible under his fingers and the Constitution on his lips guaranteed that these two achievements of the written word would be linked in the office of the presidency for generations to come.

Geoffrey Hoderath picked up the story. "After consulting with Washington, Chancellor Robert Livingston, the Grand Master of Masons of the State of New York and one of five drafters of the Declaration of Independence, who was to administer the oath of office, hurriedly sent Worshipful Brother Jacob Morton to nearby Saint John's Lodge to retrieve its altar Bible. Washington might have been playing a clever game. There were twenty-three churches in New York City. If he were to swear on a specific Bible, that church might get precedence. Instead he used a Masonic Bible, which is nondenominational. We are fortunate to have that Bible here today."

Hoderath gestured to the right of the pulpit, where three men in suits, aprons, and Secret Service demeanors stood holding a square metallic suitcase. With its shiny faces and bulging locks, the case looked like the kind of device James Bond might use to carry a portable satellite dish, a machine gun, and a spillproof container of shaken vodka martinis. The men put on white gloves and opened the top. They pulled out a sizable King James Bible, with a flaking leather front and two locks on its side. It had been printed in London in 1767 by Mark Baskett, the same printer who published the Book of Common Prayer that Jacob Duché defaced on July 4, 1776.

The Washington Bible, as it came to be called, is the most illustrious Bible in the country, and arguably the most famous single book in American history. At least five other presidents used it in their inaugurations: Warren Harding, Dwight Eisenhower, Jimmy Carter, and George H. W. Bush, and the Masons carried it to Washington, D.C., in 2001 for the inauguration of George W. Bush. The Bible was present at the funerals of Andrew Jackson and Zachary Taylor and was used at the dedication of the Washington Monument, the laying of the cornerstone of the U.S. Capitol, and the centennial celebration of the White House and Statue of Liberty. The Bible is owned by Saint John's Lodge and is used in Masonic rituals, though it spends most of its time on display at the Federal Hall museum on Wall Street, a onetime customs house built on the spot of the demolished first capitol. A gallery contains the original balcony railing and the purported slab where the president stood. I had visited Federal Hall a few months earlier and stumbled onto the tale of how the Bible was nearly destroyed one morning two centuries after it first gained fame.

At 7:45 A.M. on September 11, 2001, janitor Daniel Merced showed up for work at Federal Hall, less than a thousand feet from the World Trade Center. A first-generation Hispanic American, Daniel asked his colleague to sweep the building's front steps, and then he went to change. Just before nine o'clock, Daniel looked out the door and noticed the steps were covered in office paper, fax-transmittal forms, and debris. It was a jolt. "Didn't you sweep the steps?" he asked his colleague. Stepping outside, he cried out, "Look, there's smoke!" Daniel thought 120 Broadway was on fire and rushed to find his cousin, who worked there. Along the way he ran into a colleague, who told him, "A plane hit the World Trade Center." They hurried back to Federal Hall, and as they got inside, the building shook. "'Lock the doors,' our supervisor said. 'Another plane hit the World Trade Center.' At that point we knew what it was."

Later that hour, after securing the building and speaking with his wife, Daniel headed outside to begin walking home. "That's when the first tower fell," he said. "I saw the dust. It looked like it was alive. Soon I was covered in it." He made it back to the front door, and he and his colleagues decided to use Federal Hall as a shelter. They ushered victims inside and offered them water. Then, disaster. The second tower fell. This time the blast blew out the windows and filled the building with soot and rubble. That's when Daniel Merced thought, *"The Bible!"*

He ran to the front desk and retrieved the key to the display case. He had never opened the case before and had never touched the Bible. "I was shocked, really," he said. "It didn't feel old and fragile. It was kind of strong for a book that old." He quickly placed the book in the carrying case, raced downstairs, opened the museum's vault, and secured the Bible in the safest place in Federal Hall. "Every now and then I'll walk by the case today," he said, "and I'll think about what I did. Nobody else thought about the Bible that day. I'm proud of what I did for my country." He smiled. "People often ask, 'When something happens, what will I save?' Then something happened, and I saved Washington's Bible."

BACK IN SAINT Paul's chapel, Geoffrey Hoderath was ready for the main event. "When Washington stepped onto the balcony, he was met with rousing cheers. Back then, the cheer was 'Huzzah!' I would like you to give it a try. *Three cheers for the president of the United States!*'"

The audience huzzahed on cue. As they did, the Very Worshipful Mason playing the president-elect strode onto the pulpit, wearing a brown suit and powdered wig. The Mason playing the secretary of the Senate took the Bible and held it open, while Washington repeated the oath of office specified in the Constitution: "I do solemnly swear that I will faithfully execute the office of President of the United States, and will to the best of my ability, preserve, protect, and defend the Constitution of the United States." Some witnesses say that the president added the words "So help me God," before bending to kiss the Bible.

When the original ceremony was over in 1789, Jacob Morton marked the page where Washington rested his hand: Genesis 49:13 through 50:8. These chapters come at the very end of the first book of Moses. Abraham's grandson Jacob, who is dying in Egypt, has gathered his sons for a blessing. He enjoins them to return his bones to Hebron, where his grandfather is buried. Jacob dies and is mummified in the manner of an Egyptian nobleman. Then, in a passage rarely remembered, Joseph—Jacob's favored son, who is serving as the second-highest official in Egypt—confronts the pharaoh and asks that he be allowed to return to the Promised Land to bury his father. And the pharaoh agrees. "Go up, and bury thy father." In this peaceful precursor to the Exodus, Joseph departs for Canaan, taking along the senior members of the pharaoh's court as well as Joseph's household and brothers. "It was a very great company," the Bible says.

It's possible, as legend holds, that Washington selected this passage randomly. But there's reason to doubt this. Washington obviously knew his Bible and planned every detail of his inauguration. Genesis is the first of more than seventy books in the Mason's Bible, which includes the Apocrypha. Genesis 49 begins about one-twentieth of the way through the text. If you're looking for a random passage, why reach for a page so obviously near the front? If you're just letting the book fall open, what are the chances that it settles so close to the beginning? Or, more likely, if you believe you're standing at the beginning of a grand experiment in democracy, if you're conscious that every gesture you take, every thread you wear, every word you utter will be remembered forever as the first statement by the first president on his first day in office, wouldn't you reach for the first book of the Bible, with its epic founders and stories of Creation?

If Washington's random selection wasn't so random after all, what message was he trying to send? At first glance a passage about death, mummification, and burial hardly seems appropriate for a new beginning. But the closing chapters of Genesis are not merely about endings; they are about reconciling past rivalries and preparing for a future nation, two themes ripe for the Revolutionary generation. In the passage, as Jacob dies, he gathers his rivalrous sons and beseeches them to honor his blessing. After Jacob is buried, the sons who once sold Joseph into servitude in Egypt run to their brother and announce that their father urged Joseph to forgive them. Jacob had said no such thing.

Joseph's response is telling. "Have no fear," he says. "Am I a substitute for God? Besides, although you intended me harm, God intended it for good, so as to bring about the present result." At the height of his power, Joseph, the prime minister of Egypt and now de facto leader of Israel, declares, *I am no God. I am no king. I am your brother. We may have fought amongst ourselves in the past, but now we stand, removed from our father and cut off from our fatherland, and we must work together.* For George Washington, the consensus leader of God's New Israel, the man who repeatedly stepped between the feuding founding brothers and urged them toward reconciliation, Genesis 49 and 50 may have been a private message, but it was a powerful statement of fraternal harmony.

Even more, by insisting that he is no substitute for God, Joseph stresses the limits of his own leadership, a theme Washington emphasized throughout his career, from the Continental Army to the Constitutional Convention to the presidency. Jacob, in the blessing he gives Joseph, accentuates his debt to God, "in whose ways my fathers walked . . . who has been my shepherd from my birth to this day ... who has redeemed me from all harm." Washington echoed these words in his inaugural address, given just minutes later. "No People can be bound to acknowledge and adore the invisible hand which conducts the Affairs of men more than the People of the United States. Every step by which they have advanced to the character of an independent nation seems to have been distinguished by some token of providential agency."

On the first day of the American presidency, Washington used the first book of Moses to send a message of humility.

"Three cheers for George Washington!" the faux Robert Livingston cried. "The president of the United States."

And the two hundred people gathered in lower Manhattan rose to their feet and cheered, "Huzzah! Huzzah! Huzzah!"

AFTER THE CEREMONY I lingered in the chapel for a few minutes and visited the pew where Washington is said to have worshiped following the inauguration. Framed above it is the oldest known painting of the Great Seal, dating from the eighteenth century. Nearby is the so-called Bell of Hope, donated by the mayor of London to honor the remarkable survival of Saint Paul's on September 11, 2001, when the collapsing towers across the street filled the facility with soot and debris. A plaque explained that the bell was cast by Whitechapel Foundry, "the same foundry that cast Big Ben and the Liberty Bell."

As I was preparing to leave, a man walked up behind me and grabbed my upper arm. Before I could react, he spun me around. "Who are you?" he asked, not exactly menacing but not welcoming, either.

I was startled. I collected myself and explained that I had reached out to the Masons repeatedly, that I had heard about this event. He cut me off. "Wait here," he said. "I need to speak to the Grand Master and our public relations representative."

"Your PR rep?" I repeated.

He shrugged, as if to say the Masons had been getting a lot of negative publicity lately, then said, *The Da Vinci Code.* He huddled with some colleagues, returned, and jabbed his finger in my face. "You're coming to lunch."

The next thing I knew I was huddled onto a bus with fifty Masons, driven to the bottom of Manhattan, and led up four flights to the top of Fraunces Tavern, where Washington bade farewell to the Continental Army in 1783. Revolution-era flags hung from the rafters, and a huge deli buffet was spread across the room. Had I really penetrated the inner sanctum of America's Most Secret Society only to find it filled with Oscar Mayer bologna and Vlasic pickles?

Over the next few hours I got acquainted with Masonry. The white aprons are a symbol of purity and a tribute to the stonemasons who helped build Solomon's Temple in Jerusalem. A third of U.S. presidents have been Masons, along with thirty Supreme Court justices. When I began probing about Masonry and the Bible, I was told, "There's someone you should meet."

A few days later I walked through the revolving door of a building on Sixth Avenue and Twenty-third Street. On the wall was a giant mural depicting the all-seeing eye in a pyramid, flanked by seven men from ancient Egypt and six from colonial America. "Hmm," I thought, thirteen. After a short elevator ride, the doors opened on more frescoed walls and four marble muses.

I was greeted by Tom Savini. A forty-something man who looked like an insurance salesman (albeit one with an earring), Tom is a historian of comparative religion, a lapsed Catholic, and a Mason. He showed me around the boardroom, which contained a gilded statue of Washington in an apron and the two-story marble sanctuary, complete with gilt-edged ceiling and thronelike chairs. The entire edifice struck me as one part Buckingham Palace, one part Trump Tower. We settled in the library, and I asked Savini if he thought Masonry was a religion.

"I would call it a catalyst for religion. It's a belief system that focuses individuals on principles and patterns of living that Masonry believes are fulfilling and lead to a better society. And yet it doesn't fill in the details. Masonry tells you to worship a Supreme Being, but it doesn't ask you what you call that being. It reveres what it calls the Volume of Sacred Law but it doesn't tell you what that volume should be."

The origins of what is now called speculative Freemasonry began in western Europe in the late seventeenth century. Though the movement claims roots in antiquity, it exploded when middle-class men adopted traditions from medieval stone layers. The heart of Freemasonry is an elaborate allegory that stretches back to Mount Sinai. After handing down the Ten Commandments, God instructs Moses to place the tablets inside the Ark of the Covenant. Later, when the Israelites conquer Jerusalem, the ark is transferred to its permanent home in Solomon's Temple. But the Masons introduce a dimension of intrigue into the biblical story. The "master workman" of the temple, Hiram Abiff, is murdered for refusing to reveal some mysterious password. He's buried under green moss. Those who discover his body utter, "Thanks be to God, our Master has got a Mossy House." A shortened version of that statement, *Macbenah*, became the Mason password.

As historian Steven Bullock explained in *Revolutionary Brotherhood*, a history of Freemasonry, the use of necromancy, secret codes, and ancient wisdom appealed to Europeans in the seventeenth and eighteenth centuries caught up in the twin allures of antiquity and the Enlightenment. Like Protestants, Freemasons viewed the Middle

Ages as "ignorant" and expressed greater interest in the Hebrew Bible as a primary source of knowledge. Masonic teaching involved "reconciling Plato and Moses," said one observer. Yet Masonry insisted that wisdom could be found in all religions. Its morality plays, elaborate stage productions complete with costumes and sets, wove quotations from the Pentateuch with Newton, Pythagoras, even Shakespeare. The status that came with mastering these rituals attracted men cut off from traditional peerage. Masonry became a gentlemen's club, a civic-promotion institution, and a pan-religious body all in one. By the mid-1700s, Masonry had spread across western Europe.

The lure of education and status particularly appealed to Americans far removed from English society. Lodges were set up in the 1730s in Boston, Philadelphia, Charleston, and Savannah. Benjamin Franklin published the Freemason's code, *The Book of Constitutions*, in 1731. By the eve of the Revolution, the colonies brimmed with rebellion-minded members, including Samuel Adams, Ethan Allen, John Hancock, and Paul Revere. The movement transformed the social landscape of early America, says historian Gordon Wood. "Masonry was not only an enlightened institution, it was a republican one as well. It repudiated the monarchical hierarchy of family and favoritism and created a new hierarchical order that rested on 'real worth and personal merit.'"

Masonry suffered a backlash in the nineteenth century, as Americans rebelled against its perceived influence, but it regained popularity in the twentieth century, reaching four million members following World War II. By the turn of the twenty-first century, that number had eroded by two-thirds, forcing the Masons to fling open their doors to attract members. Tom Savini explained that he often pleads to potential members, "Our air-conditioning is nice."

I was more interested in Masonry during the founding era, specifically how the Mosaic story, working through Masonic liturgy, might have influenced the creation of American society. I asked Savini why Masons had focused so intently on Solomon's Temple.

"The temple is just a symbol," he said. "Interpreting it literally is going to drive you crazy. It represents a place where humans can live in concert with the divine. Our message is, 'You should listen to what God is telling you. You should focus on the work in front of you, as a good craftsman. And you should judge how you're doing by the stones you're laying."

"So you're a student of religion," I said. "Is that a message from the Hebrew Bible?"

"Absolutely," he said. "I don't think Masonry is self-reflective enough to say that it's definitely more Mosaic than Christian, but it is. It has no concern with the afterlife. The focus is on the here and now. It encourages action. And there's a strong element of suffering, of laboring, of caring for your brother, and working to preserve the community."

I told him I'd learned that America has a meta-narrative, an overarching story that runs through the Pilgrims, the Great Awakening, the Revolution, and beyond. It's the story of oppressed people from differing backgrounds, who tap into the idea that all humans have natural, God-given rights to dignity and freedom, then strive to create a better world, a New Israel, where they can fulfill those liberties and spread them to others. "Did the Masons help create the narrative of America?"

"I think it fits into the narrative of America, but I don't think it shaped that agenda," he said. "To give it that much purpose is to assume too much about it. No man had a greater influence on America than Jefferson, yet he wasn't a Mason."

"But what about Washington and all those Masons involved in the Revolution?"

He lifted his arms and raised his eyebrows almost apologetically. "Sorry. It might be more interesting if we had some secret control over America at the time, but we didn't. True, a lot of the generals around Washington were Masons. Masonic lodges might have been used to plot the Boston Tea Party. Nine signers of the Declaration were Masons. But so were many loyalists. Masonry was just one more social movement at that time. Just because some of our ideas correlate with the Revolution doesn't mean there's causality.

"What I would say," he continued, "is that at a time when British society was being overturned, Masonry provided a sense that an American society could replace it. Masonry contributed to the notion that you could take wisdom from ancient sources, and it stressed that honor, politeness, and order were important characteristics in society. Here's where Washington being a Mason may have been important. He emphasized certain values—fortitude, justice, humility—that are very Masonic. Masons call Washington a 'perfect ashlar,' a great stone, chiseled to perfection, that's ready for the house of God. For many Masons today, he's still the standard by which they are judged."

A FEW DAYS later I drove to Princeton, New Jersey, to further explore the connection between the United States following the Revolution and Israel following the Exodus. Since 1620, colonists had been using the Moses story as a boon to their aspirations to break away from England. But by the 1780s Americans had different concerns. Freedom was not enough. They had no organized economy, no discernible borders, and no national identity. Cut loose from their past and wandering toward their future, Americans had even greater need for a historical precedent. And once again they turned to the Bible. The Israelites provided a history for a people orphaned and afraid. Moses offered leadership for a population adrift.

The most immediate example Americans drew from the Exodus was the harsh reality the Israelites face in the desert after they flee Egypt. No sooner do the Israelites cross the Red Sea than they start to complain. The first ill words occur a mere three days into their journey. "And the people grumbled against Moses, saying, 'What shall we drink?'" Moses throws a piece of wood into some briny water and turns it sweet. Next the Israelites complain about the lack of food, and God rains down manna from the sky. But the manna, which tastes like "wafers in honey," comes with a "test," God says. The Israelites are instructed to gather one portion of the "fine and flaky substance" every day, and an extra on the sixth day for the Sabbath. Instead, the Israelites hoard the manna and the leftovers become infested with maggots. Israel flunks the test, and "Moses was angry with them."

These incidents in the wilderness have a clear theme: The Israelites are not yet truly free. They are still trapped in the slavishness of the past and unable to cope with being a liberated people. The pattern will only deepen in the years to come as the motif of murmuring becomes a dominant theme of the last four books of the Pentateuch. The Moses narrative contains at least a dozen different rebellion stories in which the people gripe about everything from water to food to their leadership to God. In many ways, these stories reflect the problems of the original Creation story in which God finds humanity corrupt and sends a flood to destroy them. In the Sinai, God again threatens to destroy his chosen people. Creating a righteous nation, the Bible suggests, is an indirect and awkward business.

In the 1780s, American preachers were particularly fond of drawing parallels between the stiff-necked rebellions of the Israelites during their desert wanderings and the moral degeneracy of the colonists during and after the Revolution. As early as 1777, Nicholas Street preached a sermon called "The American States Acting Over the Part of the Children of Israel in the Wilderness." He used as his base text Deuteronomy 8:2. "God led them those 40 years in the wilderness to humble and prove them," Street said. And while Americans are indignant about the Israelites' grumblings against Moses, we are "acting the same stupid part." He continued, "Now we are in the wilderness, i.e. in a state of trouble and difficulty, Egyptians pursuing us, to overtake and reduce us. Are you not ready to murmur against Moses and Aaron?"

Samuel Cooper, a preacher who turned down the presidency of Harvard, proclaimed in 1780 that to mention all the passages that proved the Americans were like the Israelites "would be to recite a large part of its history." Still, he mentioned a few. "Like that nation we rose from oppression, and emerged 'from the House of Bondage.' Like that nation we were led into a wilderness, as a refuge from tyranny, and a preparation for the enjoyment of our civil and religious rights. . . . And like that nation we have been ungrateful to the Supreme Ruler of the world."

In 1973 political scientist Donald Lutz undertook a comprehensive survey of American political rhetoric during the founding era. He set out with Charles Hyneman to read everything published in America between 1760 and 1805. The effort took ten years and covered 15,000 items, including 2,200 for which they recorded every reference cited. Their goal was to settle long-simmering disputes in the political-science community over the sources of the Revolution by objectively evaluating the influence of Enlightenment writers such as Montesquieu, Locke, Hume, and Hobbes, as well as ancient writers such as Plutarch and Cicero. The first sentence of their conclusion reads: "If we ask what book was more frequently cited by Americans during the founding era, the answer somewhat surprisingly is: the Book of Deuteronomy." Thirty-four percent of all references were to the Bible, compared with 22 percent for the Enlightenment and 9 percent for the classics. The Bible was cited four times as often as Montesquieu, ten times as often as Locke, and thirty times as often as Hobbes.

But why Deuteronomy specifically? The fifth of the Five Books of Moses, which scholars believe was added after the original four, is mostly a retelling of the earlier books. The name Deuteronomy, from the Greek *deuteronomion,* literally means "repeated law." Deuteronomy is Moses' closing argument. The focus of the book is a series of speeches Moses gives to the Israelites near the end of his life. In them, he reiterates the blessings that await the people when they conquer the Promised Land yet reminds them of the obligations that come with that bounty. Deuteronomy resonated so deeply in early America because while Moses celebrates the liberation of Exodus in its pages, he also tries to reassert control over a population intoxicated by its newfound freedoms. The Moses story, in other words, can play two ways: Yes, it urges antiauthoritarian actions by celebrating the confrontation with the pharaoh, but it also promotes a new authoritative order through the imposition of divine law.

And once again the books of Moses proved predictive of events in the United States. By 1787, Americans concluded that the Articles of Confederation were too weak to preserve the Union and should be replaced with a stronger federal law. Given that sectarian differences still separated the states, delegates largely chose to leave God out of the Constitutional Convention. Lutz and Hyneman, in their study of political rhetoric, found that the number of biblical citations, which was 34 percent throughout the 1780s, dropped to less than 5 percent from 1787 to 1788. "The Bible's prominence disappears, which is not surprising since the debate centered upon specific institutions about which the Bible had little to say."

America's greatest contribution to world religion—and the idea that most ensured religion's success in America—the First Amendment, which holds that "Congress shall make no law respecting the establishment of religion, or prohibiting the free exercise thereof," was passed with little sustained discussion of theology. Asked about the dearth of conversation about God, James Madison is said to have responded, "We forgot." Hardly. The ardent champion of religious liberty in Virginia purposely avoided the topic, yet he still managed to secure his point, that "religion flourishes in greater purity, without rather than with the aid of Government," into law. "One is tempted to conclude," writes Martin Marty, the dean of American religious historians, "that the 'godless' Constitution and the reticent constitutionalists helped make possibly a 'godly' people."

Yet if Moses lay dormant during the drafting process, he returned in earnest during the ratification. In June 1788, Samuel Langdon, the former president of Harvard, delivered a sermon before the Court of New Hampshire, which was considering ratification. "The Republic of the Israelites an Example to the American States" maintains that the three-branch structure of government of God's New Israel was identical to that of God's Old Israel. When the Israelites first left Egypt, Langdon said, they were a feeble patriarchy. By Mount Sinai, they had organized a body of elders and a network of judges. "The great thing wanting was a permanent constitution, which might keep the people peaceable and obedient." In response, God created a senate of elders and a body of tribal representatives and a justice system and named Moses "chief commander." "The government therefore was a proper republic," Langdon said. After his speech, New Hampshire became the ninth and deciding state to ratify the Constitution.

Even the most colorful writer of the age, Ben Franklin, joined the Exodus chorus in 1788 with a diatribe, "A Comparison of the Conduct of the Ancient Jews and the Anti-Federalists in the United States of America." Like Israel of Old, the Supreme Being has freed Americans from bondage and given the nation a constitution, Franklin wrote. Yet once again, "discontented, restless spirits" are rejecting God's law, crying, "We have freed ourselves from the slavery imposed by the Egyptians, and shall we suffer ourselves to be made slaves by Moses?" Franklin concluded that the American Constitution, like the biblical one, would eventually pass. The man who proposed that Moses appear on the seal of the United States in the wake of the Declaration now brought back his champion to save the Constitution.

The persistence of Mosaic rhetoric in the first decade of the United States testifies to the enduring elasticity of the Exodus as a trope in American identity. The fact that so many who invoked the story were members of the elite shows that reverence for Hebrew scripture ran through even the highest segments of society and was not merely for rallying illiterate masses. All ten colleges founded on American soil before the Revolution offered instruction in Hebrew. The seal of Yale depicts an open Bible with the inscription "Light and Truth" in Hebrew. The seals of Dartmouth and Columbia include Hebrew as well. The Harvard commencement included a Hebrew oration every year until 1817. Even in the face of the Enlightenment, the Hebrew Scripture stubbornly maintained its grip on the American mind. And Moses maintained his status as the Bible's chief ambassador to the United States.

MICHAEL WALZER STROLLED amiably into the main reading room of Fuld Hall on the campus of the Institute for Advanced

Study in Princeton. Famed for housing the office of Albert Einstein, Fuld Hall is a redbrick Georgian building with a cream-colored bell tower, making it the spitting image of Independence Hall. The genetically tweedy Professor Walzer, in his early seventies, had hair as gray as Einstein's but much straighter and more kempt.

In 1984, Professor Walzer, a left-leaning political theorist, published *Exodus and Revolution,* a pioneering reading of the Moses story that introduced an idea into the study of the Bible that electrified readers. Walzer's simple yet radical notion is that Moses was not merely a convenient example of how to execute a revolution. Moses *invented* the idea of revolution, at least as it's practiced in the Western world. "Since late medieval or early modern times," Walzer wrote, "there has existed in the West a characteristic way of thinking about political change, a pattern that we commonly impose upon events." That pattern, he said, is oppression, liberation, social contract, political struggle, new society. "This isn't a story told everywhere; it isn't a universal pattern; it belongs to the West, more particularly to Jews and Christians in the West; and its source, its original version, is the Exodus of Israel from Egypt."

A near-perfect example of that revolution occurred in America. In both cases, the moment of liberation—when the Israelites cross the Red Sea; when the Americans win the war—is not a moment of genuine freedom, Walzer argues. The newly freed slaves remain trapped in a web of servility; they are passive, weighed down by oppression, frightened. They have the misplaced notion that freedom means lack of responsibility. "The childish and irresponsible slave or subject is free in ways the republican citizen can never be."

The solution, Walzer puts forth, is to voluntarily commit oneself to a new form of bondage. To *reenslave oneself.* For the Israelites, this means accepting the law handed down to Moses on Mount Sinai. For the Americans, this means ratifying a new federal compact. The former victims could become free "only insofar as they accepted the discipline of freedom; the obligation to live up to a common standard and to take responsibility for their own actions." The covenant, in other words, is the linchpin of freedom. The two pillars of the Moses story—freedom and law—have been present in America since the Pilgrims were reconfirmed in America's founding decade.

I asked Dr. Walzer why the moment of emancipation is not the moment of freedom, especially because everybody believes it to be so.

"But disappointment is built into the story," he said. "The slavishness of the people. The yearning to go back to Egypt, the golden calf. It's part of the extraordinary realism of the biblical writers. They understand that there's going to be backsliding.

"Lawlessness," he continued, "is the most radical notion of freedom, but that's not a version that's compatible with any form of a common life. You might say the Israelites have no common life between leaving Egypt and Sinai. You have a group of freed slaves, with some collective memory, but without a sense of society until they assume the burden of the commandments."

I mentioned that the moment of covenant seems conservative, compared with the radical moment of liberation.

"Rousseau describes freedom as giving the law to yourself," he said. "And that's what supposedly happens at Sinai. When Moses comes down from the mountain, the people say, 'All that the Lord has spoken we will do.' That's when they become a free society. They had been Pharaoh's slaves, and now they are God's servants. In biblical Hebrew, the same word, *ebed*, is used to describe the Israelites' relationship to Pharaoh and later their relationship to God. There's a kind of bondage in freedom."

"So if that's the key moment," I said, "why is that the least cele-brated part of the story? At Passover we celebrate the crossing of the Red Sea. In America we celebrate the Fourth of July. The mo-ment of covenant is overlooked."

"Right, though in the Jewish calendar there's Shavuot"—the summer holiday that marks the giving of the Torah to Moses—"and the Constitution does take on a kind of sacred character, even if there isn't some ritual celebration of its ratification. But there should be."

"The heart of your argument," I said, "is that the Exodus is not just a model of revolution; it is a causer of revolution. If that's the case, is the Exodus a causer of America?"

"It's certainly an inspiration," he said. "It's clear to me there was an enormous excitement in reenacting the story. That feeling of being on God's side can be dangerous, as we've seen recently in American foreign policy, and as we saw with early-American texts that treat the Indians like idolaters and tried to exterminate them. But it's clear to me the Exodus was a powerful player."

"So understanding that the story can be used for good and bad, when we look back at the founding moment are we supposed to celebrate it every year, or are we supposed to be wary?"

He chuckled. "You better be wary of it, but that's probably not a reason for refusing to cheer."

AT TEN O'CLOCK on the morning of Thursday, December 12, 1799, George Washington left his home in Mount Vernon, where he was enjoying his retirement from the presidency, and rode out to review his estate. The weather darkened, from rain to sleet to slush. He remained exposed for five hours, and was so late returning that he went to dinner in wet clothes, rather than keep his guests waiting. The next day, the sixty-seven-year-old general complained of a sore throat and nausea but still ventured out into the snow to mark trees for removal. That evening he retired to his office refusing medicine, saying of his condition that he preferred to "let it go as it came." When his wife, Martha, chided him for working late, he replied, "You well know that through a long life it has been my unrivaled rule never to put off till the morrow the duties which should be performed today."

Washington's condition worsened overnight, and doctors were summoned. Unable to speak, he was fed a mixture of molasses, vinegar, and butter and became convulsive trying to swallow it. He was given vinegar and tea to gargle but almost suffocated. His doctors aggravated the situation by following medical custom and opening veins to bleed him, removing a total of five pints of blood. "I am dying, sir, but am not afraid to die," he told his doctor. Medical historians now believe he suffered from acute epiglottitis, a rapidly progressing infection at the base of the tongue that can become fatal when swelling closes off air passages. The disease, which is treatable with antibiotics, is considered an atrociously painful way to expire.

At four-thirty that Saturday afternoon, December 14, Washington had Martha summon his will, which, among other requests, freed his slaves (though not hers). Around 10 P.M. he experienced a respite. He asked that his corpse be kept for three days before being interred, a request that some consider a harkening back to fears that Jesus may have been buried alive. No preacher was summoned to Washington's side. Before eleven, he uttered his last words, "'Tis well," and his hand fell to his side. "'Tis well," Martha echoed. "I have no more trials to pass through. I shall follow him soon."

The Apotheosis of Washington, depicting the deceased president, supported by Father Time, being conducted heavenward by an angel, leaving below symbols of the American republic. Print by John James Barralet, 1800. *(Courtesy of The Mount Vernon Ladies' Association)*

Washington's will stated his express desire that his corpse "be interred in a private manner, without parade, or funeral oration." His modest request, like so many before it, went ignored. Washington's Masonic lodge in Alexandria was invited to make arrangements for a funeral march. At 3 P.M. the following Wednesday a procession set off from Mount Vernon consisting of cavalry, foot soldiers, and a military band. The general's steed walked with an empty saddle. His body was carried to a small tomb on a bluff below the mansion. The Reverend James Muir performed an Episcopal burial ceremony and members of the lodge performed Masonic burial rituals. Eleven artillery rounds were fired over the Potomac, a veil was lifted over Washington's face, and the first president of the United States was buried, Reverend Muir wrote, as "the sun was setting."

For all the dignity of this ceremony, it created a number of challenges. The new country had never lost a man of such stature, and the public craved communal bereavement. Newspapers printed special editions with black borders, women purchased commemorative jewelry, men wore black armbands. Grief was so widespread that merchants complained of shortages of black fabric as late as the following July. But the focal point of the public commemoration was a series of mock funerals. The first was held in the nation's capital, Philadelphia, on December 26. The morning began with cannon fire and was followed by a long procession of exactly the kind Washington had feared, featuring a riderless horse with an empty saddle, holsters and pistols dangling at its side, and boots reversed in the stirrups. The horse's head was festooned with black and white feathers; an American eagle was displayed on its breast. Pallbearers carried an empty bier, and Congressman Henry Lee delivered his famous valediction: "First in war, first in peace, and first in the hearts of his countrymen."

In the coming months, city after city held similar faux funerals.

Four hundred forty orations were given, many of which were published. Of those, 346 survive. Robert Hay of Marquette University
surveyed the existing eulogies in 1969 and concluded that the common perception that they drew largely on classical references was
false. "Page for page, religious themes far outnumber classical
themes," he wrote. Specifically, mourners drew on themes from the
Hebrew Bible. A study of references concluded that of the 120 biblical texts used in discourses, only 7 came from the New Testament,
and of those, 4 were references to Old Testament characters. One
figure was mentioned above all others. "Washington was compared
favorably to all the outstanding biblical, classical, and modern heroes," Hay writes, "but no analogy was so well developed as the
contention that the departed leader had truly been a Moses for
America." As many as two-thirds made this comparison.

Far from passing references to Moses, many of these orations
included extensive comparisons between the "first conductor of the
Jewish nation" and the "leader and father of the American nation."
Some went on for dozens of pages arguing that Washington "has
been the same to us, as Moses was to the Children of Israel." The
single biggest theme was that both men had been commissioned by
God. "Kind Heaven," one orator said, "pitying the servile condition
of our American Israel, gave us a second Moses, who should (under
God) be our future deliverer from the bondage and tyranny of
haughty Britain." Orations compared the births of both men, pointing out that Moses was born in Goshen, "one of the best provinces"
of Egypt, while Washington was born in Virginia, "well known for
its profusion and wealth." One preacher even argued that both men
had been mama's boys. As a baby, Moses was hidden by his mother
for three months, while "the future hero of AMERICA," fatherless
since age ten, was destined for a future of lax morals on a British

naval man-of-war. "But fortunately for himself, and for the world, he was soon released from that corrupting, hazardous employment by the earnest solicitations of his affectionate mother." Providence "snatched him from the brink of ruin, in almost as singular a manner as he did the Hebrew child."

The orations naturally focused on the parallels between the Israelites' deliverance from Egypt and the Americans' emancipation from Britain. Both Moses and Washington, eulogizers insisted, were trained in the art of war, were roughly the same age when they led their people to freedom, and conducted similar numbers to freedom. The age issue is a canard, as Moses dies forty years after the Exodus at age 120, but the population comparison is more apt. The population of the United States in 1776 was between 2.5 and 3 million, while Exodus says Moses led 600,000 men to freedom, which with women and children could easily reach the same number. But orators were more interested in poetry than mathematics. "Moses led the Israelites through the Red Sea; has not Washington conducted the Americans thro' seas of blood?" As one minister told the Masonic lodge in Cooperstown, New York, "He who had commanded Moses at the Red Sea, also inspired Washington on the banks of the Delaware."

The most frequently cited comparison was also the most problematic: the deaths of the two leaders. Moses, of course, is denied entry into the Promised Land. After a "face to face" meeting with God on Mount Nebo, he dies in the wilderness and is buried in an unmarked grave. How could Washington be compared to Moses in this regard, considering that he actually led his people into the Promised Land?

One orator offered a twist by explaining that both men were stopped just short of their respective *capitals*, invoking Washington, D.C., then under construction. "A few steps more & the Israelitish nation would have pitched their government in Canaan. A few steps more and the American nation would have pitched their government in the City of Washington." But others suggested that the difference in their deaths suggests that Washington was actually superior to his Israelite predecessor. "Moses conducted the Israelites in sight of the promised land; but, Washington had done more, he has put the Americans in full possession." One eulogizer in Massachusetts went even further, calling Moses "the Washington of Israel."

At the end of America's second century, the death of George Washington provided the country with yet another opportunity to publicly reaffirm the connection between its own destiny and the fate of the Israelites in the Bible. At a time when the country was involved in a naval war with Napoléon and a domestic political showdown between Whigs and Federalists, the mourning of Washington offered a rare moment of national renewal when anxious Americans could reassure themselves that they were still God's chosen people. If God had sent them a second Moses, surely he would uphold his end of the covenant and continue to bless the United States.

And while many of the comparisons between the two deliverers might have been stretched to make a point, one parallel between the two men is striking. Biblical Israel and God's New Israel were formed on the twin shoulders of liberation and law. In both cases, one man was present at both moments. Both men had the unusual combination of skills—leadership and humility, fortitude and diplomacy—that could serve them well in dramatic moments of confrontation as well as years of slowly building a people. Beloved founders, both could have clung to power but resisted the temptation to turn their nations into monarchies. Reticent speakers, both left behind some of the most quoted words ever spoken.

But for all their similarities, there was one enormous difference that separated them, and it's a chasm that few people mentioned in the public orations around Washington's death. Washington may have led his people from slavery to freedom, but he left a huge population living amidst the chosen people who were still being held as slaves. Somehow God's New Israel, having just left Egypt, had become God's New Egypt. If America was going to fulfill its promise in the century after its great liberator died, it first had to confront its own moral paradox and raise up a new kind of Moses.

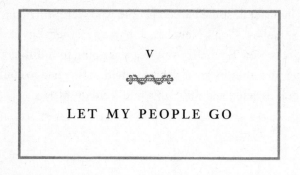

V

LET MY PEOPLE GO

T HE MUD ALONG the Ohio River has memory. Just beneath the storied town of Ripley, the dark, glutinous sludge catches everything from driftwood to tractor tires to deer antlers. Standing in the guck just after eleven o'clock on a Tuesday night in late autumn, I hear the steady ripple of crickets and birds. A sycamore hangs over the water. The bank is so steep here that I can barely see the houses along Front Street. The wind stings my face, and the weather feels like it's changing. Winter is coming, the time of year when ice flows along the shore and, on occasion, the river freezes solid. In the decades before the Civil War, these months were the time when shadowy figures emerged from the brush on the Kentucky side and made their way across the slippery surface into the free state of Ohio. For millions of Africans enslaved in the South, Ohio was the Promised Land. And the Ohio River was the Jordan. As one slave spiritual promised:

I'll meet you in the mornin',
Safe in de promised land,
On the other side of the Jordan,
Boun' for de promised land.

Ripley, in the southwest corner of the state, sits on the most famous bend of the Ohio and is the town some believe is the home
alluded to in the spiritual "Swing Low, Sweet Chariot" (*"Comin' for to*
carry me home"). Ripley also was a focal point in the use of Moses
in antebellum America. If Moses was a unifying presence during
the Revolutionary era, a generation later he got dragged into the
issue that most divided the country. Moses was born a slave. Later he
gave up the comforts of wealth to slay a wicked overseer. And still
later, he walked away from a peaceful life with his wife and son to
confront the greatest slave master who ever lived.

For slaves, Moses was more than just a figure in the Bible. He became a leader of the emerging black nation within the nation. And he
provided the blueprint for the famed living metaphor of nineteenth-
century America, the Underground Railroad. The generation-long
struggle to shuttle slaves from the South to the North is an enticing
example of American ideals and pluck. But mostly it's a human story,
of individuals, many with no historic connection to the Bible, who
took the central story of that book and transformed it into a narrative
of hope. The Founding Fathers chose the Exodus as their theme in an
attempt to make their lives better. The slaves needed it to make their
lives worth living.

God did say to Moses one day
Say, Moses, go to Egypt land,
And tell him to let my people go.

The river sounds fade as I reach the top of the bank, and the fetid smell of the mud gives way to the gentle perfume of fresh-cut grass and chrysanthemums on the porch. The wooden town houses and brick mansions that line the river are from bygone eras, Georgian, Victorian, Queen Anne. Some have lace curtains in the windows. A few have candles. I see a gas lantern. The houses remind me of patrons, dressed up in costumes from different decades, sitting in box seats overlooking the theater of the river. A light on one of the porches suddenly flashes on, and I wonder if people might begin to wonder why I'm prowling around here near midnight.

My plan is to re-create one of the more daring stretches of the

Ripley, from the Kentucky side of the Ohio.

Ripley, Ohio, as depicted in a nineteenth-century woodcut, from the Kentucky side of the Ohio River. The Rankin House can be seen at the top of the hill, overlooking the town. Originally published in 1847. (*Courtesy of The Union Township Public Library, Ripley, Ohio*)

Underground Railroad, by tiptoeing through the residences along the Ohio, slipping in between the shops of Main Street, then climbing straight up a tree-shrouded ridge to the safe house that was known across a dozen states from 1829 to 1860 for the beacon that shone in its window and its open door to fugitive slaves. But a few steps in and I'm already feeling nervous. I'm not illegal. No bounty hunters are chasing me. I'm carrying a cell phone, a BlackBerry, and a spare hundred-dollar bill to bail my way out of trouble, if necessary. Yet still I'm scared.

I have been told that alleys run in between the houses of Front Street, perpendicular to the river. They are overgrown and dark, and I'm trying to figure out which one is safe. I come across a sign that marks the birthplace of Senator Alexander Campbell, "doctor, merchant, and early anti-slavery leader." Campbell was a Virginian who moved to Ohio in 1803, freed his slaves, and served as U.S. senator. "He's considered one of the pioneers of the abolitionist movement," the sign says. If that's the case, he must have helped a fleeing victim or two. I choose the alley alongside his house.

Before I've gone fifty yards a dog starts howling. I jump back. The dog races to the fence that separates us and follows me up the alley, leaping and snapping across the barbed wire. I pick up my pace. Suddenly a light switches on. I've been on dry ground for less than ten minutes, and already I've made what would have been a catastrophic mistake. My freedom would have ended here.

I scoot out of view and soon come to a dirt road and a small barn. Each house has a small backyard and some kind of shed, cabin, or storage facility, perfect for stashing fugitives. The next paved road I come to is Main Street, Route 52, part of the Ohio River Scenic Byway that stretches from Cairo, Illinois, to Ohio's West Virginia border. In between it passes towns with names like Friendship, Utopia, and Rural. I wait beside the Ripley Museum until the few cars pass, then scurry across the street, in between the Church of the Nazarene and the Masonic lodge. Soon I come to the Presbyterian church that housed the pulpit of John Rankin, the pioneering abolitionist. His restored home is my destination.

Behind the church, I climb a small wall and find myself in an open yard. I think it's public property, but I'm not sure. Another dog barks as an American flag flutters in the breeze. A woman steps outside and invites her barking dog into the house. "Does everybody in Ripley have a dog?" I wonder. Ah, no. There's someone with a cat. I begin my hunt for the wooden stairs that will take me to the top of the hill.

For all the self-congratulation about America being God's New Israel, a bit of Old Egypt—slavery—was built into the country from its inception. The first twenty African slaves were sold to Jamestown settlers in 1619. Even before the Pilgrims spoke of breaking away from the English pharaoh, real slaves in the colonies were groaning under more immediate hardships. The African slaves became part of a larger network of enslaved Indians and even European whites, who were kidnapped and shipped to the colonies. But as rice and tobacco farming expanded in the colonies, the number of African slaves exploded, reaching 44 percent of the population of Virginia by 1750 and 61 percent of South Carolina. The "Negro Business," wrote Joseph Clay of Savannah, "is to the Trade of the Country as the Soul is to the Body." By 1790, the number of slaves living in the United States was 697,647, making up 17 percent of the population.

Few whites had illusions about the horrors of slavery. Thomas Jefferson called the institution a "hideous evil" and chastised freedom fighters "who can endure toil, famine, stripes [lashes], imprisonment, or death itself" fighting for their own liberty, but who still impose bondage "one hour of which is fraught with more misery than ages of that which he rose in rebellion to oppose." Yet Jefferson kept slaves himself, and believed that black Africans were inferior and had a "strong disagreeable odor." He even fathered children with his slave Sally Hemings.

Others, though, put their distaste into action. As early as 1641, Massachusetts forbade slavery, except for prisoners of war. By the 1780s, Quakers formed a committee for banning the "execrable traffic" of slaves. Benjamin Franklin, once a buyer and seller of slaves, became an abolitionist. A Vermont judge wrote that he would accept one person's ownership of another only with a "bill of sale from God Almighty." By the end of the eighteenth century, Delaware, Virginia, Maryland, the Carolinas, and Georgia all banned the importation of African slaves, while most northern states passed laws mandating gradual emancipation. The movement to undermine the institution was beginning to gain momentum.

I REACH THE base of Rankin Hill, where some teenagers are riding bikes. I can't believe they are out at this hour. I walk the length of the road and reach a dead end, so I double back, past the dogs and the cat, to the house with the American flag. I spot what appears to be a path and follow it. Suddenly trees envelop me. As I begin making my way up a slope, the sound of grasshoppers fills my ears and I'm moving much more slowly. I come to a patch of dead leaves, and my every step is incredibly loud. A shriek of foliage. "Where are the stairs?" I wonder.

At the end of a patch of dirt and mulch, I spot the hint of a wooden structure. I'm under a full canopy in complete darkness. This is totally foolish and a tad dicey, I tell myself. Assuming these are the stairs to the Rankin House, I begin to climb, but the treads haven't been repaired in years and some splinter beneath my shoes. Then suddenly the stairs end, and I'm back in roots and mud. I'm breathing heavily now. If anyone had been anticipating fugitives, this is surely where they would have waited. The only way to proceed is on all fours. My hands are riddled with splinters. Sweat drips into my eyes. Finally I come to a second set of stairs and start to climb, counting *one, two, three.* These steps are firmer under my feet.

Ripley, Ohio, is located 250 miles south of the Canadian border in a stretch of hilly woodlands once known as the Imperial Forest. With its plum river location, Ripley emerged as an economic powerhouse in the early 1800s. It became so wealthy that during the panic of 1837, the town sent money to help bail out New York banks. Yet Ripley became best known as ground zero in the antislavery movement, the "hell hole of abolition."

For all the hand wringing over slavery, the institution's pivotal role in the nation's economy only expanded in the nineteenth century with the growth of cotton as a major cash crop. Importing slaves was banned in 1808, but the existing population ballooned, more than doubling to two million by 1830, then doubling again by the Civil War. Though the Underground Railroad was neither unified nor centralized, it was the most comprehensive attempt to undermine this behemoth and was the greatest movement of civil disobedience since the Revolution. Modern estimates suggest that in the six decades after 1800, between 100,000 and 150,000 slaves received assistance from the network.

John Rankin was Ripley's most controversial resident and Ohio's main conductor. One scholar calls him a "moral entrepreneur," who brilliantly mined the hearts and minds of southern Ohio and molded them into an underground army. A native of Tennessee, Rankin was raised a strict Calvinist but was transformed by the revivals of the Second Great Awakening that reached across the Appalachians in

The Rankin Family, 1872: the Reverend John Rankin is seated in the center of the bottom row; his son, John, Jr., is standing immediately behind his father's right shoulder. *(Courtesy of The Union Township Public Library, Ripley, Ohio)*

1802 and 1803. "A wonderful nervous affection pervaded the meetings," Rankin wrote. "Some would tremble as if terribly frightened; some would have violent twitching and jerking; some would fall down suddenly as if breathless and lie for hours."

Rankin reacted by reading and rereading the Bible, committing large parts of it to memory. He became a minister but was pushed out of the South for using the Bible to teach "incendiary ideas" about slavery. On New Year's Eve 1822, Rankin, along with his wife, three sons, and the family's last remaining fifty dollars, boarded two skiffs and crossed the icy Ohio to Ripley. With a population of 421,

Ripley had not yet experienced the prosperity it would soon enjoy, and Rankin remained restless. "Something good would eventually come from Ripley," his wife assured him. That something came two years later in a letter Rankin received from his brother Thomas, who announced that he had come into money and purchased slaves. Rankin was disgusted and poured out his ire in a series of twenty-one letters over the next thirteen months. The letters were later printed in the Ripley *Castigator* and made their way to the man who became the country's leading abolitionist. William Lloyd Garrison credited them with his entry into the movement and reprinted them in the *Liberator*. Rankin's letters were eventually published in a book that went through eighteen different editions.

In his passionate, meticulous diatribes, Rankin attacked every known argument in favor of slavery. His first letter begins, "I consider involuntary slavery a never failing fountain of the grossest immorality, and one of the deepest sources of human misery." In coming letters, he lambastes the notion that God had designed blacks for servitude. He argues that the Israelites' slavery in Egypt was state-sponsored service and thus less heinous than owning human chattel. "When the slavery in Egypt is viewed, even in its worst forms, it does not appear to equal in cruelty that which exists among us." He twice quotes Exodus 11: "He that stealeth a man and selleth him . . . shall surely be put to death." And he adds a quotation from Deuteronomy 23: "Thou shall not deliver unto his master the servant which is escaped." In 1827, Thomas Rankin yielded to his brother's arguments and freed his slaves. Soon afterward, Thomas moved to Ohio and joined the Underground Railroad.

In 1829, John Rankin bought sixty-five-and-a-half acres of thickly forested land on a hill 540 feet above Ripley. On either side were valleys and behind him the Appalachian foothills. From his front door, Rankin could see nearly five miles of the Ohio River and well into Kentucky. In their modest, one-story house, Rankin and his wife raised at least twenty-two children, including thirteen of their own, plus others from their siblings and friends. To alert slaves that they would be welcomed, the Rankins placed a lantern in the front window every night, making it visible deep into slave territory. One slave referred to it as a "big lighthouse in his yard" and said, "It always meant freedom for a slave if he could get to this light."

In the coming decades, Ripley became a hotbed of conflict between abolitionists and slave catchers. "This was a period when men went armed with pistol and knife and used them on the least provocation," wrote John Parker, a mulatto slave who bought his freedom in 1845 and moved to Ripley in 1848. "When under cover of night the uncertain steps of slaves were heard quietly seeking their friends. When the mornings brought strange rumors of street encounters the night before, but daylight showed no evidence of the fray." Parker claimed to have aided 315 slaves in their quest for freedom. In his autobiography, he tells of numerous trips across the Ohio to help families cross. He observed a slave leave a skiff so a fellow passenger's husband could board, only to be captured moments later, "a heroic victim of his own unselfishness." He ferried women wearing four dresses and three pairs of underwear who almost drowned when they tripped on the lips of their mistresses' stolen hoop skirts and fell into the water. And he made a daring run into the bedroom of the master of a frantic couple whose baby was being held hostage. "Peeping around the foot of the bed, I saw a bundle lying close to the edge. Without waiting to see what it was, I dragged it toward me, and getting a firm hold pulled it off the bed. As I did there was a creak of the bedsprings and the next moment the room was in darkness. There was no cause for secrecy now, so I jumped to my feet and rushed to the door."

Once in Ohio, the slaves were taken to safe houses, then usually sent up the hill to the Rankin house, or similar places, where they were clothed, fed, then taken to subsequent towns, often that same night. "There would be a knock on the door," explained town historian Betty Campbell, whose great-great-great-grandfather was Ripley's first resident and whose husband is descended from Senator Alexander Campbell. "The Rankins would take the fugitives in, and their goal was to get them out of there that same night. Often one of the Rankin boys would lead them over the hills. And of course the Rankins had to be back before daylight so nothing would look amiss." If the runaways arrived too late, the family hid them in the barn, so the Rankins could plausibly deny knowledge of how they got there. Historians have identified one hundred such "stops" on the Underground Railroad in the Buckeye State alone. Ripley was stop number one.

The most famous person to make the flight across the Ohio to Ripley, and, indirectly, one of the more influential Americans of the nineteenth century, was a slave girl called Eliza who crossed on a brutally cold night in February 1838. "All the boys in town had been down on the slow ice that very afternoon," John Rankin remembered. "They knew the ice was rotten, with air holes and cracks extending almost across the river." Eliza was a mulatto with a two-year-old baby who was thought to have been fathered by her overseer. Upon hearing that her master planned to sell her child, Eliza took off north with the baby. An elderly white man who lived along the river advised her against crossing because the ice was too soft. She was ready to turn back when they heard the baying of dogs pursuing her. Relenting, the man gave her a woolen shawl to protect her child and pulled off a wooden rail from his fence for her to support herself should she fall through the ice.

Eliza hurried down the bank and onto the frozen river just as the

Eliza crossing the Ohio River, from a poster of a staged production of Harriet Beecher Stowe's *Uncle Tom's Cabin*, created by W. J. Morgan & Co. Lith., Cleveland, Ohio, 1881. *(Courtesy of The Library of Congress)*

dogs burst into the open. With her pursuers watching from Kentucky and bounty hunters eyeing her from Ohio, she placed her foot on a soft spot of ice and plunged into the frigid water, managing barely to heave her baby to safety on some solid ice. The rail worked, caught the ice, and saved her from sinking to the bottom. Grasping desperately in the darkness for her child, who had nearly come unwrapped from the shawl, Eliza rebundled the baby, pulled herself to the surface, took another step, and promptly broke through the ice again, splashing into the water. Once more she tossed the baby to refuge. She scurried to her feet, claimed her baby, then fell yet again into the water. Three times she fell through the ice that night; three times the rail saved her life. Finally she reached the Ohio side, where a bounty hunter, Chancey Shaw, was waiting. He grabbed her by the shoulder. A fugitive like Eliza was worth five hundred dollars, with more for the enslaved infant. But Shaw had been watching the horrifying scene unfold on the river. "Any woman who crossed that river carrying her baby has won her freedom," he told her. Then he sent her up the stairs to Rankin's light. "No nigger was ever caught that got to his house," Shaw said.

An hour later, warming in front of a fire, Eliza told her story to John Rankin. A year after that, Rankin was visiting one of his brothers in Cincinnati. He called upon an old friend, Calvin Stowe, a professor of biblical studies. One of the people present as Rankin retold the story was Stowe's wife. "Terrible!" she said upon hearing the tale. "How terrible!" Harriet Beecher Stowe was so moved by Eliza's story that she retold it as part of her novel *Uncle Tom's Cabin*, which became the best-selling book of the nineteenth century and the most influential piece of antislavery literature ever published. Eliza electrified the public and was quickly memorialized in paintings, woodcuts, and stage productions across the country, becoming the public face of the unbreakable humanity of the slaves. As Rankin's son, John junior, later recalled: "Strange how this unknown fugitive mother figured into the history of this country."

AS THE NUMBER of stairs nears one hundred, I break through the overhanging trees and into the open air. The moon makes the sky seem as iridescent as Times Square. My heart is pounding, and I enter an open meadow at the top of the hill. Grass slopes up from the tree line to a destination I can't quite see. I notice a stone path and some fruit trees that have lost their leaves. And at the top: a small redbrick house with white trim that reminds me of a one-room schoolhouse. It has two chimneys, two windows, two columns, and a white door. A candle is burning in one of the windows. I've reached the end of the climb. I've made it to the light in the window.

I settle onto the front stoop and let my body collect itself. A train rumbles by on the Kentucky side, and I can't believe how loud it is. Sounds carry for several states around here. I see a few cars on the Ohio River Scenic Byway, as well as a bicycle. A barge is moving up-river. From Rankin Hill, the Ohio River valley seems awash in transportation. Maybe that's why the first slaves who fled north to freedom were described as having disappeared so quickly they must have traveled on an "underground road." Later, with the arrival of steam locomotives, the phrase was replaced with *railroad* and the legendary route had its name. It occurred to me that many of the storied paths in American history run from east to west—Daniel Boone, Lewis and Clark, the Mason-Dixon line, the Oregon Trail, the Transcontinental Railroad. The Underground Railroad was one of the rare paths that ran south-north, as if a counterculture was fighting the natural thrust of American history.

I sat quietly for a few minutes and let my heart quiet down. I began to hear the sound track of the hill—the grasshoppers, a crow, an animal darting across some dried twigs. For a second I thought I heard someone singing. *When the sun comes back, and the first quail calls, / Follow the drinkin' gourd.* I chuckled, but the sound didn't go away. If anything, the deep, bass voice seemed to be getting closer. It reminded me of "Ol' Man River" from *Show Boat.*

> *For the old man is waiting*
> *For to carry you to freedom*
> *If you follow the drinkin' gourd.*

Maybe someone had left a CD on inside Rankin House.

Then suddenly a figure emerged from the side of the house and stood in shadow just a few feet in front of me. I scrambled to my feet and nearly tripped. He was bigger than me in every direction and wore a printed African shirt with white cowry shells and black stripes. He had a full white beard. He *looked* like Joe, who sings "Ol' Man River," or at least Jim from *Huck Finn,* sprung from captivity, with a few decades of home cooking inside him. "Welcome to the Promised Land, son," he said. I thought I recognized the voice.

"Jerry Gore!?" I said.

He let forth a belly laugh that could be heard halfway to Mississippi.

"Good God, you scared me to death!" I said.

"Lawd, I hope so," he said. "White boy like you tryin' to walk in my shoes." Then he resumed his song.

> *"The riverbank will make a very good road,*
> *The dead trees show you the way.*

Left food, peg foot travelin' on,
Follow the drinkin' gourd."

He gave me a hug. Jerry Gore is something of a self-appointed guardian of the Underground Railroad. A onetime professor at Morehead State in Kentucky and a great-grandson of a fugitive slave, Jerry is a collector of slave artifacts, the administrator of a small museum in nearby Maysville, Kentucky, and a walking encyclopedia of plantation life. But he's also elusive. For weeks I had been trying to confirm a meeting for the following morning. His answering machine was charming; on it he speaks like a Zulu chieftain, but I had grown tired of hearing it. In my last message I said I was going to make the trek up Rankin Hill around midnight. No one rides these rails today without a bit of conducting from Jerry Gore.

We sat on the stoop, and I asked him why every conversation about the Underground Railroad seems to end with somebody singing. He answered with a brief history lesson. The first enslaved Africans who were shipped to America brought with them their own religious traditions. For some it was Islam; for others Christianity. But most brought tribal customs and traditional gods. Once they arrived in America, many slaves were forcefully exposed to the Bible. White owners sometimes justified slavery by telling themselves they were doing the pagan Africans a favor by converting them to Christianity.

"The key to making a slave is stripping away the enslaved person's culture," Jerry said. "Ban their religion. Deny their dress. Take away their names. If you remove the essential parts of a person's culture, you can make that person do what you want."

"So was teaching the slaves Christianity an attempt to control them?"

"Very much so. The controlling part is that I'm trying to convince you that my God is the real God. In the African perspective, God is to be loved. In the European perspective, God is to be feared. You don't want to do anything that will incur the wrath of God. So if I'm your slave, and you can teach me to fear your God, then that is a form of control." In Kentucky, he said, whites built special churches where they took their slaves on Sunday mornings. The slaves were sent up ladders to special balconies—Jerry called them "nigger pews"—then the ladders were removed so they couldn't escape. "At least it's the best view!" he joked.

But the whites didn't anticipate that the slaves would take the Christian stories, mix them with African traditions, and create a potent religious vernacular. They applied African ecstatic behavior to the staid customs of Protestantism. They brought in rhythmic clapping, ring dancing, call-and-response. They integrated the body into worship, something frowned on by most Christians. By the early 1800s, when the supply of native-born Africans was cut off, this hybrid, Africanized Christianity had become the dominant cultural language in slave communities across the country. And the Bible became central to the slave experience.

"What did slaves hear about?" Jerry said. "They didn't hear news from the newspaper. Many of those men and women couldn't read. They heard news from Bible stories. And they looked at those stories and said, 'Wow. It says all God's children should be free. You've got Joshua fightin' the battle of Jericho. Moses partin' the Red Sea. Slavery may be hell, but there's still a miracle chance that I might be free.'"

"So they had a choice," I said. "Either ignore the Bible, or turn it into their own story."

"That's what the African did. He turned the Bible into his own salvation history. Even though things are terrible now, it's still gonna be all right." Jerry closed his eyes and began to sing.

> "Hold on, just a little while longer.
> Hold on, just a little bit longer.
> Everything's gonna be all right."

Or a song like:

> "I've never been to heaven
> But I've been told
> Try'n-a make heaven my home
> That the streets up there
> Are paved with gold
> Try'n-a make heaven my home."

He opened his eyes and looked back at me. "That's a coded song," he said. "It's a call to the slaves saying, 'There's a conductor here, and I'm goin' the next day.'"

Songs were not the only source of codes for the Underground Railroad. Along routes used by runaway slaves, conductors would drive nails into trees at forks in the road. The nails would be precisely three and a half feet above the ground and affixed to the right side of the tree if the right fork was to be taken, the left side for the reverse. The painted black coachmen used as hitching posts sometimes doubled as signposts. If the coachman's lantern was lighted, fugitives could consider the home a safe house; if not, they should keep running. Some scholars believe quilts were also full of codes and were hung over fence posts to guide fleeing slaves. Five square knots would indicate that a slave should travel a certain distance to a safe house. The carpenter's wheel pattern evoked Jesus and, if placed in a certain quadrant of the quilt, told the slave to head in that direction.

But the most comprehensive use of codes was in the rich canon of slave spirituals. Slave songs, as they were known, grew out of the African tradition known as the "shout," in which people would gather in a circle, stamp and clap in a carefully choreographed call-and-response. The term "spiritual" was first applied in 1909 on Saint Catherine's Island, Georgia, about fifty miles south of Savannah. As with slave religion in general, practitioners replaced African gods with biblical figures to create an entirely new form. Spirituals were potent because to the naked ear, that is, the white overseers, the songs were about reaching heavenly redemption. *Great! They're worshiping our God!* But to the slaves, the spirituals also evoked a this-worldly liberation. As Frederick Douglass, the most famous former slave in America, wrote of his own escape, when he and his fellow runaways sang *O Canaan, sweet Canaan, / I am bound for the land of Canaan,* the words had double meaning. To the outside "it meant the expectations of a speedy summons to a world of spirits, but on the lips of our company it simply meant a speedy pilgrimage to a free state, and deliverance from all the evils and dangers of slavery."

The story of the Israelites' escape from slavery and flight to freedom became the single greatest motif of slave spirituals. The Exodus was the sound track of the Underground Railroad. A partial list of titles includes: "Didn't Ole Pharaoh Get Lost [in the Red Sea]," "Turn Back Pharaoh's Army," and "I Am Bound for the Promised Land." Slave spirituals demonized the pharaoh and glorified Canaan.

> *There was a wicked man,*
> *He kept them children in Egypt land.*
> *Canaan land is the land for me.*

And they heralded the man who led the Israelites to freedom. *De rough, rocky road what Moses done travel, / I's bound to carry my soul to de Lawd.*

Moses starred as the hero in many songs, particularly in what may be the most recognized slave spiritual of all, "Go Down, Moses," which Isabella Beecher Hooker, the half sister of Harriet Beecher Stowe, called "the Negro Marseillaise." In Washington, on Thanksgiving Day 1862, Harriet and her sister visited the barracks of fugitive slaves who had joined the Union forces and were celebrating their first Thanksgiving on free soil. After the blessing, the choir sang in jubilant call-and-response style the song "forbidden to them down South," Isabella wrote. The song uses as its refrain the words Moses says to Pharaoh in Exodus 5:1: "Thus says the Lord, the God of Israel: 'Let my people go.'"

> *When Israel was in Egypt Land,*
> *Let my people go;*
> *Oppressed so hard they could not stand,*
> *Let my people go.*

> *"Thus saith the Lord," bold Moses said,*
> *"Let my people go;*
> *If not, I'll smite your first-born dead,*
> *Let my people go!"*

> *Chorus:*
> *Go down, Moses,*
> *Way down in Egypt Land.*
> *Tell ol' Pharoah,*
> *Let my people go.*

The song, which some credit to Denmark Vesey, a free black in Charleston, South Carolina, continues for twenty-four verses. Like most spirituals, it compresses time, making the daring escape of the chosen people of Israel a model for the forgotten children of Africa. The last verse captures the moment of liberation.

> *What a beautiful morning that will be!*
> *O let my people go!*
> *When time breaks up in eternity,*
> *O let my people go!*

I asked Jerry Gore why Moses was so popular to the slaves.

"It goes back to what it means to be enslaved. Once somebody breaks your will, you can be made to do anything. But as long as your will is not broken, you can always resist. You can always hope. And as long as you have hope, you're human."

"But when you're singing to Moses," I said, "he was living in Egypt. He was traveling in the desert. It seems like long ago and far away."

"No, it's not. Because what Moses went through, you're going through. What you draw on is the analogy." He gestured to the home behind us. "When I was five years old, my mother brought me up here to the Rankin House," he said. "We climbed the steps you just walked up. We sat in this very spot. I was looking out at the green hills of Kentucky, and I was thinking about how my little feet hurt. And my mama told me the story of Moses. I had never heard it before."

"So what did you think?"

"That Moses must be somethin' special to have God talk to him like that!" he said. "You gotta understand, black folk look at systems. And the system is that Moses is part of God. He's a door. Not just a door to salvation but a door to living. You walk through Moses to get up this hill. You walk through Moses to get to this light." Then Jerry Gore began to sing.

"He delivered Daniel from de lion's den,
Jonah from the belly ob de whale,
and de Hebrew children from the fiery furnace,
and why not every man?"

The National Underground Railroad Freedom Center sits on the banks of the Ohio River in Cincinnati. On the second floor is an empty, two-story log cabin, a little bigger than a boxcar. It has four small windows and a red door and is the kind of house schoolchildren imagine as the birthplace of Abraham Lincoln. But it was a slave pen, where slaves were packed for days or months at a time, some chained to wrought-iron rings still visible on the rafters. Found in northern Kentucky, the pen housed slaves as they waited out price fluctuations in the market before being shipped down the Mississippi to auction sites in Natchez or New Orleans.

"The day we found this, I stepped in here and wept," said Carl Westmoreland. A descendant of slaves from Virginia, Westmoreland is a veteran of the civil rights movement, an urban planner, and the curator of the $110 million museum, which he helped found. As folksy as Jerry Gore was, Carl Westmoreland was genteel. Nearing seventy years of age, with pale brown skin dappled with freckles, he wore a black-and-white tweed jacket, a white shirt, and an air of taut authority that came from half a century of fighting inner-city battles. I came to see him to discuss how blacks in the nineteenth century transformed themselves from a population of slaves into a "black nation" and how much that process drew on the Israelites' experience in the desert.

"The first time I came here, I had the same emotional reaction as when I went to Auschwitz," Carl said. "It reminded me of a day back in 1943, when I was six years old. I was sitting in Miss Watt's Sunday-school class at Saint Simon's Episcopal Church, and we were talking about the Exodus. After Mass, we would join our parents at the parish house, and I said to Momma and Daddy, 'The same thing happened to the Jews is happening to us! Only for us, the white people are Pharaoh.'"

"You were six!" I said.

"I was a kid in short breeches, in an all-black town," he said, chuckling. "The only white people I knew were the nuns at Saint Simon's, and I didn't like them."

"So what did your parents say?"

"They just took it up. They talked to me as if I were a college freshman. My dad explained the parallels between the Jewish experience and the black experience. He talked about the atrocities going on in Europe. He said similar things were happening to us. He said if we weren't careful, they'd lock us up, too. Why did he do it? Because he wanted me to stay in church, and school, and he knew that the two were connected."

The idea that Africans in the United States might form a cultural tradition separate from whites began almost as early as the United States. From its inception, black nationalism was modeled to a large degree on Israelite nationalism. On January 1, 1808, Absalom Jones, the first African American priest in the Episcopal Church, delivered a sermon in Philadelphia celebrating the end of the transatlantic slave trade. He opened with a quotation from Exodus 3: "And the Lord said, I have surely seen the affliction of my people." Jones declared that if blacks hoped to become a chosen nation like Israel, they also had to subscribe to the ethical standards of the Israelites. He proposed five commandments for all blacks to follow, including remembering their enslavement, expressing gratitude to God, and conducting themselves in an honorable manner. Jones also suggested a festival of "publick thanksgiving" on January 1 to remember the "sufferings of our brethren and their deliverance." In addition, more such holidays came to be celebrated in black communities: July 4, the end of slavery in New York, and July 5, the day of emancipation in the West Indies. The beginnings of a rival calendar were being formed.

Orators at these black festivals often made the direct connection between the liberation of Israel and the emancipation of black America. Eddie Glaude, a professor at Princeton, examined hundreds of these speeches, as well as sermons, newspaper articles, and letters. As he concludes in his book *Exodus! Religion, Race, and Nation in Early Nineteenth-Century Black America,* by the 1840s, metaphors of the Exodus had become "the predominate political language of African Americans." "Exodus, in effect, was no longer the story of Israel," Glaude wrote, "but an account of African-American slavery and eventual deliverance—the taken-for-granted context for any discussion of slavery and freedom." The story had become what he calls "the covenant of Black America."

What's striking about the use of Exodus language in nineteenth-century black America is how closely it parallels what happened in Puritan New England in the seventeenth century and Revolutionary America in the eighteenth century. In all three cases, the Exodus first provides a language of chosenness for a beleaguered population, then a rhetoric of mission that emboldens the aggrieved people to strive for their own liberation, and then—in a part of the story I never fully appreciated before embarking on this journey—a rhetoric of control that allows the newly emancipated community to rein in any tendencies toward excess. The Puritans did this by imposing Mosaic-inspired laws across New England. Early Americans did this by crafting the Constitution.

African Americans attempted something similar by adopting an informal covenant for the new black nation that stressed faith, work, and education. As contraband slave Brother Thornton warned his fellow refugees in 1862, Egypt may be behind them, but the Promised Land was still far away. "There must be no looking back to Egypt," he said. "We must free ourselves from the shackles of sin, especially the sin of disbelief.... We must educate ourselves and our children." Here was the true power of Exodus. It helped create a new meta-narrative of what it means to be a nation: revolution, followed by covenant, together creating an adhesive community that is both supportive of ongoing change yet resistant to it as well. This ideal manages to balance both dissent and consensus at the same time. For African Americans, this narrative created a vision of a nation within a nation in which they would try not to overthrow the American Dream but to join it. For them, the Promised Land became a place in the middle class.

"There was a mistaken belief on the part of the Anglos," Carl Westmoreland said, "that because we couldn't read English, we were illiterate. Well, we couldn't read English, but we in our own cultures knew about social justice, we had measurements of ethical behavior and heroic behavior. And I don't know how much of the story of Exodus is mythical, but I know enough to know that it's true. And in our community that story resonated, and continues to resonate. I can talk about it on the corner with drug dealers, or in a bar with alcoholics, and it will stop them in their tracks because it says to them what it said to my dad, that there is opportunity available out there.

"We would get to the lines in the 1960s," he continued, "knowing we were going to get our asses whipped. And the kids would start singing,

> 'Ain't gonna let nobody turn me around!
> I'm gonna keep on a-walkin', keep on a-talkin',
> Marchin' down to freedom's land!'

I understand how Muslims decide they're gonna die because of the power of what they believe. And I believe now, as I believed then, that I was walking in the steps, in the blood, of the folks who experienced the Exodus."

"One of the hallmarks of the Exodus story in the Bible," I said, "is the covenant. When you look at African American history, a similar theme emerges. What does that idea mean to you?"

"When blacks came north, into lower Manhattan, Philadelphia, Boston, Baltimore, we weren't well received. The covenant was the creation of self-help institutions within the church, institutions that had strict demands on how you behaved. For example, my son went to Morehouse; his great-grandmother went to Spelman right out of slavery. With his last name, he was expected to go to college and abide by a strict code of behavior, which runs counter to the inner-city neighborhood in which he was conceived and raised. He wanted to drop out of Morehouse once, and I said, 'Westmoreland men don't drop out of college. You have to earn the right to carry my last name.' White America has no idea how the majority of us think, and we got it from the Exodus."

"So from your point of view, blacks coming out of slavery understood the full dimensions of Exodus. Not just 'We want to be free' but the idea that with freedom comes responsibility."

"All of this began with the black churches in the nineteenth century. The African Methodist Episcopal Church was one of the feared institutions of its time because of its demands. And it continually reminded people that the Jews went through a period of renewal, celebrating Passover and the pain of the past. Rather than saying the Exodus was the flight of a desperate people, they drew a moral parallel and turned the paradigm inside out. We were once a people of flight, and now we've become a people of shelter. Instead of sitting on your high horse, do what John Parker did, row back across the

Ohio, and bring more people to freedom. Parker was the *sixth-richest person in Ripley*. I've read the will of his banker! And Parker was obviously influenced by the central tenet of the Old Testament."

"So what is that tenet?"

"Freedom is the right to be free, and then the obligation to accept responsibility. If you don't understand that, then ugly stuff happens. And when you do understand that, you're prepared to meet the obligations straight-on."

JOAN SOUTHGATE HAS a rule: It may be rude to reveal a woman's age, but it isn't when that age is your own. Joan tells me minutes after meeting her in Cleveland that she was born in 1929. She says it in a voice rich with wisdom and warbled with a slight quiver—imagine Carol Channing reborn as a gospel singer—as we head out one morning to the last few of Ohio's one hundred Underground Railroad stations. Joan knows these sites well, because at age seventy-three, the grandmother of four, a retired African American, inner-city-school teacher, set out on a solo, 519-mile walk retracing the Underground Railroad through Ohio, Pennsylvania, New York, and Canada. She's a modern-day pilgrim, made even more appealing by her size, four feet nine.

"For some reason, I had really been thinking about slavery a lot," Joan said of the day she came up with the idea. "I was always eager and articulate as a student. I was a teacher's pet. But when slavery was the lesson, I was suddenly ashamed of the people I came from. Then one day a few years ago I was taking my usual, stay-healthy walk, and I kept thinking, 'Who were those amazing people who walked to freedom? How could they do it? And how should I praise them?'"

With the approval of her doctor, Joan began fourteen months of training alongside her black cat, Nelson Mandela. She mapped her route and arranged safe houses in every town. And one April morning she climbed Rankin Hill and began making her way. Her goal was to walk ten miles a day. "I rarely feel old," she said, "but that first week I functioned like an old lady. Napping in the morning. Letting people take care of me." At one point she had a panic attack when she thought her damaged foot would require surgery, but one of her conductors arranged for an after-hours visit to a shoe store to get something more comfortable to walk in. "I really did hear heavenly organ music playing when I strode pain-free around the store."

For the better part of a day, Joan and her friend Fran Stewart, a journalist who cowrote Joan's memoir of her journey, *In Their Path!*, drove me from small town to smaller town, from preserved safe house to crumbling safe house. We visited the Burrell House, a semi-restored two-story home in Sheffield Village, where Captain Jabez Burrell housed twenty students from nearby Oberlin College in the 1830s. He also kept runaway slaves in his barn, where a recently un-earthed tunnel led them to the Black River and north to Lake Erie, across which lay Canada. We strolled through Oberlin, an antislavery bastion, where some students recently erected an Underground Rail-road Healing Garden consisting of eight railroad ties surrounded by herbal plants used by African Americans during the journey. These included catnip for insomnia, hives, diarrhea, and menstrual cramps; evening primrose for tumors, coughs, depression, and rashes; but-terfly weed for insect bites and poison oak; and black cohosh for heart trouble, bronchitis, and when times called for it, an aphrodisiac. I couldn't help wondering how many of those on the Underground Railroad with heart trouble and bronchitis really had the need for an aphrodisiac.

Then Joan told me something that stunned me and made me realize how close these events still were to our day. She had a personal
connection to the most famous conductor of the Underground Railroad, a woman known in her time as "the Moses of Her People."

The future Harriet Tubman was born a slave in Dorchester
County, Maryland, in 1822. In 1844 she married a free man, John Tubman. Five years later, fearing that she was about to be sold, Tubman
tapped into a local network, received two names of safe houses from
a white neighbor, and fled north toward Philadelphia. The journey
was terrifying and mystical. She navigated using the North Star; she
may have *followed the drinkin' gourd,* a code name for the Big Dipper;
and in a clear homage to the Israelites' flight from Egypt, she recalled that she felt led by an "invisible pillar of cloud by day, and of
fire by night."

In other echoes of the Exodus, she described her feeling upon
reaching freedom as solemn and lonely. "I had crossed de line of
which I had so long been dreaming. I was free; but dere was no one
to welcome me to the land of freedom, I was a stranger in a strange
land." The Mosaic theme of estrangement that had captivated both
William Bradford and George Whitefield, that would influence Harriet Beecher Stowe and the Statue of Liberty and would shape the
scholarship of Harvard's Peter Gomes and the Institute for Advanced Study's Michael Walzer, here appears almost verbatim in the
words of an uneducated slave woman from the Maryland shore.
What ensured Tubman's reputation was how she reacted to her feeling of alienation. The following year she trekked hundreds of miles
back into slave territory to free her sister and her sister's children. A
few months later she returned to rescue her brother Moses and two
others. On a third trip she intended to bring back her husband, only
to find he had taken up with another woman. She vowed at first to

"The Moses of Her People," Harriet Tubman, as photographed by
H. B. Lindsley, c. 1860–1875. *(Courtesy of The Library of Congress)*

create "all the trouble she could," but quickly resolved, "if he could do without her, she could do without him," and freed two others on that trip.

Harriet Tubman made as many as thirteen expeditions into "Egypt land," guiding seventy slaves to freedom and giving instructions to dozens more. She became infamous across the South, her name plastered on posters, and rewards offered for her capture totaled forty thousand dollars. Frederick Douglass said that with the exception of John Brown, "I know of no one who has willingly encountered more perils and hardships to serve our enslaved people." Brown himself described her as "one of the bravest persons on the continent."

From her earliest days as a conductor, Tubman employed the Exodus story. At times she used it as code to communicate with slaves still in captivity. In 1854 she wrote to her brothers that they should be ready to climb aboard "when the good old ship of Zion comes along." To avoid detection by white postmasters, she sent the letter to a free black, Jacob Jackson, and signed it "William Henry Jackson." Jacob Jackson was grilled by authorities but pointed out that he knew no one by that name. Jackson then relayed the plot to its intended subjects. Tubman also used spirituals to communicate in the middle of an operation. Once at the meeting point, she would sing one verse to announce her arrival and another to signify that the coast was clear. But she reserved one verse to warn that there was danger in the area and the slaves should stay put:

> *Moses go down in Egypt,*
> *Tell ole Pharo' let my people go;*
> *Hadn't ben for Adam' fall,*
> *Shouldn't hab to died at all.*

As her fame grew, Harriet Tubman adopted the alias Moses to keep her identity anonymous. The name became renowned across the South—beloved in the black community, cursed in the white. Newspapers reported on the clandestine activities of "Moses." The *Liberator* reported in 1860 that "Moses" spoke before an antislavery gathering in her "quaint and amusing style." Posters appeared across the upper South bearing the name "Moses" in large letters and a description of Tubman. I can think of few images more vivid in the evolving role of the Exodus in American life than the idea of posters tacked up on fence poles and shop walls across slaveholding territories of the United States saying WANTED: MOSES, DEAD OR ALIVE. Decades earlier, Washington had been hailed as the American Moses; now Americans wanted Moses locked back into shackles.

Late in her life, when Tubman was suffering financial hardships, her friends commissioned an authorized biography to help her generate some income. Originally published in 1869 as *Scenes in the Life of Harriet Tubman*, it was republished in 1886 as *Harriet, the Moses of Her People*. The author, Sarah Bradford, wrote that the title might seem a little ambitious "considering that this Moses was a woman."

But I only give her here the name by which she was familiarly known, both at the North and the South, during the years of terror of the Fugitive Slave Law, and during our last Civil War, in both of which she took so prominent a part. And though the results of her unexampled heroism were not to free a whole nation of bond-men and bond-women, . . . her cry to the slave-holders, was ever like his to Pharaoh, "Let my people go!"

During these later years, Tubman lived in Auburn, New York, near where Joan Southgate was born. "My mother knew Harriet in those years," Joan explained. "When 'Aunt Harriet' would go through the town, sometimes she would fall asleep while driving her carriage. The horse would stop, and my mother and her friends would sit on the curb and wait for her to rouse. They made sure it was just one of her sleeping fits.

"But when I was growing up," she continued, "I thought 'Aunt Harriet' meant the same as my Aunt Val or Aunt Pauline. I thought, 'Great! I'm related to Harriet Tubman.' That part turned out not to be true."

I asked Joan why she thought Harriet Tubman was so famous, especially considering she didn't save that many people when compared with others.

"Probably because she was a woman. She was bold. She risked her freedom to save others. But since she was a woman, few people thought she was smart enough. During one trip, she watched some men putting up a wanted poster for her that said she was illiterate, so she just sat down in their presence and read a book because she knew they'd never suspect her!"

We reached our final destination, the terminus of the Black River, where it flows into the Erie Canal. A sign identified the spot as Station #100, the last stop on the Underground Railroad in Ohio. On the far side of the lake is Canada, the real land of freedom for many slaves, since there they could not be claimed by bounty hunters. I had been thinking all day that Joan, an ordinary person by her own account, was connected by family, and now through her own journey, to an extraordinary chapter in American history. I was reminded how young America is. The connections that link the Puritans with the Revolution, with the Great Awakening, with the Underground Railroad—and all of these events with today—took place in less time than the Israelites were enslaved in Egypt.

But what I found most stirring is how alive these connections still seemed to people like Jerry Gore, Carl Westmoreland, and Joan Southgate. Their ancestral slaves in America were as close to them as the enslaved Israelites had been to their ancestors. For those in pain, biblical time becomes any time. Now becomes then. And the longer I thought about it, the more I realized that a similar message echoes in the Jewish commemoration of the Exodus. A chief message of the Passover story is that the Exodus is perpetually now. As the Passover liturgy puts it, "In every generation, a person should look upon himself as if he personally had come out of Egypt." We all are in pain. We are all strangers in a strange land. And the proper way to acknowledge that suffering is to relieve the suffering of others. "Befriend the stranger," says Deuteronomy 10:19, "for you were strangers in the land of Egypt."

Few people I met understood this message better than Joan. As we were leaving, I asked her how her experience affected her.

"I never thought of myself as a religious person," she said. "But once I got started, so many things I call miracles happened. In the first week, a truck driver, a white guy named Al, heard about my walk and pulled his eighteen-wheeler to the side of the road and was waiting for me. He said, 'Mrs. Southgate, I just had to stop and say thank you. I think we have not done a good job of telling our children the stories.' And then he said, 'Do you mind if we pray?' At first I thought, 'Oh, he's one of those fanatics,' but the way he spoke was exactly as I would have spoken. I kept thinking of all these people on the roads who are just like us.

"There's an African word, *sankofa*," Joan continued, "that kept coming back to me during my walk. It means 'go back and fetch it.' Step back into the past and bring it to the present, so we don't make the same mistakes. That's what I learned on the Underground Railroad. We have to keep our past alive."

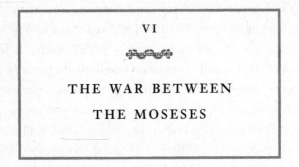

VI

THE WAR BETWEEN
THE MOSESES

I'M LOST. I'M searching for a white Victorian mansion on a hill overlooking Cincinnati. In the early years of American expansion, the house was a meeting point of East and West. In the buildup to the Civil War, it was a battleground of North and South. Today it's nearly impossible to find, trapped in a sad sprawl of abandoned car dealerships, one-room BBQ joints, and urban blight.

Between 1820 and 1840, Cincinnati was the fastest-growing city in the world and one of five American cities with a population of more than 25,000. It was also the City of Many Nicknames. "Porkopolis" was a teeming mix of swine and swindle, where southern pork farmers sold their pigs to northern packers. "The London of the West" was a fierce testing ground for American religious freedoms, where Protestants fought vicious battles with Catholics and where Jews and Mormons made early stands for legitimacy. And "the Queen City" was a tinderbox in the battle over slavery. Though nominally free, the city depended for its wealth on selling goods—including humans—from plantations in Kentucky. Cincinnati stood in the North, the saying went, but it faced the South.

All of these reasons helped make the Victorian mansion a center of intrigue. In the 1830s, the fledgling Lane Theological Seminary built the "peculiarly pleasant" house on a choice perch above town in an attempt to lure the most famous preacher in America to become its president. Lyman Beecher was the last great oak of New England Puritanism and a deacon of Old World oratory. As one contemporary recalled, "No American, except Benjamin Franklin, has given utterance to so many pungent, wise, sentences as Lyman Beecher." He was also the father of thirteen children, two of whom became central players in the dominant showdown of American identity.

The first of Beecher's prominent offspring was Harriet, his fifth child. Her novel *Uncle Tom's Cabin* was so influential in shaping public opinion that Abraham Lincoln was said to have remarked on meeting Harriet in 1862, "So you're the woman who wrote the book that started this great war!" The second of Beecher's progeny to dominate the era was his ninth child, Henry Ward, who by 1860 had become the most important preacher in the country and, according to a biographer, "the most famous man in America." Grateful for Henry's role in helping turn the English against the South, Lincoln asked the portly preacher to give a sermon at the raising of the Union flag at Fort Sumter in April 1865, the symbolic end of the war. "Had it had not been for Beecher," Lincoln said, "there would have been no flag to raise."

Harriet and Henry were reared by their Calvinist father in the most storied Christian family of the century. They shared a love of fireside debate, a passion for Scripture, and an interest in mining one

Henry Ward Beecher and Harriet Beecher Stowe, photograph, c. 1868. *(Courtesy Harriet Beecher Stowe Center)*

biblical narrative to support abolition. A chief tension in nineteenth-century America was that half the country disagreed with the Beechers but used the same Bible, the same narrative, and the same central figure to argue the opposite case.

The Civil War was a battle between North and South, between Union and states' rights, between slavery and emancipation. But it was also an exegetical battle over who controlled the Bible. The least understood dimension in the War Between the States is that it was also a War Between the Moseses. Both North and South claimed that Moses was on their side. Southerners pointed out that the Five Books of Moses are full of laws, given by God on Sinai, that govern the ownership of slaves. Why would God spend so much time regulating an institution he disapproved of? The Northern case was more indirect. It drew on the larger themes of the Bible that all humans are created in God's image, and stressed the triumph of the Exodus in which Moses leads the Israelites out of bondage. Why would God free his people from slavery only to allow them to enslave others?

When one side eventually lost the War Between the Moseses, the result was the most severe theological crisis the United States had ever seen. It took perhaps America's most Bible-quoting president, Abraham Lincoln, to try to salve the wound. In doing so, he was hailed as America's greatest Moses.

AS A MARK of the world it helped create, the Stowe House sits on Gilbert Avenue between Lincoln Avenue and Beecher Street, just a block from Martin Luther King Drive, in the once heyday thriving community of Walnut Hills. The stately home is hidden under broad trees at the top of a slope that in its heyday brimmed with locust trees, rosebushes, and honeysuckle. On this day, as on most, it's empty.

"The Beechers moved here in 1833," explained Barbara Furr, the chief docent. An African American, Barbara is not much taller than Harriet, but she's more feisty than the famed introvert. "Harriet moved out in 1836 when she married Calvin Stowe, but came back a few months later to give birth to their twins. Calvin was a biblical scholar and was off collecting books in Europe. Can you imagine? He could have took her! He just didn't want to spend all that money on a woman."

But soon that woman began earning more money than everyone else in her family combined.

The "first family of the Northern cause" were agents of change when nearly everything in America was changing. Historian Gordon Wood likens the decades after the Revolutionary era to the bursting of a dam, when society exploded in an unprecedented eruption of population and ideas. By the early 1800s, he writes, America had emerged as "the most egalitarian, most materialistic, most individualistic society" in history. Benjamin Rush, one of the signers of the Declaration of Independence, said Americans were awash in selfishness, and he lamented that he felt "like a stranger" in his native land, "a bebanked, a bewhiskied, and a bedollared" place. Like many, Rush believed the only force strong enough to hold together the fracturing country was religion. As Lyman Beecher put it, religion was "the central attraction" that could cure the country's political disarray.

Rush and Beecher got their wish. Religion boomed in nineteenth-century America, but it was not the top-down Calvinism of Beecher's youth. Instead, it was closer to the populist model introduced by the Great Awakening, in which believers could experience a "new birth" and form their own relationship with God. The Enlightenment notion of universal rights, so crucial to American politics, became equally central to religion as Americans decided they had the right to interpret the Bible for themselves. The result was the Second Great Awakening, the most sweeping wave of voluntary religious conversions since the Reformation. In 1780, one in fifteen Americans belonged to a Protestant church; by 1835, the ratio had nearly doubled to one in eight. By 1850, 40 percent of Americans defined themselves as evangelical Christians.

Baptists and Methodists, denominations that held that individuals were responsible for their own salvation, benefited the most. The number of Baptist churches grew fifteenfold during these years; the number of Methodist churches twice that. The old Puritans, meanwhile, dropped from 20 percent of the population to 4. The impact on American life was profound. As Alexis de Tocqueville observed in the 1830s, America was "the place in the world where the Christian religion has most preserved genuine powers over souls."

But American society was also "the most enlightened and most free," Tocqueville said. By midcentury, Americans realized that the idea Jefferson called the Constitution's "wall of separation" between church and state actually *spurred* religious growth rather than killing it. The First Amendment's ban on the "establishment of religion" ensured that federal money would not be directed to religious institutions. Most European countries still funded state churches, and while some American states continued this practice into the 1830s, American churches were ultimately cut off from public funds. The change forced churches to compete more openly in the marketplace of ideas and to work more feverishly to attract new members. The pressure to become more user-friendly became one of the hallmarks of American religion and one of the primary reasons religion continued to thrive in the United States, long after state-sponsored churches elsewhere began to atrophy.

And just as political freedom enhanced religious freedom, religion began to reshape politics. The first national political convention was convened in 1831, for example, by a onetime evangelical society that called on many of its revivalist techniques. The vernacular of American political campaigns—the parades, the tents, the rousing speeches, the passing of collection plates—was lifted from this era's barnstorming evangelical preachers. The government and the churches are "mutual friends," wrote a minister in 1831. The church simply asks for protection, and in return the state receives "the immense moral influence of the church."

Few men embodied this symbiotic relationship more than Lyman Beecher, a pioneer in the wave of Christian volunteer societies that swept America with a spirit of do-goodism. Beecher focused on such issues as temperance, literacy, and Sunday schools. His most successful effort was the American Bible Society, which he helped found in 1816. The society's goal was to use up-to-date printing techniques and distribution to counteract the wave of secular publications that were distracting Americans from their Bibles. The group's ambition was to have "a Bible in every household," and it came remarkably close. Capitalizing on the new printing technique of stereotyping, using lead plates to make facsimiles that could be reproduced more efficiently, the society generated an outpouring of Scripture. In 1829 alone, it printed 360,000 Bibles; in 1830, the number rose to 500,000. By the 1860s, the society was printing more than 1 million copies a year, for a population of 31 million. Americans may have been a People of the Book before, but now they could actually *own* the Book.

But the biggest movement Beecher joined was carrying the Protestant ideal of a new American Israel across the mountains into the wilderness of the West. Beecher's original objective in moving to Ohio was to "evangelize the world" and save the region from Catholicism. "The religious and political destiny of our nation is to be decided in the West," he said in a fiery 1835 speech. He and others echoed many of the themes from the Pilgrims and the First Great Awakening. And once more, they relied on the language of the Exodus.

In 1784, John Filson, a Pennsylvania schoolmaster, returned from two years across the Appalachians and published *The Discovery, Settlement and Present State of Kentucke,* a recruiting booklet designed to lure people to the region. Filson called the territory "the land of promise, flowing with milk and honey," where "you shall eat bread without scarceness and not lack any thing." His account ended with a dramatization of a real yet undistinguished trader named Daniel Boone, which helped turn the Revolutionary War veteran into the archetypal hero of the American frontier. Since Boone was a man of few words, Filson flushed out his "autobiography" with elaborate fictionalizations

George Caleb Bingham's *Daniel Boone Escorting Settlers Through the Cumberland Gap,* 1851–52. Oil on canvas, 36½ x 50¼". Mildred Lane Kemper Art Museum, Washington University in St. Louis. Gift of Nathaniel Phillips, 1890. *(Courtesy of The Mildred Lane Kemper Art Museum)*

drawn from sources ranging from Roman to Romantic. But many of the characteristics Filson gave to Boone were modeled on a figure known for venturing into the wilderness.

Like Moses, Daniel Boone leaves his family for the howling wilderness. Like Moses, he arrives traumatized but is cleansed and transformed by his immersion in nature. Like Moses, he experiences an encounter with Providence. Like Moses, he climbs a summit and overlooks an even greater paradise ahead of him. And like Moses, Boone returns to summon those left behind to migrate into the untamed territory and transform it into a new Eden.

There are differences in the two narratives, of course, but in the biblicized America of the nineteenth century, many recognized Daniel Boone as "the Moses of the West." In 1851, George Caleb Bingham painted *Daniel Boone Escorting Settlers Through the Cumberland Gap*, depicting a Moses-like Boone leading an exodus through the parted Appalachian mountains with a shaft of light in front, a trail of clouds behind, and a white horse by his side. Even the phrase that encapsulated this period, "manifest destiny," evoked for literate Americans the biblical calling for God's chosen people to settle the Promised Land. Beginning with the Puritans, the world was often referred to as God's "manifestation" and history as God's "destiny." Manifest destiny was another way of saying that God had chosen Anglo-Americans to convert the land for him—no matter who got misplaced. In the same way that colonizing America was viewed by many participants as a reenactment of the Exodus, many settlers heading west saw themselves as reliving the Israelites' flight into the wilderness to create a new American Israel.

THE ENTRANCE OF the Beecher house opens into a larger foyer, flanked by two public rooms. On the right was Lyman Beecher's study, which today contains a period secretary, a bookcase, and assorted chairs. "Dr. Beecher was not the neatest person in the world," Barbara Furr explained, "so when he wrote his sermons there were probably speeches and papers strewn everywhere." On the desk was an original leather book containing a student's lecture notes from one of Beecher's classes. I flipped through it and certain phrases jumped out: "church and state," "the duties of ministry," "the church in respect to civil government." I double-checked the date: 1845. The United States was 95 percent Protestant. James Polk was in the White House. Yet the questions about religion in America have hardly changed in the intervening thirty presidencies.

On the opposite side of the foyer was the parlor. "This is the room where Harriet gathered many of her ideas," Barbara said. "The Beechers were different because they allowed women to mingle with men. And if the men didn't have their ideas right, I'm pretty sure the women corrected them."

Though Harriet was initially skeptical about the move to Ohio, she took advantage of the relaxed mores of the West, which offered more opportunities for women. She wrote a geography book for children and, with her sister, opened a school for girls. She also joined the Semi-Colon Club, a coed literary society that focused on the growing genre of domestic literature—poetry, essays, letters. One of her fellow members was Calvin Stowe, a Lane professor who was widely regarded as the country's leading Bible scholar. A widower, Calvin was nine years Harriet's senior with a "tall, rectangular, perpendicular sort of body," she recalled, "as stiff as a poker." From this inauspicious start, their relationship never much warmed, although he did encourage her writing, in part because they needed more income.

Though Harriet gave birth to seven children before moving east in 1850, she still managed to participate in parlor society and join the fray over slavery. Both were crucial for *Uncle Tom's Cabin.* At home, Harriet was a laureate of letters; she wrote detailed accounts of her daily life and scolded others for leaving out minutiae. "I want to know if the kitchen is built & how the church progresses and about how the grapes succeeded," she wrote one cousin. These are "just the things we women like to hear." Her domestic life also fed her interest in abolition. She wrote that her greatest insight into slavery came from the experience of losing her own eighteen-month-old son, her "pride and joy," Charley, to cholera. "It was at *his* dying bed, and at *his* grave, that I learnt what a poor slave mother may feel when her child is torn away from her."

Once stirred, Harriet plunged into the topic. She visited slave-auction sites in Kentucky, read accounts of runaways, and on a trip to visit Henry in Indianapolis met an elderly former slave named "Uncle Tom" Magruder. Following passage of the Fugitive Slave Act of 1850, her sister-in-law wrote, "Harriet, if I could use a pen as you can, I would write something that would make this whole nation feel what an accursed thing slavery is." After reading the letter aloud to her children, Harriet announced, "I will write something if I live." While taking Communion a few months later, she had a vision of a Christ-like black man being viciously flogged and praying for his torturers as he died. Uncle Tom was born.

Given the importance of the Bible to her life and time, biblical themes abound in *Uncle Tom's Cabin.* The novel centers on two slaves from Kentucky: Eliza, who escapes along the Underground Railroad to Canada with her son; and Uncle Tom, who is sold to a series of owners deeper and deeper into the South. The long-suffering Uncle Tom displays many parallels with Jesus. He miraculously saves the life of a child; he tries to evangelize his masters for Christ; and the persecutors who ultimately beat him to death are so impressed by his faith that they convert to Christianity. But with slavery at its heart, *Uncle Tom's Cabin* is also steeped in parallels with the Exodus. Eliza's flight to freedom is likened to the Israelites' arrival at the Promised Land. "Her first glance was at the river, which lay, like Jordan, between her and the Canaan of liberty." Uncle Tom muses on the similarities between his own plight and that of the Israelites in Egypt. "In fact, as time went on . . . , the strength of the parallel increased." And he constantly sings spirituals with Mosaic themes. *Oh, had I the wings of the morning, / I'd fly away to Canaan's shore.*

By mixing themes from the Bible with carefully observed scenes of parlor life, *Uncle Tom's Cabin* became America's first blockbuster novel. Published on March 20, 1852, the book sold 10,000 copies within the first week and 305,000 copies in its first year. It became the first book to sell 1 million copies in the United States. It sold another million in England and was translated into Italian, Swedish, Danish, Dutch, Flemish, German, Polish, and Magyar. As Henry Ward Beecher biographer Debby Applegate puts it, Harriet "took the most unpopular subject in the country and turned it into the most popular book in American history."

Perhaps more important, she joined a long tradition of prophetic voices in America. From Columbus, through the Pilgrims, to the Revolution, breakthrough moments in American history were portrayed in the language of the Bible. The more radical the idea, the more leaders relied on the language of the Exodus to align their mission with the moral example set forth by Moses. Like William Bradford, Benjamin Franklin, and others, Harriet Beecher Stowe was encouraging her readers to support a cause that involved *breaking the law.* The only way to do that was to persuade them that God was on their side.

And Stowe succeeded. Her novel was received as American scripture, transcending the realm of fiction to become part of the nation's conscience. Long before he became a twentieth-century symbol of accommodation, Uncle Tom was viewed as a liberator sent to bring forth his people from slavery. On the page he may have been a Christian symbol of martyrdom, but once he entered the culture as the face of American slavery, Uncle Tom became a Mosaic call to action. As journalist D. B. Corley wrote after the war, "We are told that Moses was chosen as the means by which the children of Israel should be liberated from their bondage. . . . Tom was made the chosen means for the liberation of his brethren, [and] through him the colored slaves of the world have, like the children of Israel through Moses, been led to their respective happy lands of Canaan."

Harriet, of course, had anticipated this outcome. In Deuteronomy 34, Moses is described as having been buried by God in an unmarked grave, "and no one knows his burial place to this day." In chapter 41 of *Uncle Tom's Cabin* the hero is also portrayed as having been interred in secret. "There is no monument to mark the last resting-place of our friend. He needs none! His Lord knows where he lies." In a country steeped in biblical overtones, Uncle Tom became a timeless American hero, a universal symbol for the moral rightness of freedom.

He became a Moses for his time.

AS I WAS leaving Stowe House, I asked Barbara Furr what Lyman Beecher's legacy was. In 1850, humbled by his lack of success in converting the region to Protestantism, Beecher slunk back east. "Lyman was a fairly naïve person," she said. "I think he thought he could win over Cincinnati pretty quickly. But there was already a church on every corner. People resented that Beecher was trying to Yankeeize them."

One problem for Beecher is that by the 1840s, American society was becoming mired in a religious civil war that proved to be a vivid precursor to the real war that followed. As Mark Noll captured in his book *The Civil War as a Theological Crisis,* the clash over what God said about slavery in the Five Books of Moses—and what Jesus *didn't* say about slavery in the New Testament—represented a radical challenge to a fundamental pillar of American civilization: namely, "trust in the Bible as a divine revelation." By 1860, a substantial majority of Americans believed that the Bible, in addition to its religious uses, promoted republican politics, was best interpreted by ordinary people, and forecast the future glory of the United States. Yet for all its unifying power, the Bible could not heal the rift over slavery. Civil war threatened not just the union of states. It threatened the union of the United States and God.

A chief battleground in this war was a series of high-profile debates. As Walker Gollar, a professor at Xavier University in Cincinnati, explained to me, debates were becoming popular entertainment. "They would debate questions like 'Which is a greater force, love or hate?' or 'Who's been treated worse by the whites, Native Americans or blacks?'" One milestone debate was held at Lane Seminary in 1834 on the question "Ought slavery be abolished immediately?" The topic was debated for two and a half hours a night, for nine nights. Though eleven of the speakers had been raised in the South, none defended slavery. The measure passed unanimously, but the outcome so enraged Cincinnati society that forty students, dubbed "the Lane Rebels," were forced to flee north to Oberlin.

An even more contentious debate was held in Cincinnati in October 1845. On this occasion, like many, the more potent biblical argument belonged to the proslavery side. The essence of the Southern case was that if the Bible is God's word, then it is the believer's duty to heed every aspect of that revelation. And in example after example, the Bible sanctions, tolerates, regulates, and does nothing to eliminate slavery. Slaveholders collected a bevy of biblical citations they could wield like cudgels. In Genesis 12, Abraham acquires slaves in Egypt. In Genesis 17, God instructs Abraham to circumcise his slaves. In Exodus 12, God instructs Moses to invite slaves to the first Passover. In Leviticus 25, God tells Israel "it is from the nations round about you that you may acquire male and female slaves."

The New Testament also supports slavery, Southerners insisted. In 1 Corinthians 7, Paul ordains that both slave and master abide by their calling. In Romans 13, Paul insists that his followers honor the authority of their regimes. In Ephesians 6, Paul instructs slaves to "obey your earthly masters with fear and trembling." In 1 Peter, Peter orders servants to "accept the authority of your masters with all due submission, not only when they are kind and considerate, but even when they are perverse." These passages were undeniably clear and made the Bible's view on slavery abundantly transparent to the lay reader. "Don't take my word for it," the Southerner could say. "Take God's word for it." As the South's leading theologian, James Thornwell, boasted in 1861, "That the relation betwixt the slave and his master is not inconsistent with the word of God, we have long since settled. . . . We cherish the institution not from avarice, but from principle."

Antislavery activists also cited the Bible, but they were forced to sidestep these individual planks of Mosaic law and focus on larger themes, like the idea in Genesis 1 that all humans are made in God's image. Or they cited Genesis 17, in which Abraham circumcises his slaves, thereby welcoming them into the covenant, as well as Exodus 21, in which a master is ordered to free a slave if he's harmed. Or they claimed, as Harriet Beecher Stowe did, that the slavery in the Bible was different from that practiced in the South. Altogether, the biblical antislavery argument was considerably weaker. As Mark Noll concluded: "The North lost the exegetical war." Yet Northerners didn't back down, and the results were seismic. In 1837, the Presbyterian Church split along regional lines, followed in 1844 by the Methodists and in 1845 by the Baptists. If North and South could not agree on the same Bible, they could not sit in the same pews, and if they couldn't sit in the same pews, they couldn't stay in the same union. As had occurred with the Revolution, what started in religion happened next in politics.

The book that joined Americans together was being torn asunder by slavery.

The 1845 debate in Cincinnati was a sterling example of this biblical fratricide. Hosted by the Presbyterian Church in the largest room in the city, the event lasted for four days, eight hours a day, discussing "Is slave-holding in itself sinful?" The two participants were ministers. Jonathan Blanchard, a Lane Rebel and later a candidate for president, said the answer was yes. Nathaniel Rice, a well-known Southern sympathist, argued no. Blanchard went first and immediately framed the question as religious: "Whether the religion we profess is a humane or an inhuman one?" He invoked the Declaration of Independence, saying men must not be slaves, "because 'God hath created all men free and equal, and hath endowed them with certain INALIENABLE rights!'"

But Rice, going second, delivered a more nuanced argument. Sure, some slaveholders might be evil, he said, just as some farmers are cruel to their horses, but the institution itself should not be blamed. "It is not a sin to own a horse," he said. Plus, he said, Scripture agreed with him. "My position is that God expressly permitted [slavery] in the words of the Jewish law, given from himself to Moses." What made Rice's presentation so powerful was that he repeatedly used the Bible as a weapon against Blanchard. In his second speech, Rice declared: "We have heard him, during one hour and a half, labor to prove his proposition, without quoting one passage of

Scripture!" In his third speech: "He and I agree that the Bible is the only rule by which any thing can be proved sinful; and during the two and a half hours he has made not one reference to that infallible rule." In his fourth speech: "We are not about to close a discussion of *six hours*. . . . And although this question can be determined only by an appeal to the Bible, the gentleman in the affirmative has not quoted even a solitary passage from that book."

Rice's argument was a bit disingenuous because Blanchard had repeatedly cited biblical principles, but the goading worked, and on day three, Blanchard shot back with a litany of verses that he claimed opposed slavery. Jeremiah 22:13: "Woe unto him that buildeth his house by unrighteousness." Isaiah 58:6: "Loose the bands of wickedness . . . and let the oppressed go free." He attacked what he called the "slaveholders' texts": Exodus 21:21, which calls for the avenging of a man who dies striking a slave; and Leviticus 25:45, which says the Israelites can acquire "slaves" from neighboring states. The Bible says "bondmen," not "slaves," Blanchard said, and Rice was not qualified to challenge the greatest translators in the world. "His whole vaunted argument is founded in and drawn from a mistake." The irony of this exchange is that slaveholders were citing Leviticus 25, while a portion of the same verse, molded onto the State House bell in Philadelphia, was being reborn as the cri de coeur of abolitionists.

And therein lay the painful reality of the Bible in America. On the one hand, the Bible still gripped the heart of political discourse. The Blanchard-Rice debates, when published, ran 482 pages, longer than the Lincoln-Douglas debates thirteen years later. Reading the transcript, I was struck that the Bible was invoked on *nearly every page;* at least two dozen biblical books were cited; and neither Blanchard nor Rice had to explain the meaning of their quotations. Americans knew the text, and it mattered to them what the Bible said on this issue. Even more, Americans personalized the debate by equating Moses with Scripture. Control him, and you could control the debate. That's why Blanchard chose the final night to deliver his fiercest attack. My opponent's doctrine is a "slavery movement," he said, "and quoting Mosaic practice to support it is a dreadful perversion." Moses, Blanchard insisted, ended slavery. Rice was an anti-Moses. The comment was one of the few during the entire four days to earn applause.

Yet for all the importance of the Bible, these debates signaled a coming crisis for America's sacred text. Both Blanchard and Rice agreed that the Bible was the source of last resort, yet they couldn't agree on what the Bible said. As a result, Moses could no longer be the argument-ending precedent he had been for centuries. And if you couldn't wield his story in a dispute, there was only one thing left to wield. As Mark Noll summed up the impasse: "The Book that made the nation was destroying the nation; the nation that had taken to the Book was rescued not by the Book but by the force of arms."

CINCINNATI, OHIO, IS not really on the way to Gettysburg, Pennsylvania, unless you're coming from, say, Springfield, Illinois, the home of Abraham Lincoln. The three cities are virtually in a straight line—call it the Lincoln-Beecher line—and by November 1863 they were bound together by an ever lengthening thread. The "great war" that Lincoln attributed to Harriet Beecher Stowe reached its turning point at the battle of Gettysburg in July 1863. Four months later, the Kentucky-born Lincoln came to help dedicate the National Cemetery and delivered the most famous speech of the nineteenth century, one ripe with echoes of the Exodus.

Gettysburg on an early winter's sunny morning is an eerily beautiful, almost spooky place. Streaks of sun press through the peach orchard's branches near Plum's Run, and a cool mist hovers around the cannons in the Devil's Den. The gray granite monuments and somber stelae on Cemetery Ridge are so chilly they could be made from ice. Just across from Seminary Ridge is the Angle, where the Confederate forces taking part in Pickett's Charge broke through the Union lines before being felled by guns and bayonets. This spot is known as the High-Water Mark of the Confederacy and is memorialized by a giant bronze book listing the names of those who fought here. Up the slope is the summit of Cemetery Hill. It's here that Lincoln gave the speech that some consider the high-water mark of the Bible in America.

Compared with the open expanses of the battlefield, Gettysburg National Cemetery is a well-manicured place, with headstones arranged in a semicircle. The focal point is a soaring marble monument to Lady Liberty that resembles Forefathers' Monument in Plymouth. More than six thousand people, Northerners and Southerners, died in the three-day battle of Gettysburg, along with three thousand horses and mules. Many were hurriedly pushed into shallow graves that were soon opened by heavy rains. A local attorney, David Wills, organized plans for a formal cemetery to honor Union dead. But each state wanted its dead buried at the summit, so Wills arranged the tombs in the shape of a fan with each state side by side, an ironic tribute to the principle they were fighting against: states' rights. Each soldier was interred with feet facing downhill, so that if the bodies rose from the dead, they would overlook the field where they died. The move was another small gesture to the centrality of faith in the Civil War.

The showdown over the Bible that marked the lead-up to the war continued headlong into the early days of fighting. And once again, both sides claimed the mantle of Exodus. In the South, the Reverend Benjamin Palmer gave a sermon in 1861 labeling the Confederates God's chosen people and Lincoln the pharaoh. "Eleven tribes sought to go forth in peace from the house of political bondage," he said, referring to the eleven states that had seceded from the Union at that time, "but the heart of our modern Pharaoh is hardened, that he will not let Israel go." In New York, Henry Ward Beecher delivered a sermon based on Exodus 14, when the Israelites, fleeing Egypt, find themselves trapped before the Red Sea. "Why do you cry out to me," God says to Moses. "Tell the people to go forward." Beecher delivered a similar message to frightened Northerners. "Right before us lies the Red Sea of war," he said. "It is red indeed. There is blood in it. We have come to the very edge of it, and the word of God to us today is, 'Speak unto this people that they go forward.'"

Bibles and bullets had long gone together, and the Civil War was no exception. Mark Twain is said to have satirized the common claim of soldiers having their lives saved by their pocket Bibles with the story of how he was strolling down a sidewalk near a hotel one day when a Bible came plummeting toward him from an open window above. Fortunately, the Bible hit the "lucky bullet" he always carried in his breast pocket and his life was miraculously spared. On a more serious level, the American Bible Society published three million Bibles during the war, and three hundred thousand were smuggled from the North to the South. IN GOD WE TRUST was first placed on Union coins during this period; Thanksgiving became a recurring national holiday. And with 622,000 dead, heaven became a national obsession. Before the war, most people died at home, surrounded by family members, and heaven was a vague place where the deceased went to be with God. On average, the number of books about heaven published each year was not quite one. But with so many people dying far from home, and many bodies never returned, families became concerned about their loved ones. In the decade after the war, ninety-four books about heaven appeared.

Abraham Lincoln may have been the person most affected by this change. Certainly prosecuting a long, deadly, and often unpopular war seems to have affected his spiritual beliefs. Like George Washington, Lincoln was a man of no religious affiliation who loved to quote the Bible. He was born into a family of strict Calvinists who placed Scripture at the center of their existence; the Bible was probably the only book the family owned. But by the time Lincoln ventured out on his own in Illinois, he had turned hostile toward organized religion. "He entered with zest into the theological discussions of the community," a friend recalled. Yet while he enjoyed the mental exercise, "emotionally the bitterness of sectarian prejudice must have been repellant to him, and was probably the cause of his lasting reluctance to affiliate with any sect."

Lincoln's refusal to join a church and his open skepticism toward the Trinity triggered whisper campaigns that he was an "infidel," a catchall phrase meaning someone who is hostile to religion. In his 1846 race for Congress, Lincoln was forced to issue a handbill. "That I am not a member of any Christian Church, is true; but I have never denied the truth of the Scriptures; and I have never spoken with intentional disrespect of religion." Lincoln succeeded in American politics because being on good terms with the Good Book was more important than being on good terms with your pastor. And few people in American history knew their Bible better than Abraham Lincoln. He told a friend, "The Bible is the richest source of pertinent quotations." His debating nemesis, Stephen Douglas, complained of Lincoln's "proneness for quoting Scripture." As Lincoln told the country in his first inaugural address, he thought God would ultimately decide whose view of the Bible was correct. "If the Almighty Ruler of nations . . . be on your side of the North, or on yours of the South, that truth, and that justice, will surely prevail, by the judgment of this great tribunal, the American people."

But leading the country through God's trial was such a monumental chore that Lincoln's views on religion underwent a shift, captured in his three great expressions of American theology: the Emancipation Proclamation, the Gettysburg Address, and his second inaugural address. To help unpack their meaning, I went to see one of the country's most astute dissectors of Lincoln.

Allen Guelzo is the Henry R. Luce Professor of the Civil War Era at Gettysburg College, a member of the National Council on the Humanities, and a two-time winner of the coveted Lincoln Prize. An army brat and high school drum major, he showed up for our meeting with a red letter sweater featuring a giant *P* for the University of Pennsylvania. Professor Guelzo was so broad-minded and, perhaps because of his outfit, so cheerful that early in our conversation I wanted to curl up on the sofa in his dormer office and say, "Okay, start at the beginning and tell me everything that happened in American history."

The heart of Guelzo's view of Lincoln is that the sixteenth president, though undereducated, was more a man of ideas than generally credited. For Guelzo, the private Lincoln, who struggled with religion his entire life, and the public Lincoln, who practiced a staunch Whig ideology of economic advancement through hard work, self-improvement, and self-control, were intimately related.

"I think Lincoln's interest in Whig ideology is a kind of surrogate religion," Professor Guelzo said. "Whig ideas managed to appeal to both secular people like Lincoln and evangelicals like Lyman Beecher. Why? The connection is the idea of transformation." The Enlightenment was devoted to transformation, he explained. Command of scientific law gave individuals the power to alter the world. Electricity, for instance, was no longer a mysterious power; it could be named, created, and eventually used to transform life. "Lincoln loves transformation because he grew up in a dirt-poor, subsistence-farmer culture. He couldn't *wait* to get out. It's the American Dream.

"Now shift the focus," he continued. "What is evangelical Protestantism all about? It's about transformation. From sin to grace. From the slavery of selfishness to the freedom of benevolence. For Lincoln, both the scientific revolution and the spiritual conversion promise transformation."

Lincoln's greatest act of transformation was the Emancipation Proclamation, and not surprisingly, it's the first time Lincoln's personal relationship with God appears to have crept into his decision making. Initially Lincoln resisted freeing the slaves, deeming such an act unnecessary. But as the war proceeded, Lincoln focused increasingly on the moral dimension of slavery and eventually cast his decision to free the slaves as an outgrowth of his relationship with God. On September 22, 1862, following the battle of Antietam, Lincoln called a special session of his cabinet and announced, "I made a solemn vow before God," that if the Confederates were driven out of Maryland, "I would crown the result by the declaration of freedom to the slaves." The head of the navy wrote in his diary that the move was Lincoln's vow, a "covenant" with God.

Slavery. Freedom. Covenant.

Egypt. Red Sea. Sinai.

Despite his initial resistance, Lincoln had become a Moses, though he got there not by being born a slave who was raised in the pharaoh's house but by being born in poverty and working his way out.

"I think Lincoln always related to slaves," Allen Guelzo said. "He made a comment once: 'I have seen a great deal of the backside of the world.' What he's saying is, 'I came from dirt.' And that helps him believe he understands what slavery is. Frederick Douglass makes a comment the first time they met in 1863 that Lincoln was the first white man he ever met who didn't think about race, 'who in no single instance reminded me of the difference between himself and myself.' And Douglass explains why: because of the way they both had risen from humble origins. I read that and I thought, 'Aha! Abraham Lincoln as a slave.'"

"Could this be one reason he felt so attached to the Bible?" I asked.

"Oh, yes. It's also the reason he had difficulty with it. The Bible offers him hope, and snatches it away. It encourages him in his quest for transformation, and yet it tells him that the ultimate saving transformation he cannot accomplish himself. It must come from God."

I asked Professor Guelzo whether Lincoln was more interested in the Old or New Testament.

"It's the Old Testament that fascinates him. Constantly. Constantly. It's a God who's remote and hands down ways of doing things. It's a God who promises deliverance. And deliverance, of course, is the message of Gettysburg."

Lincoln was an afterthought as a speaker at the dedication of the Soldiers National Cemetery, having been added to the program only a few weeks earlier. Still, late on the morning of November 18, 1863, a dense crowd of thousands gathered on Cemetery Hill, where around thirty-five hundred Union dead were already being reburied. The Confederate dead remained haphazardly interred in the fields. Methodist chaplain Thomas Stockton gave the invocation: "Blessed be God, the Father of our Lord Jesus Christ, the Father of Moses." Edward Everett, the most famous orator in the country and a onetime U.S. congressman, senator, and vice-presidential candidate, gave a two-hour recapitulation of the battle. Finally, President Lincoln rose. He was wearing a black suit and white gauntlets and carrying a hat with a mourning band in memory of his son Willie, who had died that February at age eleven. He wore reading glasses and held his speech. He had been invited to give remarks that would console "the many widows and orphans." His address contained a sparse nine sentences and around 271 words. Counting the five interruptions for applause, it lasted about three minutes (or for all time, depending on how you count).

Four score and seven years ago our fathers brought forth on this continent, a new nation, conceived in Liberty, and dedicated to the proposition that all men are created equal.

Lincoln drew on many inspirations for his remarks, including Pericles' ode to the dead and the Declaration of Independence. And from the opening phrase, he drew deeply from the Bible. "Four score and seven years" echoes the phrase in Psalm 90: "The days of our years are threescore years and ten; and if by reason of strength they be fourscore years . . . it is soon cut off." He especially drew from Exodus. The phrase "brought forth" appears throughout the Bible, including a line from Luke that Mary "brought forth" the baby Jesus. But of the sixty-three times the expression appears in the King James translation, only nine are from the New Testament, compared with fifty-four from the Old Testament. Thirteen times "brought forth" refers to Israel leaving Egypt, including a reference that Moses "brought forth" the people to meet God at Mount Sinai.

Elsewhere, Lincoln evoked biblical themes. After opening with images of birth—"fathers," "brought forth," "a new nation," "conceived"—he moved on to images of death—"dedicate," "a final resting place," "those who here gave their lives." "In a larger sense," he said, "we cannot dedicate—we cannot consecrate—we cannot hallow—this ground." Again, the language is pure Old Testament. *Dedicate, consecrate,* and *hallow* appear a collective twenty-six times in the Old Testament and none in the New. *Hallow* is used in the phrase immediately *before* the passage of Leviticus 25 that appears on the Liberty Bell: "And ye shall hallow the fiftieth year, and proclaim liberty throughout all the land unto all the inhabitants thereof." Oh, to have been able to ask Lincoln that morning if he knew the connection to the bell that was widely believed in 1863 to have rung on that fateful July 4, "four score and seven years ago."

Finally he came to his conclusion: the rebirth of liberty. "We here highly resolve that these dead shall not have died in vain—that this nation, under God, shall have a new birth of freedom." The phrase "new birth" was first popularized by George Whitefield and was widely used during the Second Great Awakening of Lincoln's youth. By linking the *new birth* of the Civil War with the *bringing forth* of 1776, Lincoln was connecting the current struggle to the moral foundation of the Declaration of Independence. On a deeper level, he was presenting a vision for God's American Israel that reconnected it to God's original Israel. In the Creation story, the world begins as a watery chaos, God "divides the waters from the waters," and "dry land" appears. In the Exodus, the Israelites also face a watery chaos in the Red Sea, God "divides the waters," and the Israelites cross on "dry ground." Creation is the Bible's original birth. The Exodus— from the breaking of the water, to the easing through a narrow passageway, to the deliverance—is the Bible's rebirth. Lincoln understood this cycle, and the Gettysburg Address forever seared this biblical pattern—the birth, death, and rebirth of a nation—into America's consciousness. Maybe that's why one newspaper compared Lincoln that day to Moses on Sinai, saying the ruler of the nation "never stood higher, or grander, or more prophetic."

But Lincoln's most Mosaic moment may have come more than a year later, in March 1865, during his second inaugural, just a month before he died.

"At Lincoln's first inaugural, there's no mystery about what to do," Professor Guelzo said. "He's very rational. He's very confident. But by the time he gets to the second inaugural, he's crossed a fiery brook. Passion has been let loose, and events have gone in a direction that secular Whigs have no explanation for. So he switches to full evangelicalism."

The speech he gave that day at the Capitol is sometimes referred to as his last will and testament to the American people. At 701 words, it's a little more than twice as long as the Gettysburg Address but still the second-shortest inaugural address in American history. He refers to prayer three times, quotes or paraphrases the Bible four times, and mentions God fourteen times. And he invokes the mystery of God to heal the decades-long war over the Bible. "Neither party expected for the war the magnitude or the duration which it has already attained. . . . Both read the same Bible and pray to the same God. . . . That of neither has been answered fully. The Almighty has His own purposes."

"The minute you suggest that history is mysterious, you have left the Enlightenment," Allen Guelzo said. "But unlike all those people in the North who believe they are thoroughly righteous, Lincoln is more cautious. He says we don't understand God, and we're never going to understand, so we might as well give it up. History is the plaything of God."

"So if the Civil War was really a war over the meaning of the Bible," I asked, "which side won?"

"Neither. The events of the war showed that war is not skywriting from God about the virtue of one side or the other. Rather, the ambiguity of the war was evidence of the ambiguity of the American mission; maybe we're not the chosen people we thought we were. Remember that Lincoln, even in 1861, describes Americans as the 'almost-chosen people.' By the end of the war, he's lost confidence even in that measure of chosenness. It would almost be like Moses on top of Mount Nebo saying, 'Hey, guys, I'm not so sure that leaving Egypt was a good idea.' Imagine how that would have gone over! Abraham Lincoln at the end of his life is America's Moses, but he's not sure about the Promised Land. The only thing he's sure of is the need for 'malice toward none and charity toward all.'"

"Given this ambiguity," I said, "is it safe to say that Lincoln represents the beginning of the end of the Bible in America?" I had been thinking about this idea for a few weeks now and was eager to test it. "Lincoln uses biblical language, but he separates it from religion. He views the Bible as just another source of knowledge but not as the ultimate truth. Can't we call him a bridge—the last of the religious people, and the first of the secular people?"

Professor Guelzo didn't hesitate. "No," he said.

"No?" I repeated.

We both laughed.

"I think this is because American culture really has two souls. And it's not a question of whether the culture becomes secularized. The culture never becomes one thing or the other. The culture is always two. The culture is always William Bradford and Jonathan Edwards. The culture is always Benjamin Franklin and Thomas Edison. America was born just in time to have two mentalities. We're like Jacob and Esau struggling in the womb. Secular people want to believe that we are a nation of the Enlightenment, and because of the Founding Fathers and the Constitution that secularism will supersede religion. Religious people want to believe that through the revival religion will supersede secularism. And both are wrong.

"What's going to happen," he said, "is that there will continue to be a constant dynamic and tension between the two, running side by side.

And they're going to keep on being about that for as long as there's an American identity worth talking about. Lincoln does not throw a switch; we're on one track and now we're on the other. He is symptomatic of both. There are in American history people who are examples of one or the other. But every now and then you get these remarkably creative people who are crossovers. Those are the people who are really fascinating. Abraham Lincoln is one of them."

NOT LONG AFTER Lincoln's second inauguration, the president sent his request to Henry Ward Beecher asking him to deliver a sermon at the ceremony celebrating the Union's recapture of Fort Sumter in South Carolina. The April 14 event would mark the end to the war four years after its first shot in April 1861. The invitation was so momentous that Beecher's friends and neighbors in Brooklyn Heights deluged him with requests to attend, forcing his patrons to hire a second ship. In early April, what seemed like half of Brooklyn sailed for Charleston.

By 1865, Beecher's name was on everyone's lips in America, and his hands were in half the petticoats of Brooklyn Heights. Once teased for having a voice that sounded like there was pudding in his mouth, the jowly Beecher with thinning white hair tucked behind his ears—imagine Franklin without the spectacles—had transformed himself into an electrifying speaker. Rejecting the wrathful God of his father, Beecher emphasized the warm embrace of God's love. "It is love the world wants," he preached. "Higher than morality, higher than philanthropy, higher than worship, comes the love of God." He filled his services at the massive Plymouth Church with music, his sermons with jokes, and his pulpit with flowers. And the public responded by filling his pews. Every Sunday throngs would take barges from Manhattan called "Beecher Boats." He made a fortune speaking around the country. And he gave a series of antislavery speeches in London that even Robert E. Lee said had turned the British against the Confederacy. "Abraham Lincoln emancipated men's bodies," one admirer wrote. "Henry Ward Beecher emancipated their minds."

But as much as he was adored by abolitionists, he was reviled by Southerners. He was accused of being a "nigger worshipper." His house in Brooklyn was vandalized. Even one New York paper called for him to be hanged for treason for agitating against slavery. And whispers had already begun over what would become one of the biggest scandals of the century, a public trial in which Beecher was accused of committing adultery with a friend's wife. (A jury discussed the eye-popping testimony for six days but reached no verdict.) I live a few blocks from Plymouth Church today, and as I walk around my neighborhood, I often imagine Beecher hopscotching from one brownstone to the next, preening his plumage in parlors far more elegant than the one he grew up in in Cincinnati, and inching his fingers up the silk stockings of his most ardent admirers. Being a Beecher in the Beecher Century did have its perks.

By the time the ships reached South Carolina, Robert E. Lee had surrendered at Appomattox, and the symbolic party at Fort Sumter suddenly became a real party indeed. On Good Friday morning, April 14, every floating vessel for miles made its way to Charleston Harbor, decked from bow to stern in banners and flags. The ruined fort filled with soldiers and color guards, including a brigade of African American soldiers led by Henry Beecher's brother James, who marched under a banner designed by Harriet with a sun and the word LIBERTY in huge crimson-and-black letters. Having scripted the preamble to the war, the Beechers would define its coda as well.

After the familiar litany of proclamations, the flag was raised and Beecher rose to speak. "Hail to the flag of our fathers!" he said. "Glory to the banner that has gone through four years black with tempests of war!" The flag was like Moses, Beecher continued, whom God sent into the wilderness after he killed the Egyptian overseer in an effort to prepare him to lead God's children to freedom. "When God would prepare Moses for emancipation," Beecher said, "He drove him for forty years to brood in the wilderness. When our flag came down, four years it lay brooding in darkness." But then the flag understood the sin of slavery and once more "dedicated itself to liberty." Once more Moses helped define America's preeminent symbol. Left off the Great Seal following the Revolution, during the Civil War Moses became Old Glory.

After the speech, the crowd went to an old Charleston mansion for a ball, complete with what some regarded as the un-Christian activity of dancing, followed by fireworks over the harbor. A few guests returned to their rooms early. A little after 8 P.M., Abraham Lincoln left the White House for the equally un-Christian activity of going to see *Our American Cousin* at Ford's Theatre. Just as William Bradford at the end of his life studied Hebrew to draw closer to his biblical heroes, Lincoln was imagining life after the presidency and dreamed of drawing closer to the book that had shaped his language since childhood. In their box, Lincoln told his wife, Mary, that after their time in the White House they would "go abroad among strangers so I can rest." He would like to "visit the Holy Land," he said. His last words, Mary later recounted, were that "there is no city on earth he so much desired to see as Jerusalem." Moments later, he was shot.

The following day, with no clue about events in Washington, Beecher and his party went sightseeing. With railroad and telegraph lines severed by the war, Charleston still did not know about Lincoln's passing. On Sunday morning, as the Brooklyn delegation was preparing to sail for Savannah, they finally heard the news. "It was not grief, it was sickness that I felt," Beecher recalled. He immediately ordered the ships back to New York.

Across the country, meanwhile, Easter morning drew millions to church, where worshipers listened to an outpouring of sermons about the martyred president. Given the unavoidable symbolism that America's savior had been shot on Good Friday by a rebel who felt that Lincoln had betrayed God's will, many preachers used their Easter pulpit to compare Lincoln to Jesus. Lincoln's death was "the aftertype of the tragedy which was accomplished on the first Good Friday, more than eighteen centuries ago, upon the eminence of Calvary in Judea," said one preacher in Connecticut. "Jesus Christ died for the world, Abraham Lincoln died for this country." In biography after biography about the sixteenth president, including Allen Guelzo's, the equating of Lincoln with Jesus is presented as the overriding image of Lincoln's funeral orations.

But a close inspection of the sermons indicates that another comparison may have been used even more frequently. In 1998 the Candler School of Theology at Emory University scanned the full text of 57 eulogies into a database. The sermons came from all regions and denominations. Sixteen compare Lincoln to Jesus; 34 compare him to Moses. The sermons contain 42 references linking Lincoln with Jesus and 113 linking him with Moses. Separately, 23 Lincoln funeral sermons preached in Boston were gathered in a book; 10 compare Lincoln to Jesus, 11 to Moses. In a similar compendium from New York, 6 of the 21 analogize Lincoln with Jesus, 10 with Moses. In a detailed analysis of 372 Northern eulogies, Charles Stewart shows that "nearly half the sermons compared Lincoln to Moses."

Many of the comparisons were similar to the ones made on the death of George Washington: Lincoln was a humble leader, chosen by God, to lead America into the Promised Land. Lincoln's relations to the American people "bear a striking analogy to those which Moses sustained to the children of Israel," said a Connecticut preacher.

"What was the work which Moses was called to do? It was nothing less than to deliver his race from slavery. The work before our late beloved president was the same. God called him to free the nation." Eulogizers saw similarities in Lincoln's and Moses' impoverished births, though they sometimes had to stretch their midrashic skills to equate Lincoln's log-cabin upbringing with Moses' life in the pharaoh's court. "If Moses was of humble parentage, so was [Lincoln]," said a Philadelphia minister. "If Moses derived from his mother those sentiments and feeling which formed the bases of his exalted character and success, the same may be said of the late president."

Orators saw parallels in the rebellions both leaders faced. "When his own people lost heart and confidence, and found fault with him," one preacher said, Moses "never once thought of giving up. . . . How like Moses, in these respects, was our late President?" Unlike Washington, Lincoln was not a universally beloved figure at the time of his death, and a number of speeches tweaked the late president by pointing out that, like the Israelites, Americans might have a better chance of reaching the Promised Land with a new leader. Moses was fine for the wilderness, but Israel needed a Joshua to finish the job. "In Abraham Lincoln God gave us just the man to take us safely through the last stages of the rebellion," said a reverend in Boston. "But the nation had now reached the Jordan, beyond which were sterner duties." He concluded: "We have passed the Red Sea and the wilderness, and have had unmistakable pledges that we shall occupy that land of Union, Liberty, and Peace which flows with milk and honey."

While these speeches were being delivered, Henry Ward Beecher was sailing back to New York. He finally delivered his highly anticipated eulogy in an overflowing Plymouth Church on Sunday, April 23. He began with a long recitation of the final chapter in the

Five Books of Moses, Deuteronomy 34:1–5: "So Moses went up from the plains of Moab unto the mountain of Nebo, to the top of Pisgah, that is over against Jericho." God then gives Moses a face-to-face tour of the full dimensions of the Promised Land—from the fields of Galilee in the north, to the Negev desert in the south, to the Mediterranean in the west. "This is the land of which I swore to Abraham, Isaac, and Jacob," God says. "I have let you see it with your own eyes, but you shall not cross there." Moses sees the land. He is close enough to see that God has fulfilled his promise. But he will not enter. The parallels with Lincoln were rich.

"There is no historic figure more noble than that of the Jewish lawgiver," Beecher continued. "After so many thousand years, the figure of Moses is not diminished, but stands up against the background of early days distinct and individual as if he had lived but yesterday. There is scarcely another event in history more touching than his death." Until now, Beecher suggested. "Again a great leader of the people has passed through toil, sorrow, battle, and war, and come near to the promised land of peace, into which he might not pass over. Who shall recount our martyr's suffering for this people!"

Four score and nine years after Thomas Paine likened America's independence to the Israelites' flight from Egypt, and two-thirds of a century after George Washington was eulogized as America's Great Liberator, Americans once more turned a national tragedy into an opportunity to bind their story to the three-thousand-year-old narrative of nation building forged in the wilderness of Sinai. And once more Americans likened their leader to Moses. The persistence of Mosaic imagery at nearly every major turning point in the country's formative century shows how clearly the themes of chosenness, liberation from slavery, freedom from authority, and collective moral responsibility had become the tent poles of American public life.

But in the case of Lincoln, was the analogy apt?

Before leaving Allen Guelzo's office, I asked him which comparison he would have chosen—Jesus or Moses—if he had been invited to give a eulogy for Lincoln. He clapped his hands together delightedly and rocked back in his chair. "Hmmm," he said. Then he thought for a full minute.

"I think it goes back to what we think Lincoln's greatest achievement was," he finally said in a whisper. "If Lincoln's greatest achievement was emancipation, then we're going to talk about him as Moses. If we think Lincoln's greatest achievement was redeeming the country from the onus of slavery, then we're going to talk about him as Christ."

"I would have thought Jesus was a much more influential figure in America," I said. "But I'm starting to believe the themes of Moses may echo more."

"Put it this way," Professor Guelzo said, "the story of Jesus is extremely important. What is surprising is how persistently important the story of Moses remains. After all, if you take this from the point of Protestant theology, Moses is great but Moses is the old covenant. But that's not how it plays out. The real story is not why Christ is so attractive, but how did Moses get on the stage. And why is he still here?"

"So what's your answer?"

"I think it's a message about American identity. It's like kids identifying themselves with baseball players. Cultures do the same. Our icons tell us who we are. In this case, the Moses-Jesus track comes down to which is more important: deliverance or redemption?"

"That brings us back to the question," I said. "If you had to compare Lincoln with Moses or Jesus, which would you choose?"

"It depends on how much I knew about Lincoln," he said. "If I knew a lot about Lincoln personally, I'd probably say he was more interested in redemption. But if I only knew him as the president, the guy in Washington, the man of emancipation, I'd say he was more focused on deliverance. The private Lincoln is more like Jesus, but the public Lincoln is more like Moses."

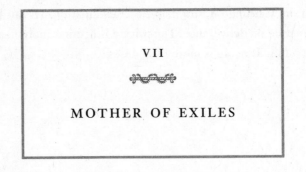

VII

MOTHER OF EXILES

I STEP OUT of the Bowling Green subway station in lower Manhattan, stride past the battered sphere sculpture salvaged from the World Trade Center, and pass through security at Coast Guard Headquarters. The guard directs me to a pylon at river's edge, and suddenly I'm in a different world. The dock is a tangle of buckets, ropes, barnacle-crusted buoys. A seagull flutters in the briny air. To my left is a four-story orange ferryboat, *Miss Liberty*. Across the inland chop is a giant air vent for the Brooklyn Battery Tunnel, and between us is a never-ending crisscross of water taxis, tugboats, and garbage barges. Far from the glittering lights of Fifth Avenue, this is industrial New York. The harbor as infrastructure. The city as work.

To my right, framed by the slate sky and a tangle of steel cranes, is the ultimate icon of industrial age America. The towering giant of copper and steel was conceived as a pagan symbol, meant to exude

Old World muscle. But by the time the New World got through re-interpreting it, the 305-foot colossus had become the standard-bearer of America's escape from tyranny, its commitment to freedom and law, and its role as the new Promised Land. Just when America's connection to Moses was tarnished by its association with the losing side of the Civil War, along came the country's most captivating symbol yet and a renewed link to its Mosaic past.

Along came the Statue of Liberty.

THE *ROSEMARY MILLER,* a small coast guard vessel, docks at the pier, and a half-dozen commuters walk up the short plank and gather in the open air at the stern. Many carry brown-bag lunches or crumpled plastic sacks. One wears a hard hat. Ignoring the wind, a few are trying to talk on cell phones or listen to iPods. These workers are taking the morning commute to Liberty Island, and as the boat pushes off from the shore, all of them are leaning against the rail or huddled in small groups, looking north. The statue is south. I had been invited by the monument's chief historian to take the staff boat to the island, and my first impression is that if you are exposed to the statue often enough, even the country's beacon of hope can become a mere backdrop. As the boat splashes into the harbor I risk exposing myself as a newbie when I defiantly look south.

At the close of the Civil War, the country's most profound shock may have been the damage to its self-image as a chosen people, selected by God to create a biblical kingdom on earth. Even more destabilizing, the closing decades of the nineteenth century brought a dizzying barrage of intellectual movements, economic transformation, and scholarly invention that collectively constituted the biggest threat to the Bible's authority in its nearly two millennia of influence. Charles Darwin published *The Origin of Species* in 1859, initiating a direct assault on the biblical idea that God created the world in six days. Also, literary critics exploded the traditional view of who wrote the Bible. Custom held that Moses wrote the books that bore his name; David wrote the psalms; and the prophets wrote their books. Scholars now argued that different authors composed the stories, often long after the events described. Educated people were forced to accept that the Bible may contain the word of God but also contains the work of scribes. Overnight, everything known about the Israelites was open to question. Did Moses really turn the Nile into blood? Did he really part the Red Sea? Did he even exist? And what about God?

God's New Israel particularly felt the impact of these changes. In less time than the Israelites are said to have spent in the desert, the United States went from a predominantly rural nation to a highly urban one, from a mostly agricultural economy to a heavily industrialized one, from a deeply religious society to a more secular one. The "age of belief" gave way to a "scientific revolution." The grip of evangelicals gave way to wave after wave of Catholic and Jewish immigrants. By 1900 it became clear that if the nineteenth century had been America's Protestant century, the twentieth century would be something else entirely. And that raised a question: If America's focus on the Bible was diminishing, would its attachment to Moses lessen as well?

ON A GRAY approach from Manhattan, the Statue of Liberty doesn't quite stir the soul as the postcard images would suggest. Her mint color seems more chilly than star-spangled. She faces south, meaning that for much of the ride you're viewing her from behind. The shadows in her folds look streaked in soot. From the rear, she appears to be sagging under the weight of her gown. Not until the boat passes under her feet does my heart skip a beat at her Olympian splendor: her firm grip on the tablet in her left arm, the seven bolts of light from her crown, and the erect majesty of her right arm, with the twenty-karat flame managing to brighten the gloom. The shock of gold in the otherwise dreary environs reminds me of the Dome of the Rock in Jerusalem.

Barry Moreno was not what I had expected. On the phone, the chief historian of the Statue of Liberty and Ellis Island sounded like a pencil pusher who wore a green visor and toted a tuna fish sandwich to the island every day. I would have pegged him for balding and fifty. In person he looked like a backup singer for Madonna. He wore fashionably flared jeans, trendy shoes, and a yellow, polka-dotted dress shirt with unbuttoned French cuffs. The son of an Egyptian mother and a Cuban-Italian father, he also has long, lithe fingers that he bends back in the manner of a yoga instructor.

"I first visited the statue in 1988 when I was hired as a temporary ranger after college," Moreno explained. "I took a train from California. I had never been to New York, and I was stunned by the statue. She was so historic. Not quite as great as a monarch, but something close to the glory of a king."

He never left. A first-generation polyglot American and a sponge for languages, Moreno was a perfect Boswell for *Liberty*. He has since written one book and one encyclopedia on the subject in English and was cowriting another in German, and in order to examine all the immigrant documents that came into the library, he had managed to learn French, Italian, Spanish, Arabic, Dutch, Swedish, Norwegian, Afrikaans, Romanian, Portuguese, and Catalan. "They're all related," he said nonchalantly, as if the task was as simple as collecting his mail.

Moreno led me up the broad sidewalk, through the tightest security I'd ever seen, and into a small museum at the base of the statue.

A giant, life-sized mask of *Liberty's* face peers out from the entrance, not as serene as the *Mona Lisa,* more sternly serious. Alongside it are some of the wooden molds used to hold the 200,000 pounds of molten copper, which were pounded into 310 sheets, each two pennies thick. Nearby is a model of the steel interior designed by Gustave Eiffel, which anticipated the Eiffel Tower that was built the following year. *Liberty's* pageantry may be American, but her infrastructure is pure French.

"When I was growing up, I knew the statue as a great symbol of the United States," Moreno said. "But when I first came here, many aspects of her origin were simply fuzzed over. The Park Service didn't want us to do our own research. It was not until I started doing my own digging that I really understood the story."

The birth of the Statue of Liberty grew out of the death of Abraham Lincoln. The news of Lincoln's assassination arrived in France at a time when the country was rent by a generation-long struggle between republicanism and monarchism. In the spring of 1865, under the regressive regime of Emperor Napoléon III, French liberals were struggling to articulate a viable model for representative democracy, and they turned to the United States. The approaching centennial of the Declaration of Independence offered the ideal time to hail American liberty, remind the world of France's role in bankrolling that freedom, and forever align the two countries. At a meeting outside of Versailles, Americaphile Édouard de Laboulaye, the author of a history of the United States and an avid abolitionist, conceived the idea of presenting a monument to the United States as a gift. At least one man in the group thought it was a good idea.

Frédéric Bartholdi was not exactly an Americaphile. But the thirty-three-year-old sculptor was a classicist, a lover of Egypt, and likely a Mason, since he had put his face on a Masonic sculpture in Paris and sculpted Washington and Lafayette in a supposed Masonic handshake. He also loved grand gestures, all of which made him uniquely suited to tackle the complexities of raising money for a work modeled partly on the Colossus of Rhodes, one of the original Seven Wonders of the World. In back-to-back trips to Egypt and the United States, Bartholdi honed the idea of a tribute to liberty that would draw its size from pharaonic monuments of Rameses II and be placed in New York Harbor. It should be seen "from the shores of America to the coast of France," Bartholdi said. To boost sagging fund-raising, Bartholdi sent a model of the torch to Philadelphia in 1876, then to New York. Joseph Pulitzer helped with the final push by appealing to readers of the *World*. On August 11, 1885, the *World* showed Uncle Sam bowing down to Lady Liberty on the occasion of topping one hundred thousand dollars in donations. The torch was being passed to a new American symbol.

But what did the statue, officially called *Liberty Enlightening the World*, represent?

"To me, she's a Roman, pagan goddess," Moreno said. He had brought me to a spot deep in the pedestal where the original torch is displayed. "Nearly everything about the statue is Greek or Roman. She's dressed in totally Roman garb. Her hairstyle is from that time. She strides forward in a neoclassical way."

"But France and America were largely Christian," I said. "Were people offended?"

"Bartholdi knew that no figure customarily represented the American people. On maps, female Indians had been used to sym-bolize the United States. But classical imagery had been popular in Europe for centuries, and even in America, our courthouses and post offices were built as Greek and Roman temples. Plus, she does have a lot of non-pagan influences."

"So let me ask you about a few of those," I said. "Is it significant that Bartholdi was a Mason? He met with Masons when he came to

THE GREAT BARTHOLDI STATUE.
LIBERTY ENLIGHTENING THE WORLD.
THE GIFT OF FRANCE TO THE AMERICAN PEOPLE.
TO BE
ERECTED ON BEDLOE'S ISLAND, NEW YORK HARBOR.

Liberty Enlightening the World, with ships and New York Harbor in the background. Lithograph published by Currier & Ives, c. 1886. *(Courtesy of The Library of Congress)*

New York. Masons raised a lot of the money, and Masons actually constructed the pedestal."

"Bartholdi believed that Masons had some secret to democracy," Moreno said. "They were connected to the breakdown of the authoritarian models of government and hierarchical, ritualistic religions. Plus they supported new interpretations of the Bible and the idea that certain elite people share a secret message of freedom."

I ticked off a series of the statue's prominent symbols and asked Moreno what they represented. A number seemed as if they were taken directly from the Bible. I started with the chains and shackle at Liberty's feet.

"Ostensibly they symbolize independence from England, but secretly they mean other kinds of servitude—slavery, tyranny, any kind of oppression in the world. That's why immigrants and refugees legitimately saw the statue as a symbol of their freedom."

The crown. Roman depictions of Liberty often showed her with a soft red bonnet, called a Phrygian cap, given to Roman slaves when they were freed. The U.S. Capitol was designed with a Liberty on top wearing one of those bonnets, though the statue was renamed *Freedom* and the cap replaced with a helmet of an eagle's head. Bartholdi scuttled the cap in favor of a nimbus, a gold circle of light in the shape of a crown with seven pointed sun rays, one for each continent, or ocean, or day of God's creation. As Moreno noted, the Roman sun god Helios was also shown wearing a spiked crown, as were Roman emperors, even Constantine. The motif of a halo around the head of a significant person was commonly used in medieval and Renaissance art, especially for Jesus.

But the notion that light should envelop the head of an exalted figure is introduced in the Hebrew Bible, predating all of these uses. In the first sentence of Genesis, God is associated with light as he utters the earliest words ever spoken: "Let there be light." God later appears to Moses in an illuminated burning bush, and he appears to the Israelites encamped at Mount Sinai as "a consuming fire on the top of the mountain." The first human to have his presence infused with God's light is Moses. In Exodus 34, when Moses descends from forty days on Sinai carrying the "two tablets" of the covenant, he "was not aware that the skin of his face was radiant, since he had spoken with the Lord." The Israelites shrink from Moses because his face is luminous and he veils himself to protect them. The story of the Exodus predates the Byzantine, Christian, and classical Greek and Roman eras, so Moses—not Helios, Nero, Jesus, or Constantine—introduces the nimbus into Western imagery. A misinterpretation of a Hebrew expression in this scene, *karan orh pahnav*, which can be read "ray of light" or "horn," produced the idea that Moses had horns. Michelangelo memorialized the horns in his statue of Moses, and they are echoed in the spikes around the forehead of Bartholdi's *Liberty Enlightening the World*.

Was Bartholdi aware of this lineage? Did he purposefully connect *Liberty*'s nimbus to Moses?

"I'm not sure where he came up with this idea," Moreno said. "Was it the Hebrews, the Greeks? But it seems to me that he probably got it from Judeo-Christian sources, because the nimbus constantly resonated in European thought. Even if Bartholdi himself didn't go to Rome to see Michelangelo's *Moses*, his friends did. And they were sharing ideas."

The statue's most unusual symbol may represent its most direct link to Exodus. Traditional depictions of Roman Libertas show her left arm down at her side, holding a broken jug, signifying the slaves' release. Bartholdi's earliest clay model includes a jug, which he later replaced with a broken chain. The final statue shows Liberty holding a singular rectangular tablet, inscribed with JULY IV MDCCLXXVI, or

July 4, 1776. Tablets were not common in classical art and were introduced into European art in conjunction with one story, Moses carrying the Ten Commandments down Mount Sinai.

In Exodus 24, God summons Moses up Mount Sinai and promises to give him "the stone tablets with the teachings and commandments which I have inscribed." Exodus 32 says that the tablets were inscribed on both sides. The tablets are elsewhere referred to in the text as tablets of stone, testimony, or law, and are often translated as the *tables* of stone. But the Bible never describes their composition or shape. Traditional Judaism suggests they were made of blue sapphire as a reminder of God's heavenly throne; others believe they were transparent. As for shape, some commentators have said they were sharp-edged cubes; others that they were separate pieces of oblong stone. Michelangelo's *Moses,* for instance, sculpted in 1513, holds two stacked rectangular tablets. The familiar depiction of side-by-side, flat stone tablets with semicircular tops containing the first five commandments on one face and the second five on the other face is not found anywhere in the Bible. These round-top tablets seem to have entered Christian art in the Middle Ages to reflect the diptych, a popular form of writing tablet in which two waxed boards were joined together by a hinge.

Regardless of their shape, Moses lugs the tablets down the mountain, but upon eyeing the Israelites frolicking with the golden calf, he "hurled the tablets from his hands and shattered them at the foot of the mountain." The move is shocking: Moses purposefully destroys the only physical manifestation of God's commitment to protect his people. But he goes further. He burns the golden calf, grinds the charred remains into powder, sprinkles the ashes into water, and forces the Israelites to drink their infidelity. Suddenly the great liberator has become a fanatic. "Whoever is for the Lord, come here!" he announces. The Levites step forward, and Moses sends them on a purge. "Go back and forth throughout the camp, slay brother, neighbor, and kin." Having completed his own God-like version of the tenth plague, Moses then returns to the mountain and asks God to forgive the remaining people. God adds his own unspecified plague but ultimately accepts Moses' plea. The covenant between God and humans is restored. God asks Moses to carve two more tablets, and once more he inscribes them. This new set of tablets is stored in the wooden ark that Moses constructs; this ark is then installed in the temple that Solomon builds in Jerusalem; and this vault later becomes the "lost ark" that goes missing for more than two thousand years.

The significance of the Statue of Liberty holding a tablet of law has not been lost on commentators over the years. French historian Pierre Provoyeur wrote that Bartholdi must have conceived the statue as a "second Moses." "*Liberty* carried the Tables of the Law in her left arm, while her forehead shone with light like the prophet's on Mount Sinai." Marvin Trachtenberg, in his definitive account of the statue, writes: "*Liberty*'s tablet—particularly the way it is borne forward—is an unmistakable allusion not only to political events but to the great Mosaic tradition." He adds, "Not only does she carry the tablet of the patriarch but her radiant crown also may allude to the 'rays of light' about his face after revelation." The statue, he concludes, is "a seer and a prophetess."

I asked Barry Moreno if he agreed.

"Even though the outer form of the statue is pagan," he said, "she was devised in a Judeo-Christian society in which the traditions of the Jewish Bible are richly powerful. The tablet is suggestive of the twelve tablets of Roman law as well as the Code of Hammurabi, but in Western society, the great symbol of the law is Mosaic. So to me, the tablets symbolize constitutional law. The goddess of freedom promises to enlighten the world with freedom, but then she has this tablet of law, reminding us that there are strict precepts. There is no absolute freedom, but rather limitations."

"But doesn't the tablet say 1776, not 1787?"

"Yes, it clearly invokes the Declaration of Independence. But to me the statue has external symbols and internal symbols. There are the ostensible reasons, and there are the secret meanings the statue conveys. Freedom from England is one of the outward messages, but freedom from slavery, whether the Exodus or the Civil War, is one of the more subtle messages."

"The Moses story is about the tension between freedom and law," I said, "between the exhilaration of the Exodus moment followed by the constriction of the Sinai moment. And it seems to me that you can see this tension in the Statue of Liberty, from the broken chain at her feet to the tablet in her arm to the light around her head. She perfectly embodies the American story—and the Mosaic story."

"Precisely," Moreno said. "That's what Laboulaye was trying to say, and he's the real intellectual force behind the statue. His main goal was to increase freedom in France but not so much that it led to anarchism, violence, and coups d'etat. He looked to America and saw a totally open society, yet one that had prevented disorderly conduct. Even with the Civil War, Americans had somehow managed to preserve the Constitution without a revolution. It was a miracle."

"So even before Americans set about reinterpreting the statue, the French viewed the United States as a Promised Land."

"Yes, I think they felt Americans had achieved the promise."

THE PEDESTAL IS an engineering marvel nearly equal to that of the statue. Built over a massive, tapering block of concrete fifty-two feet tall and ninety-one feet square at the bottom, the six-story pedestal is probably strong enough to withstand nuclear attack. Its walls are eight to nineteen feet thick, made entirely of concrete, covered with Connecticut granite. It narrows to forty-three square feet under the statue's feet. The pedestal's labyrinthine interiors, a Rube Goldberg–like maze of black staircases, elevator shafts, and steel beams, remind me of underground bunkers from the Cold War. The base involved by far the largest use of concrete at the time— twenty-seven thousand tons—and is said to have marked a turning point in the revival of Roman-style concrete as a popular building material in the United States.

Barry Moreno led me to a narrow staircase and we began climbing the 156 steps. Giant conical bolts and sixteen steel tie-rods fill the walls and open spaces, securing the 450,000-pound statue to the pedestal. Steel cables and a glass elevator shoot up through the middle. The effect is rather like rock climbing through a pocket watch. I felt a little light-headed from the sharp turns and elevation. Even more unsettling was that every gust of wind outside causes the tie-rods to reverberate like twangs on a mouth harp. The statue was generations ahead of its time with a tension-flex system that lets the body sway five inches and the arm up to eight. *Liberty* has withstood two category-three hurricanes, and Barry believes it could weather a category-five.

As we climbed, we talked about how the statue had become a symbol of immigrant America. The reason for that belongs largely to a poem that linked the Statue of Liberty with the Mosaic tradition of her adopted homeland.

Emma Lazarus, the poem's author, was an unlikely champion of "huddled masses, yearning to breathe free." The daughter of one of the wealthiest Jews in New York City, the Portuguese sugar tycoon Moses Lazarus, the never-married Emma lived with her six siblings in elegant, Judaism-free splendor in New York society. Though she was raised to keep Mosaic law, she told Ralph Waldo Emerson's daughter that her family "no longer keep the law, but Christian institutions don't interest her either." All that changed on July 29, 1881, when a steamer arrived in New York Harbor containing 250 Russian Jews fleeing pogroms triggered by the assassination of Czar Alexander II. Nearly 170 Jewish communities were attacked and 20,000 Jewish homes destroyed. The events spurred the largest mass migration of Jews since the Exodus. Between 1881 and 1914, 2 million eastern European Jews, most from Russia, Romania, and Austria-Hungary, arrived in the United States.

By December 1881, Wards Island, a dilapidated asylum in the East River, had become the dumping ground for hundreds of these refugees. The following March, Emma Lazarus made her first visit there. Her impressions were recorded the following day in the *New York Times*. Never before were prayers of gratitude more genuine, wrote the reporter, believed to be Lazarus, "when after a new exodus, and a new persecution . . . , these stalwart young representatives of the oldest civilization in existence met to sing the songs of Zion in a strange land." The visit sparked an emotional Jewish awakening in Emma. "The Jewish Question which I plunged into so recklessly & impulsively," she wrote a friend, "has gradually absorbed more and more of my time & heart—It opens up such enormous vistas in the Past & Future and is so palpitatingly alive at the moment." She began studying Hebrew; she joined delegations to the State Department on the Jewish question; she helped found the Jewish Technical Institute. And she composed a series of sixteen letters, published as "An Epistle to the Hebrews," that called for two new exoduses—one to the Promised Land of old, in the Middle East; the other to the new Promised Land, in America.

In two divided streams the exiles part—
One rolling homeward to its ancient source,
One rushing sunward, with fresh will, new heart.

In late summer 1883, the thirty-four-year-old Emma returned from a trip to Europe and received an invitation to contribute a poem to a fund-raising exhibition for something called *Liberty Enlightening the World*. She gave her stock reply: She was "unable to write for order." But a writer friend pressed her. "Think of that Goddess standing on her pedestal down yonder in the bay, and holding her torch out to those Russian refugees of yours you are so fond of visiting." Emma lit. The result was "The New Colossus."

Not like the brazen giant of Greek fame,
With conquering limbs astride from land to land;
Here at our sea-washed, sunset gates shall stand
A mighty woman with a torch, whose flame
Is the imprisoned lightning, and her name
Mother of Exiles. From her beacon-hand
Glows world-wide welcome; her mild eyes command
The air-bridged harbor that twin cities frame,
"Keep, ancient lands, your storied pomp!" cries she
With silent lips. "Give me your tired, your poor,
Your huddled masses yearning to breathe free,
The wretched refuse of your teeming shore.
Send these, the homeless, tempest-tost to me,
I lift my lamp beside the golden door!"

Even before the statue was complete, Emma performed a deft turnabout of the tensions between the goddess's pagan ancestry and the Hebraic iconography of her accoutrements. With her opening salvo, "Not like the brazen giant of Greek fame," Lazarus smashes the godless idol of the "old Colossus," the Greek god Apollo who stood astride Rhodes. Then she rechristens—or, more accurately, re-Judaizes—the statue as "Mother of Exiles." One of the Hebrew Bible's consistent themes is that humans encounter God most intimately when they are in exile. Abraham forms his alliance with God when he leaves his native land and his father's house to go forth to the land God promises him. Moses encounters God in the burning bush during his self-imposed exile, after he leaves his native land and his surrogate grandfather's house and flees into the desert. The Israelites form their covenant with God during their forty years in exile, after departing their native land and their fathers' homes and crossing into the wilderness. The pattern is later repeated in Babylon, Persia, Greece, and Rome.

But exile is not just a physical state, the Bible suggests; it's a moral one. At Mount Sinai, God specifically uses the Israelites' exile in Egypt as a foundation of their identity and a core reason that they should be compassionate toward others. "You shall not oppress a stranger," God says in Exodus 23, "for you know the feelings of the stranger, having yourselves been strangers in the land of Egypt." The idea that people who were once exiled have a moral imperative to care for future exiles is the primary lesson Emma Lazarus drew from the Israelites. Her genius was to fuse this biblical value with the story of America, then attribute both to the Statue of Liberty. As the great prophet of exiles, Moses becomes a bridge linking the Bible with *Liberty*, the mother of exiles. Emma Lazarus, a Sephardic aristocrat with little identification with the Jews, who returns from her own exile from her faith to become a passionate leader of her people, bears so many similarities with Moses that the connection becomes even more profound.

Lazarus's "Mother of Exiles" also channels Moses' showdown with the pharaoh. Just as the exiled Israelite cries to the mighty superpower, "Let my people go," so *Liberty* has a similar confrontation with entrenched status: "Keep, ancient lands, your storied pomp." A society must gauge its worth not by power, the statue insists, but by how it treats its strangers. Rejecting the "conquering limbs" of the past, *Liberty* offers an outstretched arm. "From her beacon-hand / Glows world-wide welcome; . . . 'Give me your tired, your poor, / Your huddled masses yearning to breathe free.'" Like Moses, the Mother of Exiles becomes the reborn child of privilege leading her "wretched," "homeless" "refuse" of a people out of bondage into freedom. Lazarus's poem is a masterful act of redefinition, rejecting the "brazen," imprisoning godlessness of the past with the welcoming beacon of moral-centeredness in the future. A "mighty woman" heralds the dawn of God's New Israel and lights its greatest "flame."

WE REACH THE top of the pedestal and light floods in from all sides. Above, a plate-glass window shows the molded interior of *Liberty*'s gown. Outside is a 360-degree walkway. The wind whistles against copper, creating a kind of sound cocoon. I mention 9/11, and Moreno explains how a colleague, seeing a plane flying abnormally close to the statue, hurried up the pedestal and took one of the photographs of United flight 175 crashing into the second tower. Since then, visitors are not allowed to enter the body of the statue. From the pedestal, the hole in Ground Zero is still visible, and the cavity in the skyline is its most notable feature. The nearest icon is the Brooklyn Bridge, which was under construction when Emma Lazarus wrote her poem, a detail she captured in her line "the air-bridged harbor that twin cities frame."

Liberty Enlightening the World was dedicated on a rainy October 28, 1886. Lazarus's sonnet, which had earlier helped raise a paltry fifteen hundred dollars, was not read and not missed. Still, a number of speakers did draw connections between *Liberty* and the Exodus. Renowned orator Chauncey Depew, the day's main speaker, said the statue was the "inspiration of God" who elevated "the conquered" to the "full measure" of freedom. Earlier he had said the statue "would for all time to come welcome the incoming stranger." John Greenleaf Whittier's official poem also likened Americans to enslaved Israelites whom Moses freed from the shadow of the Pyramids.

> Unlike the shapes on Egypt's sands
> Uplifted by the toil-worn slave,
> On Freedom's soil with freemen's hands
> We rear the symbol free hands gave.

José Martí, the Cuban patriot, described the statue on its opening day as advancing forward "as if to enter the Promised Land."

Lazarus died from cancer the following year, unlinked to *Liberty*. Not until 1903 did a wealthy friend place a plaque containing "The New Colossus" inside the pedestal. Still, it wasn't until the late 1930s, with Hitler compelling Jews once more to flee Europe, that a Slovenian American immigrant named Louis Adamic began a one-man campaign to resuscitate the sonnet and renew *Liberty*'s role as a Mother of Exiles. This time it worked. New biographies called Lazarus the "Woman with a Torch"; Alfred Hitchcock ended *Saboteur* (1942) in the statue's crown with the heroine quoting the sonnet to an enemy agent; Irving Berlin used the poem's final words in the lyrics of his Broadway musical *Miss Liberty*. By midcentury, Lazarus's vision of the Statue of Liberty as a beacon of freedom to heal a broken world had become its dominant cry. Emma Lazarus gave a voice to the statue that could not speak.

While we were standing outside the pedestal, I asked Barry Moreno why he thought Lazarus's interpretation had become the prevailing one.

"I think it has something to do with the biblical ties of the statue," he said, "and how much that related to the American experience. And to the Jewish experience. Jews were attracted to the New World, yet many of them felt attached to the world they were leaving behind. They felt compelled to come here. I think America, and the Statue of Liberty, helped persuade them into accepting a new life."

"So the statue's biblical iconography helped make them feel welcome?"

"Even the tablet itself may have been strong enough to overcome doubt. They were looking to escape their awful past—the poverty, the shtetl. Then when they get to the golden land, they see the Statue of Liberty, and they have a sense that this place also views itself as having a special role and being home to a special people. That idea had been in America from the very beginning, of course, but it took a Jewish poet to reignite it."

As if to reinforce that image, Ronald Reagan came to the statue on its centennial in 1986 and made the connection explicit. Weaving Emma Lazarus and Abraham Lincoln together with the signers of the Declaration of Independence, he rooted the Mother of Exiles in the earliest Americans, the Puritans. "We sometimes forget that even those who came here first to settle the new land were also strangers," Reagan said. "I've spoken before of the tiny *Arbella,* a ship at anchor just off the Massachusetts coast." As the ship reached shore, Reagan continued, John Winthrop reminded his fellow Puritans that "they must keep faith with their God, that the eyes of all the world are upon them, and that they must not forsake the mission that God had sent them on." Reagan failed to note that when Winthrop quoted these words he attributed them to their source, "that faithful servant of the Lord, in his last farewell to Israel." Moses. At the centennial of the Statue of Liberty, the union of state and symbol was complete. In the elegant, biblical phrasing of Ronald Reagan:

> I have always believed there was some divine providence that placed this great land here between the two great oceans, to be found by a special kind of people from every corner of the world, who had a special love for freedom and a special courage that enabled them to leave their own land, leave their friends and their countrymen, and come to this new and strange land to build a New World of peace and freedom and hope.

BACK ON THE water heading home, I was struck by how much the statue's story mirrored that of the Liberty Bell. An object made for one purpose was reimagined to signify another. In both cases, the power of the American story, with its grand themes of slavery and freedom, oppression and hope, had become so muscular that even objects with little transparent connection to Moses could be reforged in his image. The sacred story lines of America had long paralleled the central themes of the Exodus.

Then, just as the Bible seemed to be peaking in influence, something unexpected happened. Until now, the idea of linking America with Moses had been done almost entirely by Protestants. As Peter Gomes pointed out to me back in Plymouth, Christians easily cast themselves as inheritors of the Jewish role as the chosen people when no real Jews were present. But suddenly at the turn of the twentieth century, millions of real Jews showed up in America, eager to claim their place as heirs to their own story. Efforts by Jews to interact with Christian America would become one of the dominant undercurrents of the coming century and one of the greatest reasons why Moses endured as a defining figure in the American identity.

To help understand the role of Jews in creating modern America, I went to see Jonathan Sarna, the leading historian of American Jewry. Sarna's father, Nahum, was a pioneer student of biblical archaeology, and I had carried his books with me when I retraced the Bible through the Middle East. Now I was doing the same with his son's books. Jonathan Sarna is a compact man, with a tidy beard, spectacles, and a small *kippah* on his head. He holds himself very still when he talks. Like Barry Moreno, he seems perfectly cast for a man of precision, but his mind is grand and his writing brims with joy.

I began by asking him to characterize the importance of Moses to Jews.

"In traditional Judaism," Professor Sarna said, "Moses is the central figure to whom God gives the Torah. The assumption was that all the law, written and oral, was handed down at Sinai to Moses. The rabbis call this *halachah le'Moshe mi'Sinai,* the 'law that goes back to Sinai.' Cantors say that certain ancient melodies go back to Sinai. Jewish brides and grooms get married in the name of Moses. Moses is the human who comes closest to God, so everything is mediated through him."

Given that importance, it's not surprising that when Jews came to America they tried to link Moses with their adopted homeland. Their task was made easier because Moses was already here.

Jews made spotty appearances in the New World among early settlers, and the first significant community was established in New Amsterdam in 1654. But as late as the Revolution, Jews were still a microscopic presence, totaling fewer than 2,000 people. One hundred Jews are known to have fought during the War of Independence. Still, the Constitution's support of religious tolerance, and the elimination of state-sponsored churches, encouraged European Jews to view the United States as offering greater opportunity. By the start of the Civil War, America's Jewish population had reached 150,000.

As early as the 1820s, Jewish leaders in Europe and the United States had begun referring to America as the new Promised Land, but the analogy was not always positive. Many Jews echoed Moses' warning to the Israelites in Deuteronomy not to succumb to sinful temptations. As one teacher warned a couple leaving for Ohio in 1839, "You are traveling to a land of freedom. . . . Resist and withstand this tempting freedom and do not turn away from the religion of your fathers. Do not throw away your holy religion for quickly lost earthly pleasures." Again the words echo Winthrop.

Protestants were ambivalent about these Jewish immigrants. Anti-Semitism ticked up during these years, but Jews were mostly perceived as less threatening than Catholics, who had grown from 2 percent of the population in 1830 to 10 percent by 1860 to 16 percent by 1910. Americans' love-hate attitude toward Jewish immigrants was on display in an extraordinary edition of the satiric magazine *Puck* in 1881. The issue contained a two-page color cartoon showing Uncle Sam in red-and-white trousers, a blue coat, and a red cape, standing on a rock in the middle of the Atlantic, wielding a wand labeled "Liberty." In an image that looks both back to Daniel Boone and forward to Charlton Heston, Uncle Sam spreads his arm and splits the Atlantic, while a stream of Jewish immigrants, many with hooked noses and kinky hair, dressed in top hats and formal gowns, crosses on dry ground to America. The editorial compared Jewish and Catholic immigrants on the question of who fit better in the Protestant Promised Land. The writers urged hooligan Catholics to act more

"The Modern Moses." Cartoon depicting Moses dressed as Uncle Sam, splitting the Atlantic Ocean and allowing Jewish immigrants to cross to the new Promised Land. Drawn by Frederick Burr Opper and Joseph Keppler. *Puck,* December 1881. *(Courtesy of The Library of Congress)*

like the Jews but cautioned Jews not to believe they could have free rein in America. "Who is competent to decide the question?" the editors ultimately asked. "Uncle Sam, as the modern Moses, will decide it."

Up to this point, Uncle Sam had not been a particularly religious figure. He is thought to have earned his name when "Uncle" Samuel Wilson, a meat packer in upstate New York in the 1810s, teased that the initials "U.S." on barrels of pork bound for American troops referred to him. The joke stuck. By the Civil War, Uncle Sam was being depicted as an old man with white hair and a goatee. He was often shown as a male companion to the Statue of Liberty. And like her, Uncle Sam emerged during the immigration debates in the late nineteenth century as a kind of surrogate Moses. As Emma Lazarus did with *Liberty*, the editors of *Puck* imagined Uncle Sam addressing Jewish immigrants.

> I don't invite you Jews to come here because you are Jews, but because I want a lot of intelligent and ill-used people to become citizens of my glorious Republic. As my ancient predecessor, Moses, did with the Red Sea, I do with the Atlantic Ocean. The waters are divided, and you can safely pass through them to the land of liberty, and leave oppression, persecution, and brutality behind you.

In the tradition of nearly every great American icon—the seal, the flag, the Liberty Bell—Uncle Sam now took a turn as Moses. The Hebrew prophet had become so ingrained in the country's consciousness that he served as a kind of American Hamlet, a role that every actor, in order to be considered great, had to play at least once.

Jews, too, began converting Moses into a pillar of American identity, a kind of supra–Founding Father. As early as Thanksgiving 1852, a Philadelphia rabbi preached that "with the spangled banner of liberty in one hand, and the law of [Sinai] in the other, we will continue as faithful citizens in this glorious republic." A Cincinnati rabbi created a bookplate that portrays Moses on the left and George Washington on the right, with the American flag and the Ten Commandments in front. The founder of Reform Judaism, Isaac Mayer Wise, said at the centennial of Washington's inauguration in 1889 that Moses and Washington are "the two poles on the axis about which the history of mankind revolves."

I asked Jonathan Sarna why Jews worked so hard to show that Moses went hand in hand with America.

"Jews' greatest fear was that America would become a Christian nation," he said. "That there would be a Christian amendment to the Constitution. And that that would undermine everything that made America special for Jews. By emphasizing Moses, they showed that Jews belonged here as well. Jews were fortunate that so many American Protestants were Old Testament–focused."

The movement among American Jews to stress their kinship with Moses had another benefit. Liberal Jews wanted to return to the Mosaic roots of Judaism and downplay the myriad of laws governing food, dress, and prayer that rabbis had imposed over the years. Judaism should scrap these archaic ideas and modernize, they said. The back-to-Moses movement went so far that some prominent left-wing Jews actually proposed changing the name of Judaism to Mosaism, in part because Moses was perceived to be a more appealing figure to Christians.

"Many Jews had a sense that the words *Jew* and *Judaism* had negative connotations," Sarna explained. "The hope was that if you could come up with a more positive term, you would transform the way people would view Jews. I think that Jews also saw that Christians emphasized Jesus, and Moses gave Jews an opportunity to point to a similar figure in Judaism, who of course precedes Jesus, was a human figure, and didn't claim to be the son of God."

Exactly when the United States was becoming more religiously diverse, Jews subtly redefined what it meant to be American. Instead of a Christian country, they insisted, America was a *biblical* country. Moses played a key role because he resonated with Protestants and Jews. Jews belonged in the United States, they said, because America and Judaism had the same source: Moses.

In his book *American Judaism,* Sarna discusses how Jews used the holidays of Thanksgiving and Passover to stress that they had played starring roles in the defining moments of American history. The 1922

Reform *hagadah,* the book used during the Passover service, calls for an American flag to be placed on the seder table. "Why?" a child is instructed to ask. "America is the child of the Old Testament," the leader of the service is told to answer.

> It is the "Moses and Prophets" of modern times. The Pilgrim Fathers landed here inspired by Israel's wandering to go out even to the wilderness and worship God. The immortal Declaration of Independence is the Great Charter announced before Pharaoh by Moses. The Abolitionists are the product of the Bible. . . . The Fourth of July is the American Passover. Thanksgiving is the American Feast of the Tabernacles.

Several *hagadah*s even called for Jews to end their seders by singing "America (My Country, 'Tis of Thee)." Fitting into America had become such a priority that American Jews not only imported Moses into American celebrations, like Thanksgiving, they exported America back into Moses' chief celebration, Passover.

Sarna said that Jewish immigrants likely did not know they were continuing a pattern of connecting Moses and America that had been occurring since the 1600s. Still, I asked him how seventeenth-century Protestant separatists, eighteenth-century deist revolutionaries, nineteenth-century enslaved Africans, and twentieth-century Jews could all possibly have the same hero.

"What's fascinating about America," he said, "is that it's much more formless than Europe, therefore its imagery is much more open to be changed and molded. Just look at what Jews contribute to American culture. You've got the melting pot, that's a Jewish idea. You've got cultural pluralism, that's a Jewish idea. Like other groups before them, Jews are able to take an existing culture and help shape it in their image.

"On the other side," he continued, "the Bible is also formless. The lessons of these stories can be applied in different ways. So Moses became like a Rorschach test. He provided a common text for Americans. Today when we don't have a common text, it's very hard for people to realize that once upon a time we did."

"With Moses so interwoven with the American story by 1900, was his presence a reason America was so hospitable to Jews?" I asked.

He thought for a second. "The problem with that theory is that we certainly know that even early Americans who accepted the biblical story saw Jews as interlopers. The Puritans couldn't be more Hebraic, but they didn't make it particularly comfortable for Jews who arrived here. Precisely because they saw themselves as God's New Israel they were quite ambivalent about Jews who made a similar claim."

"But if I were going to press this case," I said, "I'd point out that whether they liked Jews or not, they still laid the foundation that America was built on the Moses story. And once you do that, once Benjamin Franklin and Thomas Jefferson say Moses should be on the Great Seal, once the slaves start singing 'Go Down, Moses,' you begin to say that standing up to authority, leading people out of oppression into an unknown world, then rebinding them under universal law, are central values of our country. And once that happens, the Jews can come along hundreds of years later and say: 'Hey, that's our story! We belong here, too.' Moses helps force the country into being pluralist whether that had been the Puritans' original intent or not."

"I agree," Sarna said. "You had plenty of places in Europe where the Bible was restricted to the elite. In America, the Bible was made available to everyone. Once that happens, the biblical story becomes much more important here than elsewhere. And it's not just the Bible; a lot does focus on Moses. Because of his presence, it becomes much easier for Jews to link themselves to America. And it becomes easier for America to see itself as a pluralistic nation, something that seemed impossible almost everywhere else in the world."

A FEW DAYS after I spoke with Professor Sarna, Jews around the world celebrated Yom Kippur, the Day of Atonement, which Leviticus 23 refers to as a day of "self-denial," designed to achieve expiation before God. My wife and I attended services at Brooklyn Heights Synagogue, which we had recently joined. The sanctuary cannot handle the crowds on the holiest day of the year, so services are held a few blocks from our home at Plymouth Church, the mammoth facility that was built for Henry Ward Beecher in 1850.

The exterior of the building—which was the largest in Brooklyn in Beecher's day—is lined with red brick. A garden features a statue of Beecher and a bas-relief of Abraham Lincoln, who visited in February 1860. Both works are by Gutzon Borglum, who later sculpted Mount Rushmore. Inside, the Yankee-white sanctuary was designed to enhance Beecher's dramatic style. Like a theater, it has curved pews, and no center aisle, and the proscenium pulpit is surrounded on three sides—church in the round. Though the windows were undecorated in Beecher's time, today they are filled with majestic stained glass that tells the history of American religion. Three focus on the Pilgrims: John Robinson launching the *Speedwell,* the signing of the Mayflower Compact, and William Brewster landing on Plymouth Rock. The First Great Awakening is honored with Jonathan Edwards, the Second with Lyman Beecher. Harriet appears with her sister Catharine in a tribute to women's education. Abraham Lincoln peers down on the pulpit, gripping the Emancipation Proclamation. I whispered to my wife, "It's the story of my book!"

When the time came for the Torah to be read, the rabbi called the half-dozen new members to the pulpit. He handed me one of the scrolls and asked me to carry it to the back of the sanctuary, then pass it on. I leaned it against my shoulder, and the velour cover spread warmth across my chest. The rabbi chanted in Hebrew, "This is the Torah that Moses gave to the people of Israel, from the mouth of God." For a second the blood rushed to my head. I began to walk down a side aisle, and people pushed forward, reaching out a prayer book or the corner of a prayer shawl to kiss the Torah.

Afterward, members of the synagogue took turns chanting the Torah portion for the day—sections of Deuteronomy 29 and 30—which are taken from Moses' farewell speech to the Israelites on Mount Nebo. "You stand this day, all of you, before the Lord your God," the passage begins, "to enter into the covenant of the Lord." The reading ends with Moses' great admonition to choose good over evil. "I call heaven and earth to witness against you this day: I have put before you life and death, blessing and curse. Choose life." This passage is sometimes referred to as the climax of Israel's constitution. From John Winthrop to Ronald Reagan, it has become part of America's national story line.

A rabbinic student, Tom Gardner, discussed Moses' remarks in his sermon that morning. He talked about whether religion could continue to have a role in a modern society that is dominated by science. "I'll tell you how bad it is," he said. "*I* don't like telling people I'm religious, and I'm studying to be a rabbi!" Gardner noted that in his speech, Moses seems to be saying that "if we listen, if we look, religion will make sense to us." *See, I have set before you this day. If you do not listen . . . , you will perish.* The Israelites on Mount Nebo should have found it easy to see and hear, he pointed out. Their ancestors had seen God send the plagues and split the Red Sea. They had seen the manna and water pour from rocks. They had heard God speaking from Mount Sinai. But still they doubted God.

Religion, Gardner continued, gives us eyes to see and ears to hear in ways that science simply cannot. "With our scientific eyes we can distinguish between true and false. With our religious eyes we can distinguish between right and wrong. When we see with our religious eyes, we live in a world of meaning."

After services, my wife and I walked home along the promenade that overlooks the East River and lower Manhattan. The stone esplanade has become something of our backyard. It's where we let our girls take their first steps out of their strollers, where they began to push dolly strollers of their own, and where we were now teaching them how to ride a scooter. Behind us was the Brooklyn Bridge, with its side-by-side pairings of Gothic arches. In front of us, across New York Harbor, was the Statue of Liberty. Between us was a shimmering boulevard of water.

Water. From the very beginning, I had seen my journey as a tale of water, though I didn't know quite why. Part of this, no doubt, is the importance of water to the Moses story: his birth in the watery Nile Delta, his rebirth in the wicker basket on the Nile, the pharaoh's daughter naming him Moses because she "drew him out of the water." Later, a number of the key events of his life involve water: meeting his wife by a well, leading the Israelites across the Red Sea, being denied entry into the Promised Land for improperly extracting water from the rock. Even his farewell speech in Deuteronomy 30 makes reference to the coming crossing of the Jordan. For a desert people, Moses may have been the ideal leader. He was drawn from water.

One reason Moses resonates so deeply in America may be the importance of water to the American narrative. There are the obvious parallels: the colonists crossing the Atlantic, Washington crossing the Delaware, the slaves crossing the Ohio, the immigrant steamers crossing under Lady Liberty. But beyond that, geography has been central to American history in ways that are strikingly similar to Israelite history. Both nations were bred in exile, by people who traversed a watery threshold, found a way to survive in the wilderness, and built a society of laws. And that pattern never went away in America. Moses has endured in American culture in large measure because his story spoke to the twenty million immigrants who arrived on America's shores in the first three decades of the twentieth century as much as it did to the one hundred who landed in Plymouth in 1620.

Moses' stark warning to his people in Deuteronomy became a kind of national slogan for both Israel and America because it captures the fear, experienced by each generation of outsiders, that by going to such a formless place, they will succumb to formlessness. They will forget the values of their native land and be lured by the worship of false gods. Moses' message to the Israelites is to remember where they came from—the wilderness. Remember what they formed there—a community of laws. And remember how they survived there—with water.

For the exiles, water becomes more than something to cross in order to get into the wilderness. It becomes a surrogate for their covenant. After his farewell speech, Moses gathers the Israelites one more time, in Deuteronomy 32 and reads a poem to them. It opens with these words:

> May my discourse come down as the rain,
> My speech distill as the dew,
> Like showers on young growth,
> Like droplets on the grass.
> For the name of the Lord I proclaim;
> Give glory to our God.

Stopped short of one final crossing, Moses tries to spread his watery blessing to his people. Like *Liberty*, Moses achieves his ultimate pose on that perch, light emanating from his head, the law in his arms, water beneath his feet. *Liberty* and Moses both stride forward, but both fail to reach their destination. They are beacons of promise precisely because they are unburdened by the compromises that come with the land. And their message is the same: Even when you reach your ultimate destination, don't forget the obligations that come with your freedom.

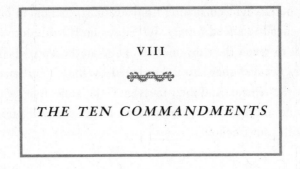

VIII

THE TEN COMMANDMENTS

AMERICA'S STREET OF Dreams, Sunset Boulevard, stretches twenty-two serpentine miles from downtown Los Angeles to the Pacific Ocean. In the eastern slums, the road has been renamed Cesar Chavez Avenue to honor the Mexican American union organizer. In the glitzy western highlands, Sunset has seen some of Hollywood's juicier past: F. Scott Fitzgerald had a heart attack here; Greta Garbo lived here as a recluse; Howard Hughes kept suites here for his various girlfriends; and it was here that Jean Harlow had an affair with Clark Gable while on her honeymoon with someone else. Humphrey Bogart and Lauren Bacall lived on Sunset for a time, as did John Wayne, who is said to have kept a cow on his apartment balcony so he could have fresh milk every morning. And 10086 Sunset Boulevard was the address of Norma Desmond, the demented silent film diva who murders her captive boyfriend at the end of *Sunset Boulevard,* before uttering the immortal line, "All right, Mr. DeMille, I'm ready for my close-up."

Early one Monday, I was heading toward 8148 Sunset to view the private memorabilia collection of the same Mr. DeMille—Cecil Blount, or C.B. to his friends—whose 1923 and 1956 film extravaganzas *The Ten Commandments* did more to define Moses for twentieth-century Americans than anyone since King James. The two films were also landmarks in how American popular culture reflected and shaped the country's evolving views of God. DeMille used Moses to promote a specific political agenda—anticommunist, pro-morality. In the process, he helped transform the biblical prophet into the figurehead of a strong-armed, open-minded America that DeMille believed could lead the world to a Promised Land of peace and prosperity. If the twentieth century was America's century, DeMille tried to turn Moses into its public face.

In many ways, DeMille was working against his times. The undermining of the Bible as the central plank of American life that began in the late nineteenth century did not abate in the early decades of the twentieth century. Even as World War I triggered a temporary surge in faith, and Darwinism and other forms of modernity led to a blossoming of fundamentalism, the Bible continued to recede as the ultimate source of authority in contemporary life. Americans attended church in extraordinary numbers and espoused a near-universal belief in God, but they relied less on the Bible as the chief source of public rhetoric. By the close of the 1930s, one scholar wrote, Americans had grown accustomed to using "a secular rather than theological vocabulary when issues really seemed worth arguing about."

While this transition might have signaled the disappearance of biblical figures from everyday discourse, something unexpected happened. Moses, along with Jesus and a few others, was decoupled from the Bible and moved into the realm of popular culture. In something akin to their own literary exodus, these figures left the bondage of the biblical narrative and set out into the wilderness of make-believe. Moses, in particular, became a star of American belles lettres. In 2004, Brian Britt, a scholar of religious studies at Virginia Polytechnic Institute and State University, analyzed every American literary work featuring Moses. He counted thirty-five, from J. H. Ingraham's novel *The Pillar of Fire* in 1859 to Lynne Reid Banks's *Moses in Egypt* in 1998. More than half were written between the Civil War and World War II, including novels by Zora Neale Hurston, Robert Graves, and Thomas Mann, an opera, two plays, and several books of poetry. The story lines touch on major themes, from Christian-Jewish relations to Freudian self-discovery. Freud wrote *Moses and Monotheism,* a "historical novel" published in 1939, which portrayed Moses as an Egyptian and claimed that the Israelites murdered him in the desert and sublimated their rebellion, thereby creating Jewish guilt.

Unmoored from the Bible, Moses became a polemical figure in the great debates of the day, which is one reason he stayed relevant. America was once again in a period of spiritual realignment. Could a fictionalized Moses help lead the way?

METROPOLITAN ART STORAGE may have an address on Sunset Boulevard, but its entrance is on a side street, a block away. I was greeted there by Helen Cohen, a vivacious costume designer who for twenty-five years has been the caretaker of the DeMille estate and the public face of the very private Cecilia Presley, Mr. DeMille's granddaughter and principal heir. I had to follow a meticulous protocol that seemed one step removed from Buckingham Palace to gain entry into this inner sanctum of Hollywood royalty. First Helen screened me, then I had to submit an application. In time I was invited to view the collection, then have an audience with Mrs. Presley, who had been on the set of *The Ten Commandments* in Egypt and had a much-discussed love affair with Yul Brynner's chariot driver.

Helen turned a key and opened the door into a room a little smaller than a one-car garage. It had fluorescent lights and a concrete floor and was covered from floor to ceiling with Hollywood artifacts: dusty plumes, faded trapeze costumes, the occasional chariot wheel, and several Roman helmets. It was like walking into your grandfather's attic, if your grandfather had directed seventy films, including some of Hollywood's grandest spectacles—*The Crusades, Samson and Delilah*, and *The Greatest Show on Earth*, which won the Oscar for Best Picture in 1952. One of the first objects that caught my eye was a corroded Golden Globe that DeMille also won for his circus epic.

For the next hour, Helen pulled objects from the collection and told me about the man dubbed "the Barnum of the movies." Cecil B. DeMille was born on August 12, 1881, to Henry DeMille, an Episcopal lay minister and playwright from North Carolina, and Matilda Samuel, a Sephardic Jew who converted to her husband's faith. In his autobiography, DeMille lingers over the $175 college scholarship his father received from a society to promote religion. "When I sign the contracts involving millions of dollars," he wrote, for *The King of Kings*, about Jesus, or *The Ten Commandments*, "and still more when I receive letters from all over the world, witnessing the religious values of these pictures . . . I like to think the good men who voted that grant might not be displeased." He fondly remembered his father teaching Bible classes in their home every Sunday and reading a chapter of the Old and New Testaments every night. But nowhere in his book does DeMille reveal that his mother was Jewish.

After dabbling in acting, DeMille joined with playwright Jesse Lasky and producer Sam Goldwyn in 1908 to enter the nascent film industry. They went on to pioneer a number of screen inventions, from indoor lighting to publicizing stars to the sneak preview. But DeMille became best known for using the big screen to promote biblical morality. His fifty-first film, the silent *Ten Commandments*, produced in 1923 for the staggering cost of $1.4 million, was his initial foray into religious spectacle. The film uses the story of Moses as a prologue to a modern parable in which two brothers have differing attitudes toward the Ten Commandments.

DeMille was part of a new wave of writers and artists trying to use the Bible to effect social change. As early as the 1890s, ministers began advocating the so-called prosperity gospel, which suggested that the Bible wanted you to be rich. Soon, biblical figures were turned into Horatio Alger–style models of success. In 1925 advertising honcho Bruce Barton published *The Man Nobody Knows*, depicting Jesus as the ultimate entrepreneur and Moses as a cunning executive. *The Man Nobody Knows* was the number four best-selling book of 1925 and the number one best-selling book of the following year. It earned Barton a coveted job as a consultant to Cecil B. DeMille. In 1927 the popular *Notebook of Elbert Hubbard* claimed that Moses was the ultimate adman. "Out of all the Plenipotentiaries of Publicity, Ambassadors of Advertising, and Bosses of Press Bureaus, none equals Moses." That same year, the Metropolitan Casualty Life Insurance Company published the lavishly illustrated *Moses, Persuader of Men*, a book that called Moses "one of the greatest salesmen and real-estate promoters that ever lived."

Yet capitalists weren't the only ones to embrace Moses as their hero. Communists did, too. The left's answer to the prosperity gospel began with the social gospel. It was based on the idea that in the exploding business climate many Americans were being left behind.

In 1906, Charles Reynolds Brown, a Congregational preacher, wrote *The Social Message of the Modern Pulpit,* which presented Moses as the ultimate advocate for the poor against the robber barons. He even labeled John Rockefeller's Standard Oil the "modern pharaoh." Brown homed in on Moses' line to the pharaoh; "Let my people go." "The very heart of the whole industrial question is contained in that brief sentence," he wrote.

The most extraordinary use of Moses during this time came from Lincoln Steffens, the celebrated muckraking journalist. In 1919 Steffens visited Russia and returned to make the infamous comment "I have seen the future and it works." In 1926 he published *Moses in Red,* which identified the Exodus as the model for revolution and Moses as the archetypical revolutionary leader. "Think of Moses as the uncompromising Bolshevik; Aaron as the more political Menshevik; take Pharaoh as the ruler who stands for the Right, and the children of Israel as the people—any people. Read the book of Moses thus and they will appear as a revolutionary classic." For a figure whom Benjamin Franklin, Thomas Jefferson, and John Adams once proposed to grace the seal to be a plausible candidate for the founding father of modern communism suggests he was the only one who could sell a new social movement to Americans. The Bible may have been under assault, but Moses was still the go-to figure of choice.

In 1923, DeMille viewed Moses as a perfect vessel to restore America's values. His was not *Moses in Red,* it was *Moses in Red, White, and Blue.* Moses had been a film favorite since the earliest days of the medium. In 1907 the Pathé company made *Moses and the Exodus from Egypt,* and in 1909 the Vitagraph Company spent fifty thousand dollars on a five-reel version of Moses' life. At a time when theaters were still considered places of sin, the film industry embraced biblical story lines to show that they could be virtuous and should be allowed to have screenings on Sundays. DeMille got the idea for his film from a contest Paramount Pictures drummed up to solicit subjects. An oil manufacturer from Michigan wrote and suggested a tribute to biblical values. His letter began, "You cannot break the Ten Commandments—they will break you." As DeMille recalled, "Here was a theme that stirred and challenged in me the heritage of being Henry DeMille's son, a theme that brightened memories of his reading the Bible aloud to us and teaching his sons that the laws of God are not mere laws, but are the Law."

Filmed in black-and-white, the 1923 *Ten Commandments* is presented in two parts. The first relates the liberation of the Israelites from Egypt, their trek across the desert, and their receipt of the Decalogue. The Exodus scenes were filmed in the sand dunes of Guadalupe, California, and DeMille transported hundreds of Orthodox Jews from New York, because he believed that "in appearance and in their deep feeling of the significance of the Exodus, they would give the best possible performance as the Children of Israel." But on their first day on set, the extras were forced to fast because the commissary served ham for dinner.

The bulk of the film focuses on a modern family. One brother keeps the commandments and is rewarded; the other is a cheat, has an adulterous affair, and listens to jazz on the Sabbath. When his mother reprimands him, he announces, "We'll break all of your old Ten Commandments, we'll finish rich and powerful with the world at our feet!" But when he builds a church with cheap materials, the church crumbles and kills his mother. Her dying words could have come from Henry Ward Beecher: "It's all my fault. I taught you to fear God instead of love Him—and LOVE is all that counts."

At the height of Jazz Age flamboyance, Cecil B. DeMille tried to reclaim the importance of law and morality. His Moses was not a radical figure, nor was he a beacon of antiauthoritarianism as he had been for the Pilgrims, slaves, and immigrants. Instead, he was an authority figure. Gone was the emphasis on the liberation of Exodus; now the focus was on the stern dictates of the Ten Commandments. As the film's opening cards put it:

> Our modern world defined God as a "religious complex" and laughed at the Ten Commandments as OLD FASHIONED. Then, through the laughter, came the shattering thunder of the World War. And now a blooddrenched, bitter world—no longer laughing—cries for a way out. There is but one way out. It existed before it was engraven upon Tablets of Stone. It will exist when stone has crumbled. The Ten Commandments are not rules to obey as a personal favor to God. They are the fundamental principles without which mankind cannot live together.

THE FURTHER WE dug into the shelves at the back of Metropolitan Storage, the more interesting the items became. Helen Cohen directed me to two black, 1950s-style snap-ring binders that looked like the ones my mother uses to collect recipes. They were DeMille's personal casting books in which he chronicled every film he watched, every screen test he viewed, and every interview he conducted. His secretaries typed up his whims in different-colored ink, at a time when that meant changing ribbons on their typewriters.

"James Stewart: 9 August 1950, Screened *Winchester '73,* originally Mr. DeMille had discussed him for the part of Coco in *The Greatest Show on Earth,* but after seeing him in this thought he could play Brad." (Stewart was eventually cast as the clown.)

"Natalie Wood. 21 September 1950. Screened *Our Very Own.* You thought the little girl, about 11 years old, was very good and wanted to be reminded of her."

"John Derek. Tested for the part of Joshua. He knows nothing about the Bible."

"Audrey Hepburn. Not pretty but a very cute personality. Very expressive eyes. Gives the impression of being smaller on screen than she is." DeMille tested Hepburn for Nefretiri, Moses' love interest, but her breasts were deemed too small for the voluptuous costumes, and the part went to Anne Baxter.

DeMille's analysis of Charlton Heston was especially tough. "Has a sinister quality," he wrote in 1950. "He's sincere. You believe him. But he's not attractive." He goes on, "Find out if he has some humor. Everything I've seen him in he's dour. He has a funny way of speaking. It's an artificial way."

"When Heston did get the part of Moses," Helen said, "DeMille invited him up to the house every Sunday for acting lessons. DeMille would put pebbles in his mouth to get him to talk naturally."

On a nearby shelf, she pointed to another gem, a script from DeMille's remake of *The Ten Commandments* in 1956. It opened with a manifesto: "All these things are as I have found them in the Holy Scriptures, the Glorious Koran, the ancient Hebrew writing, and in the annals of modern discovery. CBM." To give his film the veneer of authenticity, DeMille had his personal researcher, Henry Noerdlinger, spend years reading all the midrashic retellings of Moses, as well as every known volume of biblical archaeology. Noerdlinger's research was later published, which gave DeMille great pride, though the seventy-three-year-old showman never seemed to hesitate about tossing out the findings when it suited him. Noerdlinger reported, for instance, that camels had not been domesticated at the time of Moses, but DeMille insisted that the audience expected camels, so camels he gave them.

Even more unusual, DeMille poured his research, along with plentiful quotes from the Bible, into a handful of scripts for close aides. The result, never published, is one of the most ornate depictions of the Moses story I've ever seen. Each line of dialogue is accompanied by an individual frame of celluloid from the final film. When the voice of God calls out from the burning bush, the Bible simply says Moses hid his face, "for he was afraid to look at God." DeMille, the master of overstatement, thought this wasn't enough, so he flushed out the scene. "Moses makes a subconscious move to comply with the order but is awe-smitten. Eyes look down. And beads of sweat start from his brow. The scene subfuses with light of unearthly, vibrant quality. From within the corona of flame, spectrum rays are pulsating like an Aurora Borealis."

The scene in which Moses parts the Red Sea is particularly vivid:

As the thunderheads grapple in the darkened sky, Moses raises his staff and turns to the turbulent sea. He stretches his rod above the waters, the voice of God speaking through him. "Behold His mighty hand!" ... From the darkening sky comes the rumbling howl of a hurricane that strains the robe against Moses' body. A second seething rush of air screams over the surface of the waters. The two cloudbanks collide with a thundercrash in a titanic impact that fuses them for instants before detonating downward in a maelstrom's swirl.

That DeMille recorded these descriptions in a handful of private scripts suggests how committed he was to the Bible. He was using the power of cinema to reach large numbers of people who otherwise might not read the text. In church, his mother once said, his father could reach thousands of souls; in theater, hundreds of thousands; then a new form came along, "the motion picture, and I was able to reach hundreds of millions."

Moses' robe, worn by Charlton Heston in *The Ten Commandments,*
including photographs of Heston splitting the Red Sea and Heston
with director Cecil B. DeMille; the actor wears the robe in both.
From the private collection of the Cecil B. DeMille Estate.
(Photograph courtesy of the author's collection)

The last item Helen pulled from a shelf was a white box labeled "MOSES ROBE." She opened the top as if it contained the Shroud of Turin. Inside was a museum report: "Overall clean excellent condition. Five intact tassels on hems, slightly matted, cotton tule stripes have been intentionally distressed, spot of black paint 22.5 inches from hem." She unfolded the tissue paper and there was the burnt-orange robe with the vertical tan-and-brown stripes that Charlton Heston wore during the splitting of the Red Sea. The fabric had the burlappy feel of African mudcloth, and Noerdlinger's research claimed the colors, white, black, and red, represented the Levite tribe, a detail not in the Bible. More likely DeMille chose the color because he knew darker colors would prevent the actors from blending into the sandy background.

At Helen's suggestion I slid it on and found that at nearly six feet two, I was roughly Heston's height. I resisted the temptation to spread my arms. My first impression was how well made the garment was. Fifty years later, it seemed ready for another grueling desert shoot. But my next impression was how quaint it was. DeMille may have boasted that every aspect of his film had been taken from ancient sources, but those sources were written over a millennium after Moses would have lived. The pretense of accuracy seems very Hollywood, but it also reflects the self-confidence and reliance on science that dominated America in the postwar era. DeMille didn't believe he was making an interpretation of Moses' life. He was making *the definitive account*. In the process he made a film that says more about America in the 1950s than it does about Egypt in the 1250s B.C.E.

THE IDEA THAT Moses might help promote American ideals abroad did not begin with Hollywood. In the country's formative centuries, Moses was most often used as a role model for outsiders' claims that they were escaping oppression and trying to create a new Promised Land. The Pilgrims, patriots, and slaves all used Moses in this way. But by the twentieth century, America began to change, and so did Moses' role in the country's imagination. As the country secured its strength at home, it increasingly began to project its influence abroad. Once again, Moses provided the narrative.

As early as 1850, Herman Melville called Americans "the Israel of our time; we bear the ark of Liberties of the world." During World War I, Woodrow Wilson was hailed as Moses for his efforts to covenant the world under the League of Nations. Later Franklin Roosevelt was compared to Moses for leading Europe out of fascism.

Using Moses as a counterweight to Nazi Germany was particularly popular during World War II. Thomas Mann wrote a novel about Moses in 1943 as part of the anthology *The Ten Commandments: Ten Short Novels of Hitler's War Against the Moral Code.* The anthology's editor hoped to turn it into a film modeled on DeMille's 1923 *Ten Commandments.* A similar idea colored *Brigham Young,* the 1940 biopic of the Mormon leader known as "America's Moses." The connections between Moses and Mormonism run deep. The religion was founded in 1830 by Joseph Smith, a Mason who published *The Book of Mormon* and other scriptures that he claimed augmented the Bible. A central feature of Smith's theology describes how Jesus visited the Americas after his resurrection and preached to descendants of the Lost Tribes. Smith had a fascination with Moses and stated that the Hebrew prophet appeared to him in 1836.

Brigham Young tells the story of Smith's mob assassination in 1844, after which Young leads an exodus of Mormons from Illinois to the Great Salt Lake. To help get the controversial film made, producers played up the parallels between Mormons in America and Jews in Germany. As one of the filmmakers put it, *Brigham Young* could be "an antidote to the increased spread of fascism and anti-Semitism." The film repeatedly links Mormons with the Israelites. Smith's dying words anticipate a deliverer who will "lead my people as Moses led the children of Israel across the wilderness." Young later declares of the exodus, "I doubt that there's been anything equal to this since the children of Israel set out across the Red Sea." And when the people complain about the barrenness of Utah, Young says, "I don't claim to be a Moses, but I say to you just what he said to the sons of Levi, 'Who is on the Lord's side? Let him come unto me.'" The quote is from Moses after he discovers the golden calf.

The most influential use of Moses as pro-American propagandist during these years may be the least known. It comes from two bookish Jews in Cleveland, Ohio, who in 1938 channeled their religious anxieties into a cartoon character they modeled partly on the superhero of the Torah. Jerry Siegel and Joe Shuster were born twelve blocks from each other in Cleveland. They met while working on their high school newspaper and shared a passion for science fiction. In 1938, a five-year-old proposal they had submitted under the Gentile-sounding pseudonym Bernard J. Kenton was chosen as the cover feature of a new series, *Action Comics*. The first cover showed a man with bulging muscles, blue tights, and a red cape lifting a wrecked car to save a passenger. The story followed a klutzy reporter with spectacles who led a double life; he used X-ray vision and extrahuman strength to fight for social justice. The character's name was Superman.

Superman drew from many sources, including Greek mythology, Arthurian legend, and the science fiction of Edgar Rice Burroughs. But many of its principal themes are drawn from the Hebrew Bible, and its backstory is taken almost point by point from Moses. Just as

Moses was born into a world in which his people faced annihilation, Superman is born on the planet Krypton, which is facing extinction. Just as baby Moses is put into a small basket and floated down the Nile by his mother, baby Superman is placed into a small rocket ship by his mother and father and launched into space. Just as Moses is rescued by the daughter of the pharaoh, Superman is rescued by Jonathan and Martha Kent in a midwestern cornfield. Like Moses, Superman is raised in an alien environment where he has to conceal his true identity. Just as Moses receives a calling from God to use his powers to liberate his people from tyranny, Superman receives a calling from his father to use his great strength "to assist humanity."

Even Superman's name reflects his creators' biblical knowledge. Moses is the leader of Israel, or *Yisra-el* in Hebrew, commonly translated as "one who strives with God." The name comes from Genesis 32 in which Jacob wrestles with a mysterious man who represents God. *El* was a common name for God in the ancient Near East and appears in the Bible in names like *Elohim* and *El Shaddai*. Superman's original name on Krypton was Kal-El, or "Swift God" in Hebrew. His father's name was Jor-El. Superman was clearly drawn as a modern-day god.

To help understand what all these connections meant, I went to see Simcha Weinstein. A thirty-two-year-old Orthodox rabbi from Manchester, England, Simcha grew up, by his own admission, short, shy, and pimply, not unlike the inventors of Superman. "I'd walk out of Hebrew school," he explained, "take off my *kippah,* and shove it in my pocket. I was always scared of the big, non-Jewish kids on the corner. They'd ask my name, and instead of saying Weinstein, I'd say Jones or Smith." He took solace in pop culture, especially comic books. "I related to the double identity. With Clark Kent, who's weak and unsure of himself; with Peter Parker, aka Spider-Man, because he can't get a job or get the girl. Yet they can still save the world. On the one hand, you read all these stories about Moses and the chosen people, and on the other hand, you walk down the street and there's a swastika on the synagogue and everyone's bashing Israel." Simcha moved to America, donned the black hat of Hasidism, and eventually wrote a book, *Up, Up, and Oy Vey!*, about how Jewish culture shaped the comic-book superhero.

"Today, *Action Comics* number one with Superman on the cover sells for over a million dollars," said Weinstein, who lives in Brooklyn with his wife and two children. "But in those days it was a joke. For Jewish artists, getting into advertising was hard, getting into highbrow art was harder. But with comic books, the barriers to entry were nothing. So people like Siegel and Shuster started drawing these superheroes who were metaphors for their own lives."

A similar thing happened in the film business. As Neal Gabler described in *An Empire of Their Own*, many of the pioneering moguls of Hollywood, including the founders of Universal, Paramount, Warner Bros., Fox, and Metro-Goldwyn-Mayer, came from eastern European Jewish immigrant families. Beyond their religious background, what united these men was a desire to reject the oppression they left behind and embrace their new Promised Land. Assimilation was hardly new, Gabler wrote, "but something drove the young Hollywood Jews to a ferocious, even pathological, embrace of America. Something drove them to deny whatever they had been before settling here." A similar dynamic took hold in comic books, where a small coterie of Jewish artists created Superman, Batman, the Green Lantern, Captain America, Spider-Man, the Incredible Hulk, the Fantastic Four, and the X-Men.

One expression of these writers' Jewish point of view was their characters' double lives—the awkward public self striving for accep-

Superman battles a thinly disguised Adolf Hitler, as shown in *Look* magazine, February 27, 1940.

tance and the heroic private self that still felt the tug of the old country and hoped to defeat the perpetrators of evil. A number, including Superman, even took their battles abroad.

"The superheroes fought Hitler before the Americans did," Weinstein said. "And coming from Jewish immigrants who are getting wrenching letters from home about their families, the effect is poignant." In *Superman* number one, published in 1939, Clark and Lois Lane travel to a thinly disguised Nazi Germany, where Lois ends up in front of a firing squad, until Superman rescues her. In *Superman* number two, also from 1939, Clark Kent visits faux Germany again and meets Adolphus Runyan, a scientist clearly modeled on Adolf Hitler, who has discovered a gas so powerful "it is capable of penetrating any type of gas-mask." The front cover of *Captain America* number one, published in March 1941, shows the hero smashing Hitler across the face.

"These writers are tapping into the stories they grew up with," Weinstein said. "But even more, they're tapping into their own frustrations with America and its inability to stand up for what's right."

Americans may or may not have noticed Superman's Jewish identity, but Hitler sure did. As early as April 1940, Hitler's chief propagandist, Joseph Goebbels, denounced Superman as a Jew. The weekly SS newspaper lambasted Jerry Siegel as "an intellectually and physically circumcised chap who has his headquarters in New York. . . . The inventive Israelite named this pleasant guy with an overdeveloped body and an underdeveloped mind 'Superman.'" Goebbels went on, "Woe to the American youth, who must live in such a poisoned atmosphere and don't even notice the poison they swallow daily." And swallow they did: One in four American soldiers carried a comic book in his back pocket during World War II.

But while it makes sense that young Jews might identify with these superheroes, why did they resonate so much with Americans as a whole?

"Neal Gabler has a line in *An Empire of Their Own*," Weinstein said. "'The American Dream is a Jewish invention.' It's a profound idea, because once Hollywood, comics, and other pop media invent this idea, they help make it a reality."

"But why isn't Jesus part of this?" I asked. "Or David, or Abraham? Why is Moses the foundation of so many of these stories?"

"Because Moses is the greatest prophet," he said. "And the story of Moses is the story of the hero. He's weak. He's fleeing his past. He can't speak so well. Yet he becomes the greatest leader in the history of the Jewish people. If you look at any narrative—in film, theater—there's an element of Moses in it. It's the ultimate journey.

The hero starts out doubting himself—'I can't do it. I can't be a leader.' Yet he rises to the occasion and saves the day."

"So if you think back to yourself as a boy," I asked, "have you been saved by this story?"

He smiled. "The rabbis say that when Moses was standing at the burning bush, he saw in the fire all of the pain, all of the suffering that befell the Jewish people. And he also saw their greatness. That's the dichotomy of Moses, and that's the dichotomy of Clark Kent and Superman. And I think every one of us taps into that. Sometimes I'm standing at the pulpit, and I can't connect. I feel nothing. But other times, I'm standing there and I *really* connect. I'm prepared. I'm spiritual. I feel like Moses the leader.

"The word for Egypt in Hebrew is *Mizraim*," he continued, "which means 'to constrict.' Every one of us faces constrictions every day. We live in our own Egypt. Yet every one of us aspires to escape that. We can save the world."

SAVING THE WORLD was a central reason behind Cecil B. De-Mille's decision to remake *The Ten Commandments* in the 1950s. To help understand why, I went to see Katherine Orrison, a one-woman library of DeMille's final creation. The fifty-something author has been obsessed with *The Ten Commandments* since she saw it as a nine-year-old girl in Anniston, Alabama. She eventually moved to Hollywood, befriended Henry Wilcoxon, DeMille's longtime deputy who also acted in the film, and wrote two books about the movie. She also provided the commentary on the fiftieth-anniversary DVD. She lives in Hollywood in a home filled with overstuffed sofas, mountains of velour pillows, and multiple cats, along with never-before-seen mementoes, including a painting of DeMille and company in the Sinai.

As Orrison explained, DeMille chose to revisit *The Ten Command-ments* because he was motivated by a desire to promote morality and religious freedom both at home and abroad. The director told guests at a luncheon in 1956, "I came here to ask you to use this picture, as I hope and pray that God himself will use it, for the good of the world." In the conservative 1950s, Hollywood embraced the familiar, with westerns, musicals, and biblical epics all experiencing a revival. For six of the twelve years between 1950 and 1962, a religious historical epic was that year's number one box-office draw, including *Quo Vadis*, *The Robe*, and *Ben-Hur*. Paramount had resisted DeMille's entreaties to make another film about Moses, but his longtime rival, Adolph Zukor, an assimilated Hungarian Jew, overruled his staff. "I find it embarrassing and deplorable that it takes Cecil here—a Gentile, no less—to remind us Jews of our heritage! What was World War II fought for, anyway? We should get down on our knees and say thank you that he wants to make a picture on the life of Moses."

"Zukor and DeMille had been like little dogs growling at each other for twenty years," Orrison said. "The fact that Zukor ultimately backed the movie showed it was the right movie for the right time. Jews had almost been wiped off the face of the earth in the Holocaust. McCarthyism was rampant in Hollywood with the blacklist. The Cold War was raging. Everybody was scared." She paused. "But DeMille wasn't scared."

A conservative in a town of liberals, DeMille used his film to promote his political views on everything from communism to race relations. In an extraordinary gesture, when moviegoers went to see *The Ten Commandments*, the curtains parted and DeMille himself appeared on the screen. "Ladies and gentlemen, young and old, this may seem an unusual procedure, speaking to you before the picture begins." He went on to tell viewers what his movie was about. "The theme of this picture is whether men ought to be ruled by God's law or whether they are to be ruled by the whims of a dictator like Rameses. Are men the property of the state, or are they free souls under God? The same battle continues throughout the world today."

In the midst of the Cold War, DeMille's message was clear: Moses represented the United States; the pharaoh represented the Soviet Union. To drive home his point, DeMille cast mostly Americans as the Israelites and mostly Europeans as the Egyptians—Rameses II was Russian; Sethi I was English; Moses' adoptive mother was Dutch. (Moses' love interest, naturally, was American. No cavorting with the enemy!)

DeMille pressed his ideas in other ways throughout the film. The movie opens with a baby Moses being floated down the Nile, then being rescued by a daughter of the pharaoh. The Bible leaps immediately to an adult Moses discovering his heritage, but DeMille sexed up the story, adding a love triangle among Moses, his stepbrother, Rameses II, and Nefretiri, the throne princess. Moses is put in charge of building a treasure city, and he eases the workload of the Israelite slaves, though he doesn't yet know he's their kin. A jealous Rameses II tells the pharaoh that Moses must be the Hebrews' deliverer. Moses then learns his heritage but announces he's unashamed: "Egyptian or Hebrew, I'm still Moses." At a time when many Jews still struggled with assimilation, Moses' open embrace of his faith was a powerful statement of self-confidence.

Moses spends time among the Israelites and murders one of their taskmasters. Brought in chains before the pharaoh, Moses declares it evil that people are oppressed, "stripped of spirit, and hope and faith, all because they are of another race, another creed. If there is a God, He did not mean this to be so!" Again, the emphasis is on inclusion; God accepts all faiths, all races, all creeds. Rameses II banishes Moses to the desert and then marries a heartbroken Nefretiri. Moses also marries and is a peaceful shepherd in the desert until one day he spots a bush awash in flames. DeMille had become intrigued by a rabbinic commentary that said that the voice Moses heard from the burning bush was his father's. In the scene, DeMille used Heston's own voice slowed down and deepened. (When Moses receives the Ten Commandments, God's voice is a mixture of Heston's, DeMille's, actor Delow Jewkes, and DeMille's publicist, Donald Hayne. Perhaps one reason DeMille got such good press is that he allowed his publicist to play God!) Even more telling: When Moses speaks to God in the bush, DeMille omitted Moses' words from the Bible that imply he was a stutterer. In the Hollywood of the 1950s, the hero did not stutter.

"They originally shot the burning bush scene in the Sinai," Orrison said, "but they had to reshoot it in Hollywood because Charlton Heston couldn't pull off modesty. He couldn't do humble—*no matter what*. But the scene does work in the end. The Moses we get in 1956 from Charlton Heston is the way America wanted to think of itself at that time. The country's no longer humble. The country's a superpower. And it sees itself as God's chosen place. So Heston becomes the profile on the coin that says IN GOD WE TRUST. That Rushmore visage. Now the hair is white, the beard is longer. He becomes a Founding Father—at least the way we were taught our Founding Fathers looked."

The mixture of Hollywood magic and 1950s politics is perhaps best on display in the fan favorite of *The Ten Commandments*—the ten plagues. The Bible gives enormous weight to the plagues. Moses' birth, adoption, flight into the desert, marriage, and firstborn son are all dispensed with in only one chapter of the text. The ten plagues take nearly seven. Moses' brother, Aaron, directs the first three plagues—turning the water into blood, an inundation of frogs, and lice. For a superpower so completely dependent on water for irrigation, transportation, and religious ritual, Egypt would have been traumatized by the attack on its water supply. But just when the pharaoh is ready to relent, his stubbornness returns. Moses takes over and pilots the next six plagues—insects, pestilence, and boils, followed by hail, locusts, and darkness. Again, for a culture in which the highest deity was the god of the sun, darkness would have been particularly devastating. "The Egyptians could not see one another, and for three days no one could get up from where he was; but the Israelites enjoyed light in their dwellings." Pharaoh begs Moses to take his people and leave, but Moses insists that the pharaoh first make a sacrifice to God. The sides are at a standoff, and God announces plans for one final plague.

DeMille, working with primitive special effects, faced enormous challenges in converting the plagues into believable cinema. He chose to show only three: turning the water into blood, hail, and killing of the firstborn sons. For the blood, prop maestro William Sapp built a section of the Nile in a soundstage and stood in the river with a garden hose just beneath the surface. When Heston touched the water with his staff, Sapp pulled away the nozzle, causing red water to spew forth. DeMille found the first take too slow, so the next day Sapp turned up the pressure and pulled the hose away faster. For the hail, mothballs were considered too toxic and too fragile. So with Heston and Yul Brynner standing together in a Hollywood soundstage, Sapp and his colleagues huddled in the rafters with giant bags of popcorn. The kernels were perfect stands-ins because they could be easily swept up after each take. (Sapp also hand-made one hundred latex frogs with mechanical feet for another plague, and they taped Anne Baxter's reaction, but her feigned horror was deemed over-the-top and DeMille managed to do what the pharaoh couldn't: stop at least one infestation.)

In the biblical account, the final plague follows a celebration of the first Passover. God instructs each Israelite family to take a lamb, sheep, or goat and slaughter it at twilight. "They shall take some of the blood and put it on the two doorposts and the lintel of the houses in which they are to eat it. They shall eat the flesh that same night . . . with unleavened bread and bitter herbs." Moses instructs the Israelites to spread the blood with a hyssop branch and stay indoors until morning. God will see the blood, he tells them, and "pass over the door."

In the film, Moses gathers his Hebrew family around an abundant table and celebrates a Passover meal. DeMille lingers over the scene, which includes the Egyptian princess who pulled him from the water and, in a bold political statement in pre–civil rights America, a band of black attendants. The Egyptians were left outside, Katherine Orrison stressed, where they would be exposed to God's wrath; blacks were invited inside, where they were protected.

The tenth plague was often portrayed in art as an angel with a bloody knife, but DeMille thought the image wasn't scary enough. "The most frightening thing in the 1950s was the atom bomb," Orrison explained. "Everybody was told that radiation could permeate every nook and cranny of every house or shelter. You couldn't see it, you couldn't smell it, you couldn't feel it. But it could kill you." Sapp came up with the idea of a green fog that swooped down out of the sky in the shape of a claw. The idea for the claw came from a menacing cloud formation one of DeMille's secretaries had seen over the San Fernando Valley.

Did Americans understand the connection? "I certainly did," Orrison said. "I'm a firstborn. I'm sitting in Anniston, Alabama, watching this movie, and I'm terrified."

"Even as a child you thought it was radiation?" I said.

"You couldn't get away from it. Remember, we were doing duck-

and-cover drills every week. I knew I wasn't one of the chosen people. I was Episcopalian. But thank God Moses let those African slaves inside his house. Because what it said to me was you can be black, you can be white, you can be a nonbeliever, but Moses is a universal guardian. I think the reason baby boomers embraced the movie is that it spoke directly to our childhoods."

"What I find fascinating about the Passover scene," I said, "is that when Moses is in the slave quarters, he's suddenly human. He's not that wooden prophet who confronts the pharaoh."

"Yes! Thank God! He's the great father. The father of our country. And for me, as a child of divorce, he was *my* father."

"Your father?"

"If I was going to live through what my parents were doing to me, I needed a surrogate parent. Divorce is no big deal now, but I was in a small southern town, and I was the only divorced child in my school. And I can remember the day my mother said, 'Don't tell anybody. You'll lose your friends.' And she was right. I lost all my friends."

"But there were lots of people you could have latched onto as a father figure," I said. "Why Moses?"

"I was the right age. And I thought, 'God loves me, even though I'm not a Jew. If I can get into that house with Moses, I'll be safe. I may not have a father, but Moses is everyone's father.'"

"But why not Jesus?" I asked.

"Jesus couldn't be my father. He was above me. Jesus was divine. Moses is a family man. He's a leader. He was so real to me that the first Passover after I saw the movie, I went to our refrigerator, took out some lamb chops, and spread the blood on our front door."

My jaw dropped.

"I've done it in every place I live," she said. "I do it here!" And with that she stood up, led me to the front porch of her Hollywood home, and pointed out two faint, reddish brown streaks on either side of her front door. I thought of Exodus 12: "You shall observe this day throughout the ages, as an institution for all time." Moses was still alive in the Valley of Sin.

"So what did your mother think?" I asked.

"She said, 'Kathy, we're not Jewish.'"

"But you did it anyway."

"I thought I needed to be saved," she said. "I thought, 'If I follow God's law, and I listen to Moses, then my life will be okay.' I wasn't sleeping at night! Thinking about Moses was the only thing that brought me peace."

CECILIA PRESLEY LIVES in the desert, nearly three hours east of Los Angeles. After all the back-and-forth to get to her, she welcomed me to her lagoon-front home near Palm Springs as if I were an old friend. *Call me Ceci. How about a drink? Excuse me while I let out the dogs.* I wondered how honest she would be about the man she calls Grandfather, but I quickly discovered she had lost little of the spunk that had caused DeMille to have her chaperoned in Egypt. It didn't work. She fell so hard for Abbas El Boughdadly, the cavalry officer hired to wrangle the horses and camels, that she married him and moved to Cairo. The news caused such a scandal that it was reported in *Time* magazine.

"It wasn't a scandal in my family," Presley said. "Of course they were sorry to see me go, but he was a marvelous man. It didn't work. I shouldn't have done it. Grandfather was my life. But when I came home after a few years, he said, 'Now I can like Abbas again.'"

She eventually remarried, took over the family foundation following her grandfather's death in 1959, and became an ardent philanthropist and film preservationist. I was interested in whether her grandfather, whom Billy Graham dubbed "the prophet in celluloid," was a religious man himself.

"God was alive to him," she said. "The Bible was alive. But religion was not. He found it too narrow. He went to church, but he would go when they were empty and sit in them."

"Was he one of those people who was a lifelong searcher?"

"His fundamental belief was that Jesus Christ was a messenger, but he never stopped searching. He was fascinated by scientists—from Edward Hubble to Albert Einstein. He was working on a film on space exploration when he died. To him, religion and science were not incompatible."

"But if he was so interested in Jesus, why remake *The Ten Commandments* and not *King of Kings*?"

"Because Moses is a more universal story than Jesus, and in the fifties a more relevant story. Moses is the antithesis of communism, and Grandfather *hated* communism. He said terrible things happened to countries who had no god."

I asked her if she thought those views were reflected in the film.

She looked at me stupefied. "It *is* the movie—from the beginning to the end. When Pharaoh enslaves his people, that's communism. When he punishes at will, that's communism. When he's the divinely chosen king, that's communism. You don't have to spell it out. In fact, spelling it out would be preaching. But people pick it up."

Just in case, DeMille did spell it out—in his introduction, in interviews, and, in an unprecedented move, in the streets of the United States. As part of his plan to spread biblical values, DeMille actually paid to put the Ten Commandments in public squares across the country. The idea had its roots in 1946 when juvenile judge

E. J. Ruegemer of Minnesota offered to suspend the sentence of a sixteen-year-old boy who had stolen a car if he promised to keep the Ten Commandments. "What are the Ten Commandments?" the boy asked. Working with the civic group the Fraternal Order of the Eagles, Ruegemer distributed 100,000 framed prints of the law of Moses around the country over the following years, along with 250,000 comic books that recount the story. DeMille heard about the effort while he was working on *The Ten Commandments*. He contacted the judge and offered to up the stakes. He then persuaded Paramount's promotion department to pay for granite monoliths of the Ten Commandments to be placed on courthouse lawns, in city halls, and in public squares in every city where the film played. Over more than four thousand were made, and DeMille dispatched Heston, Brynner, and other stars to attend the dedications. One of these monuments, in Austin, Texas, later became the basis for the Supreme Court decision in 2005 that allowed the Ten Commandments on public property but banned them from courtrooms. A publicity stunt for Paramount became the basis of landmark U.S. law.

And the ploy worked. *The Ten Commandments* was released on October 5, 1956. Reviews for the three-hour-thirty-nine-minute film ranged from respectful to savaging. One critic tagged it "Sexodus," another "epic balderdash." The *New Republic* deemed it "longer than the forty years in the desert." But audiences loved it. The film earned $34 million in its first year, second only to *Ben-Hur* for the decade. By 1959, it had been seen by 98.5 million people. Today, its inflation-adjusted total ranks fifth on the all-time box-office list, behind *Gone With the Wind*, *Star Wars*, *The Sound of Music*, and *E.T.*, and ahead of *Titanic*, *Jaws*, and *Ben-Hur*. When its annual network screening on Easter is calculated, it would easily be the most viewed film of the 1950s.

"And the letters we got!" said Mrs. Presley. "One man wrote Grandfather that he had been a Nazi prison guard in Poland and had beat a Jewish prisoner senseless. 'See, now you look like the rest of the Jews who were in your Bible,' the guard said to his victim. But when he saw *The Ten Commandments* and looked into the face of those Jews, the man wrote Grandfather for absolution."

As this letter suggests, DeMille's biggest impact may have been in the area of interfaith relations. The 1950s represented a breakthrough in America's relationship with God, when the starkly drawn denominational lines of the past began to fade. True religion was under threat, wrote historian Will Herberg in his landmark 1955 study, *Protestant-Catholic-Jew*. Instead, religion had been replaced with what he called a watered-down "faith-for-faith's sake" attitude, where "familiar words are retained, but the old meaning is voided." Religion now meant little more than maintaining a positive attitude in life and believing in everything you do. Dwight Eisenhower became an emblem of this denuded devotion. America, he said, "is founded in a deeply felt religious faith—and I don't care what it is." Eisenhower's 1953 inaugural parade was led by a generic "float for God." In 1954 "under God" was added to the Pledge of Allegiance; in 1956 "In God We Trust" became the national motto; in 1957 it was added to the back of the one-dollar bill, in between the two faces of the seal.

The Ten Commandments, with its blend of Jewish and Christian themes, fit perfectly into this moment. Despite the Hebraic subject, the film is replete with New Testament references, from Moses saying after the burning bush, "He revealed his Word to my mind and the Word was God," an echo of the Gospel according to John, to a delinquent Moses appearing before the pharaoh yoked to what appears to be a wooden cross, to the playing of "Onward, Christian

Soldiers" during the Exodus. The film reflects the larger merging of Christian and Jewish strands of American life into what came to be called the Judeo-Christian tradition. Though the phrase first appeared in 1899, "Judeo-Christian" did not become widely used until after the Holocaust as an expression of the two traditions' shared values of morality, freedom, and law. In the 1952 speech where Eisenhower proclaimed America's religious foundation, he explained, "With us of course it is the Jud[e]o-Christian concept . . . a religion that believes all men are created equal."

As arguably the most influential film of the 1950s, *The Ten Commandments* both mirrored and molded the mainstream acceptance of different faith traditions that began to emerge in late-twentieth-century America. DeMille was decades ahead of his time when he included Islam in the list of great religions that belonged in the American public sphere. In the film, Moses repeatedly stresses the universality of God, who was "not the god of Israel or Ishmael alone, but of all men." Ishmael is the progenitor of Muhammad and a central prophet in Islam. Also, DeMille had his cast and crew read the Koran and often said the strongest encouragement to make the film came from the prime minister of Pakistan, "who saw in the story of Moses, the prophet honored equally by Moslems, Jews, and Christians, a means of welding together adherents of all three faiths against the common enemy of all faiths, atheistic communism." DeMille's genius was to make Moses a projection not just of American strength but also of American pluralism.

I asked Ceci Presley how much DeMille's interest in interfaith relations might have been influenced by learning later in life that his mother was Jewish.

"Grandfather identified with Judaism his whole life," she said. "But with his father being a lay minister and having grown up reading the New Testament, he could no more have been a Jew than I could have been a Muslim. Still, he was far ahead of his time in so many ways, and the thing he hated most in his life was bigotry. *The Ten Commandments* is his attempt to show how America can save the world with a universal notion of God."

That union of America, God, and Moses is most vividly displayed in the final scene of the film. Moses stands on Mount Nebo with his family, about to be summoned to his death. He blesses his

```
                     MOSES
           Go - proclaim liberty through-
           out all the lands, unto all the      (Levit.
           inhabitants thereof.                  25:10)

G-118   MEDIUM LONG SHOT - SEPHORA, JOSHUA, LILIA, MERED AND
        ELEAZAR - THE GREEN LAND OF CANAAN SEEN BEYOND THEM

        Their eyes full of love, pride and sorrow, as they
        watch the ascent of Moses 'whom the Lord knew face
        to face' (cf Deut. 34:10).

G-119   VERY LONG SHOT - MOSES

        As he ascends the Mountain.  "Thus he ascended into
        immortality, summoned by the Father, Who transmuted
        his earthly being into a single unity of Mind and
        Spirit, pure as the sunlight - radiant as Truth."
        (cf Philo 593:6).

        He raises his arm and it seems that the eternal light
        of the Glory of God blinds him from the eyes of men.

        FADE OUT.
```

Close-up of the final scene of *The Ten Commandments,* as shown in Cecil B. DeMille's private script, complete with cell of the finished film, in which Moses utters the phrase depicted on the Liberty Bell, from Leviticus 25:10: "Go—proclaim liberty throughout all the lands, unto all the inhabitants thereof"; from the private collection of the Cecil B. DeMille Estate. *(Photograph courtesy of the author's collection)* successor, Joshua, hands over the Five Books of Moses, then proceeds a few steps toward the summit. Then he turns, raises his arms to swelling music, and intones in his most sermonizing voice, "Go, proclaim liberty throughout all the land unto all the inhabitants thereof." The words inscribed on the Liberty Bell come not from this moment in Deuteronomy, of course, but from Leviticus 25. Yet De-Mille understood their significance in American history. Noerd-linger's research had uncovered not just the Mosaic connection to the Liberty Bell but also the story of Moses on the seal. A publicity illustration released with the film showed Charlton Heston holding up the Liberty Bell as if it were the Ten Commandments.

Moses then continues to the peak of Mount Nebo, and as "the eternal light of the Glory of God blinds him from the eyes of men," Charlton Heston turns back toward the camera and raises his right arm in a perfect tableau of the Statue of Liberty. In the final shot of his valedictory film, DeMille crowns his paean to the greatest prophet who ever lived by parading him through the medley of American icons to which he had been compared over the years—the Liberty Bell, Lady Liberty—until he becomes the embodiment of America enlightening the world. The closing image on the screen is the tablets of the law themselves, surrounded by the light of the burning bush, emblazoned with the words "So it was written—So it shall be done."

Before leaving, I asked Presley whether she thought her grandfather identified with Moses personally.

"He visited Churchill in 1957," she said. "Churchill was his hero. He called him 'the greatest man of the twentieth century.' Churchill received him in bed, and Grandfather told him the story of Moses as if Churchill was Moses—Churchill led his people to freedom, Churchill fought back the Nazis. And the old man burst into tears.

"And I think DeMille, through telling that story," she continued, "wouldn't have been conceited enough to think that he was such a figure. But he would have been hopeful enough to think that he had played a small part in doing what Moses had done in helping his country escape the boot of communism."

IX

I'VE SEEN THE
PROMISED LAND

ONE DAY I realized I had stumbled into a little-known curiosity of American history: The stained glass in New York City's churches must be the most unusual in the world. At Plymouth Church in Brooklyn, the twenty-three windows include such non-ecclesiastical figures as Oliver Cromwell and Abraham Lincoln. The stained glass at Manhattan's Riverside Church includes sixteen images of Jesus and seven of Moses but also the Magna Carta and the Declaration of Independence; the gramophone and the telegraph; tributes to Taoism, Buddhism, and Confucianism; and a window depicting Muhammad, something forbidden in mosques. The Episcopal Cathedral Church of Saint John the Divine, the largest church in New York, contains images of a radio and a television, a hockey player and a bowler, as well as Christopher Columbus, Washington's inaugural, the Gettysburg Address, and the sinking of the *Titanic*. Behind the lectern are nineteen stone carvings, including figures of

Martin Luther King, Jr., in a never-before-published photograph, delivering his sermon "The Death of Evil Upon the Seashore" at the Cathedral Church of Saint John the Divine, New York, May 17, 1956, during the Montgomery Bus Boycott. *(Courtesy of the Archives of the Episcopal Diocese of New York at the Cathedral Church of Saint John the Divine)*

Moses and Paul, Washington and Lincoln. The final niche has been left empty, awaiting a suitable figure from the twentieth century.

Odds are it will be Martin Luther King, Jr.

On Thursday, May 17, 1956, the twenty-seven-year-old pastor of the Dexter Avenue Baptist Church in Montgomery, Alabama, rose to the pulpit of Saint John the Divine to deliver a sermon at a special interdenominational service in honor of the second anniversary of the landmark *Brown v. Board of Education* Supreme Court ruling, which outlawed segregation in American public schools. The little-known preacher had come to national prominence six months earlier as the head of the Montgomery Bus Boycott triggered by Rosa Parks's refusal to give up her bus seat to a white man. The 381-day boycott was still going on at the time of King's address.

The title of his sermon was "The Death of Evil Upon the Sea-shore." Standing before an overflow crowd of ten thousand people, he began with a quote from Exodus 14: "And Israel saw the Egyptians dead upon the seashore." The verse comes from the very end of the Exodus, after the Israelites have crossed the Red Sea, when they look back and see that the Egyptian army has been killed by the returning waters. King's message was that the Egyptians represent evil "in the form of humiliating oppression, ungodly exploitation and crushing domination." The Israelites symbolize goodness "in the form of devotion and dedication to the God of Abraham, Isaac, and Jacob." He continued, "The Hebraic Christian tradition is clear, that in the long struggle between good and evil, good eventually emerges as the victor."

King went on to compare the plight of the Israelites in Egypt and that of colonized Third World residents. At the dawn of the twentieth century, King said, more than half the world's population lived under the yoke of oppression, including 400 million people in India and Pakistan, 600 million in China, and 200 million in Africa. The world is now seeing the victory of freedom in this struggle, he said. "The Red Sea has opened, and today most of these exploited masses have won their freedom from the Egypt of colonialism and are now free to move toward the promised land of economic security and cultural development. As they look back, they clearly see the evils of colonialism and imperialism dead upon the seashore."

Martin Luther King was not always a spellbinding public speaker. In Atlanta, I went to a museum exhibition of the King papers. One item that jumped out was his transcript from Crozer Theological Seminary in Pennsylvania. In his first semester in 1948, King got a B+ in preaching and a mere "Pass" in public speaking. The next semester he got a C+ in public speaking, and the following semester a C. He kept getting worse. I wondered, "How would you like to be the teacher who gave Martin Luther King a C in public speaking?"

Scholars have shown that King drew heavily on speeches given by others. "The Death of Evil Upon the Seashore," for example, has deep parallels with "Egyptians Dead Upon the Seashore," a sermon given by nineteenth-century abolitionist Phillips Brooks.

Brooks: The parted waves had swept back upon the [Egyptians]. . . . All that the escaped people saw was here and there a poor drowned body beaten upon the bank, where they stood with the great flood between them and the land of their long captivity and oppression. It was the end of a frightful period in their history.

King: The parted waves swept back upon the [Egyptians]. . . . As the Israelites looked back all they could see was here and there a poor drowned body beaten upon the seashore. . . . It was the end of a frightful moment in their history.

As literary scholar Keith Miller describes in *Voice of Deliverance,* a book about King's rhetoric, multiple sections of King's speech were taken nearly verbatim from other sources, especially Harry Emerson Fosdick, the so-called "Moses of Modernism," who was the preacher at Riverside Church. King also drew from sermons he gave with his father in Atlanta applying the lessons of Moses to African American life. But King's chief source, Miller concludes, was not the published works of others but the folk tradition of American slaves, passed down through oral history. "His equation of black America and the Hebrew people revived and updated the slaves' powerful identification with the Israelites suffering under the yoke of the pharaoh."

A century after the Underground Railroad, King once more tapped into the long love affair between Americans and Moses. "Many years ago the Negro was thrown into the Egypt of segregation," King declared at the climax of his speech. "For years it looked like he would never get out of this Egypt. The closed Red Sea always stood before him with discouraging dimensions. There were always those pharaohs with hardened hearts, who, despite the cries of many a Moses, refused to let these people go." But then, he continued, a new Moses rose up to liberate blacks, and he mentioned an institution that had likely never before been compared to the Hebrew prophet: the Supreme Court. "One day, through a world-shaking decree by the nine justices of the Supreme Court of America," King said, "the Red Sea was opened, and the forces of justice marched through to the other side."

The reaction to King's New York debut was instantaneous. King labeled the evening "one of the greatest experiences of my life." The dean of the cathedral called the talk the "greatest sermon" he had ever heard. As the country headed into another deadly showdown over race, America had a new prophet on its hands, and a new question to ponder: Was Martin Luther King America's next Moses?

THE HOUSE ON Auburn Avenue in Atlanta where King was born in 1929 has been turned into a small museum. It has a parlor and a study and is just steps from Ebenezer Baptist Church, where Martin Luther King, Sr., served as pastor and where young "M.L." found his voice as a leader of God's New New Israel. Sweet Auburn was one of many middle-class enclaves across the South that blacks in the early twentieth century considered the land of milk and honey. But the laws of the South were promulgated by Jim Crow, not Moses, and blacks once more went looking for a narrative of hope. And once more they turned to the Exodus.

"Fifty years brings us to the border of the Promised Land," one minister said in 1912. "The Canaan of our citizenship is just before us and is infested with enemies who deny our right to enter." But fear not, black preachers said; God will hear our suffering and send a Moses to lead the way. As one black pastor recalled, "Our ministers held forth about Moses using the rod to part the waters of the Red Sea. More than once the minister would go on to suggest that there were some 'Black Moseses' in the making."

One of the more vivid black Moseses of the twentieth century was invented by novelist Zora Neale Hurston, a central figure in the Harlem Renaissance. While a student at Barnard College, Hurston studied ethnography and discovered that Moses had been a preeminent figure in voodoo as well as other religions across the Caribbean and Africa. "The worship of Moses recalls the hard-to-explain fact that wherever the Negro is found," she wrote in 1937, "there are traditional tales of Moses and his supranatural powers that are not in the Bible." These reverent tales did not spring up spontaneously, she added. "There is a tradition of Moses as the great father of magic scattered all over Africa and Asia. Perhaps some of his feats recorded in the Pentateuch are the folk beliefs of such a character." Moses did not become an African American icon because he was featured in the Bible, Hurston suggested; he became a biblical icon after he was featured in African stories.

Hurston flushed out this theme in a 1939 novel, *Moses, Man of the Mountain*, featuring Moses as a voodoo priest. The book opens with a DeMille-like statement from the author: "Moses was an old man with a beard. He was the great law-giver. He had some trouble with Pharaoh about some plagues and led the Children of Israel out of Egypt and on to the Promised Land." That is the common concept of Moses, she said. But unlike DeMille and many other whites, Hurston wasn't interested in Moses as a figure of authority; she was interested in Moses as a person who *breaks* the law. Her Moses was a man of confrontation. "All across Africa, America, the West Indies, there are tales of the powers of Moses and great worship of him and his powers," she wrote. "But it does not flow from the Ten Commandments. It is his rod of power, the terror he showed before all Israel and to Pharaoh."

In Hurston's telling, Moses becomes an instrument of black power, the first civil rights activist. He first appears as an Egyptian prince, who earns his reputation as a man of violence and war. But at the crucial moment when he kills the Egyptian overseer for beating a Hebrew slave, Moses changes. "He found a new sympathy for the oppressed of all mankind. He lost his taste for war. . . . Henceforth he was a man of thought." Twenty years before Martin Luther King, Jr., Hurston's Moses becomes a pioneer of nonviolence. He further foreshadows King when, at the moment the pharaoh frees the Israelites, they shout a line from a famed spiritual, "Free at last! Free at last! Thank God Almighty, I'm free at last!" King would later use these same words to conclude his speech at the March on Washington.

Hurston wasn't alone in anticipating King. C. L. Franklin, arguably the most influential African American preacher through the 1940s and early '50s, spoke often of the need for a Moses figure to emerge from the black community. Franklin was known as "the Man with the Million Dollar Voice" and was the father of "the Queen of Soul," Aretha. He was based in Detroit but traveled widely around the country, and he often brought along his daughter to sing. Franklin was among the first to sell his sermons on records, and one of his more famous was "Moses at the Red Sea." "In every crisis God raises up a Moses," he said. "His name may be Moses or his name may be Joshua or his name may be David, or his name, you understand, may be Abraham Lincoln or Frederick Douglass or George Washington Carver, but in every crisis God raises up a Moses, especially where the destiny of his people is concerned." His message: Blacks should not wait for others to lead the way but should seize their own destiny. "The power of deliverance is in our own possession," he said. "The man who stands and simply cries will never go over his Red Seas."

Few men put this message of self-reliance into practice more than Franklin's spiritual protégé, Martin Luther King, Jr. Throughout his career, King stressed that liberation alone was not the destination for blacks. They must also develop standards of dignity and self-respect. "As we struggle for freedom in America," he told four thousand people in Montgomery that November, "there is a danger that we will misinterpret freedom. We usually think of freedom from something, but freedom is also to something. It is not only breaking loose from some evil force, but it is reaching up for a higher force. Freedom from evil is slavery to goodness." And this "slavery to goodness," he insisted, comes with certain duties—to respect others, to respect yourself, not to strike back, and to practice non-violence. Freedom, in other words, comes with responsibility. Liberation with self-restraint. Exodus with Sinai. The twin message of America's founding—revolution paired with constitution—now becomes the watchword of America's refounding. And once again the language comes from the same source.

"You can't overemphasize how important Exodus was to us at the time," said Robert Franklin, one of the leaders of a new generation of African American preachers who grew up during the civil rights era. A native of Illinois (and no relation to C. L.), Franklin is a Phi Beta Kappa graduate of Morehouse College, King's alma mater in Atlanta, who earned a master's in divinity from Harvard and a doctorate from Chicago. Though he's taller, with a broader repertoire of languages (including Arabic), Franklin's narrow mustache, receding hairline, and easy smile lend him a striking similarity to his hero. A week after I visited him in his office, Franklin was named the tenth president of Morehouse.

"Part of the appeal of Exodus is that the story was often enacted in our church plays and vacation Bible schools," he continued. "The drama of the pharaoh, of Egypt and all of its political might, just represented for us America. You had leaders, like northern mayor Richard Daley or southern governor George Wallace, who represented for us these pharaoh-like, hard-hearted, unflinching symbols of the biblical text. So when we acted out the story, we brought to it a contemporary emotion.

"And of course the big question," he added, "was who would get to play Moses, because we all wanted to be him. Number one, that imperfect figure. And number two, that reluctant figure who finally gets pushed onto the stage and says, 'Okay, dammit, I'll do this.'"

"So did you ever get to play Moses?" I asked.

"I never played Moses," he said forlornly. "They were always the older guys who were taller and better-looking!" And with that he laughed a huge Santa Claus laugh.

"But what about Jesus?" I asked. "What role did he play in your worldview?"

"Moses and Jesus were costars in our salvation story," Franklin said. "Jesus had his highlights—Easter and Christmas. But the rest of the year, we're in this struggle, and Jesus wasn't leading people to challenge political authority. Yeah, we need Jesus for personal salvation, and for comforting our pain. He was the suffering servant. But the idea of God coming to the aid of the *entire* people was a more powerful idea for us, so the rest of the year belonged to Moses."

"Were you ever concerned that the Exodus happened thirty-two hundred years ago and you were in a struggle now?" I asked. "What if the parallels weren't true?"

"Yeah, we understood that," he said. "But there's no way you can limit this story to one historical era. Charles Long, the great African American scholar, talks about the hundred-year cycle of history, that there's a great revolution and cataclysm every century—1776, 1861, the 1960s. In this cyclical sense of time, we can reach down into the trove of memories and experiences of our ancestors. And we think of the figures in the biblical story as our ancestors. That is our story. The fact that it's a Jewish story is kind of irrelevant. It's our book. Our people. And they're echoing through the annals of time, trying to offer us lessons."

That sense of drawing the past into the present was memorably displayed during the March on Washington in August 1963. The stated purpose of the event was to press for civil rights legislation in Congress, but the result was the largest gathering to date in the nation's capital. It culminated in a series of performances in front of the Lincoln Memorial by Marian Anderson, Bob Dylan, and others, as well as a speech by James Baldwin read by Charlton Heston. (Asked why he was chosen to lead the Hollywood contingent, Heston said it was probably because of his service to the Screen Actors Guild, "or maybe just because I'd gotten all those folks through the Red Sea.") Describing the crowd of 250,000 people, gospel singer Mahalia Jackson said the scene looked like another Exodus. "It was like the vision of Moses that the children of Israel would march into Canaan." Organizers distributed song sheets for "Go Down, Moses" and other spirituals.

King's late-afternoon speech was the highlight of the event. Seven years after he spoke at Saint John the Divine and a few months after his "Letter from Birmingham Jail," the thirty-four-year-old preacher had become the voice of civil rights. His talk wove together many of the iconic themes from the 350-year merger of the Hebrew Bible and America. He evoked the Pilgrims: "Land where my fathers died, land of the pilgrims' pride." He paid tribute to Lincoln and his use of Psalm 90: "Five score years ago, a great American, in whose symbolic shadow we stand today, signed the Emancipation Proclamation." He linked blacks with the Mother of Exiles: "One hundred years later, the Negro lives on a lonely island of poverty in the midst of a vast ocean of material prosperity. One hundred years later, the Negro is still languished in the corners of American society and finds himself an exile in his own land." He even echoed Lincoln's phrase that America was "an almost-chosen people" by suggesting that America was a broken-promised land. The Declaration of Independence and the Constitution represented "a promise," King said, "that all men, yes, black men as well as white men, would be guaranteed the 'unalienable Rights of Life, Liberty, and the pursuit of Happiness.' It is obvious today that America has defaulted on this promissory note."

But the climax echoes America's preeminent symbol of freedom and one of its greatest tributes to the Exodus: the Liberty Bell.

Let freedom ring from the prodigious hilltops of New
  Hampshire.
Let freedom ring from the mighty mountains of New York.
Let freedom ring from the heightening Alleghenies of
  Pennsylvania!
Let freedom ring from the snowcapped Rockies of Colorado!
Let freedom ring from the curvaceous slopes of California!
But not only that; let freedom ring from Stone Mountain of
  Georgia!
Let freedom ring from Lookout Mountain of Tennessee!
Let freedom ring from every hill and molehill of Mississippi.
From every mountainside, let freedom ring.

In what is arguably the most famous speech by an American since
the Gettysburg Address, Martin Luther King fused together Jefferson and Lincoln, Pilgrim and slave, Emma Lazarus and the Old State
House bell, to set up his defining message from that "old Negro
spiritual" that Zora Neale Hurston had put into the mouths of the
Israelites as they set out for the Promised Land: "Free at last! Free at
last! Thank God Almighty, we are free at last!"

I asked Robert Franklin whether he viewed the King era as a sacred time.

"Without a doubt," he said. "There was enormous optimism, that
grew week by week. And on those occasions when the Supreme
Court acted, or a local magistrate, we saw that as validation. As God
in history, pushing us on, saying, 'Keep struggling. Don't lose hope.
You're making progress and I am with you.' Time was infused with
a sense of sacred presence in the air. That we should be good and
prepare ourselves for new life, because we were moving toward the
Promised Land.

"And the fact that we weren't sitting behind desks," he said, "but were walking, making a claim on public space, was important. We were reenacting the Exodus on a smaller scale. But we flipped the script. Whereas many people saw America as the New Israel and the Old World as Egypt, we said, 'No, America is Egypt, and blacks are the New Israel. We are the Jews.'"

"So if you take your experience and turn it toward the Bible," I asked, "what theme is most important from Moses' life?"

"It would be leadership," he said. "As C. L. Franklin used to say: Absent leadership, people can go on as slaves. You accommodate yourselves. You find those narrow spaces where you experience some measure of liberation. We were doing that, and along came these leaders, like Martin Luther King, Andrew Young, and others. Impatient. Angry. Yet not so consumed with anger that they don't offer a sense of reconciliation. The kind of leader who says, 'God is not happy with the arrangement. It must change, and God is on the side of those who are going to change it.'

"A leader," he continued, "has to articulate that vision, then get people to vote with their feet and start marching. For while the Moses figure embodies the collective aspirations of the whole, he can't do it alone. For me, the Exodus is a story about how a leader describes the possibility of a better community, then mobilizes the people to achieve it."

ANDREW YOUNG WORKS today at the top of a bank building in the heart of the city he served as a congressman, a mayor, and a secret weapon behind Atlanta's securing the 1996 Summer Olympics. Born in New Orleans in 1932, Young graduated from Howard University and later earned a divinity degree from Hartford Theological

Seminary. In a nod to his rudderless early years, he describes his graduation from Howard as "not magna cum laude but 'Oh, thank you, Lordy.'"

While serving as a minister in Alabama in 1957, he read Gandhi and was invited to meet the young star of the Montgomery Bus Boycott. Young expected long hours of philosophical and strategic conversations. In his memoir, *An Easy Burden,* he describes the meeting as an "extreme disappointment": "Martin was not inclined to discuss anything philosophical. He was more interested in talking about [his new baby]. . . . He was moody and into his more private self, and he didn't feel like acting out the role of the Reverend Dr. Martin Luther King, Jr." Young later realized he had been expecting too much from a casual meeting and learned to appreciate King's sometimes brooding, sometimes clownish, private side. Eventually Young moved to Atlanta and became one of King's chief deputies. He was jesting with his friend from the parking lot of the Lorraine Motel in Memphis on the night King was assassinated in April 1968.

I wanted to know what Young thought about the role Moses played in the civil rights movement and the fascinating, if fragile, alliance between blacks and Jews that was built in part on their shared use of the Exodus. I began by asking what role the Bible played in his early life.

"My grandmother was blind from the time I was eight years old, and every night she had me read the Bible to her," he said. "I also learned the stories in chorus. But I went through a period in college when I pretty much abandoned religion. We used to say as Congregationalists, 'You can't get to heaven unless your subject and verb agree.' The emphasis was so much on learning and proper speech that they forgot the spirit."

In his late seventies now and involved in international charitable work inspired by his years as U.N. ambassador, Young was dressed

crisply in white shirt and tie. He spoke deliberately and was notice-
ably heavier than the former track star who marched alongside King,
a reminder that the carefully scrutinized leaders of the civil rights
movement were merely young men at the time—in their late twen-
ties and early thirties.

"But all that Sunday-school training came back to help me in the
movement," he continued. "All the songs we sang were about the Old
Testament. *'When Israel was in Egypt land, Let my people go.' 'Joshua fit de
battle of Jericho, and the walls came a-tumblin' down.' 'There's a balm in
Gilead, to heal the sin-sick soul.'* Martin used to say that black men and
women took Jeremiah's question 'Is there a balm in Gilead?' and
straightened out the question mark into an exclamation point. 'There
is a balm in Gilead to heal the wounded whole!'"

"Did you know that singing those songs would lead to revolution?"

"Absolutely. Because in addition to being born into that biblical
environment, fifty yards from where I was born was the German
American Bund. From my porch I could hear people heiling Hitler.
Plus, a lot of my father's dental suppliers were Jewish, so the talk in
my house was constantly about these Nazis on the corner. And my
father's mantra was 'Don't get mad, get smart.' He took me to see
newsreels of Jesse Owens in the 1936 Berlin Olympics where Hitler
refused to shake his hand. 'See, that's the way to deal with white
supremacy. Jesse Owens didn't get angry. He just went out and
beat them.'"

In recent years, Young has come under attack by some Jews for
remarks he made about Jewish merchants taking advantage of blacks.
It was another wound in two decades of deteriorating relations
between blacks and Jews over such issues as Louis Farrakhan, Israel,
Palestine, economic development, and anti-Semitism. But in the
fifties and sixties, Jews were among the staunchest supporters of

civil rights. A number of the founders of the NAACP were Jewish. Two-thirds of the Freedom Riders in 1961 were Jewish, as were 50 percent of the Mississippi Summer volunteers of 1964. Half of the lawyers who brought civil rights cases to trial were Jews, and the Civil Rights Act of 1964 and the Voting Rights Act of 1965 were both drafted in the conference room of the Reform Jewish movement in Washington. When I asked Ambassador Young, whose grandmother was half Jewish, whether a shared allegiance to the Exodus was a factor in this relationship, he said, "Always." Then he cited the example of Abraham Joshua Heschel.

Beyond sharing grand, operatic names, Abraham Joshua Heschel and Martin Luther King, Jr., formed one of the more unusual partnerships in twentieth-century American history. One was a Baptist preacher with roots that stretched into slavery, the other a Polish rabbi and émigré from Hitler's Europe whose ancestors were among the founders of Hasidism. The former was colorful and rousing, the latter pious and earnest. But Heschel, whose hair looked like Einstein's and beard like Freud's, shared with King a common interest in the overlapping narratives of Judaism and Christianity. At a time when few others were saying it, King wrote openly about the Jewish roots of Jesus: "The Christian Church has tended to overlook its Judaic origins, but the fact is that Jesus of Nazareth was a Jew of Palestine." As America's leading Jewish theologian, Heschel wrote openly that Jews ought to acknowledge the "eminent role" that Christianity plays in God's plan for human redemption.

But the foundation of Heschel and King's partnership rested on mutual respect for a different story. "The preference King gives to the Exodus motif over the figure of Jesus certainly played a major role in linking the two men intellectually and religiously," explains Heschel's daughter, Susannah, a scholar of Jewish thought at Dartmouth. "For Heschel, the primacy of the Exodus in the civil rights movement was a major step in the history of Christian-Jewish relations."

The two men met in early 1963 at the Chicago Conference on Religion and Race, an unprecedented ecumenical gathering of one thousand religious leaders. Heschel opened his speech by comparing modern America with ancient Egypt. "At the first conference on religion and race, the main participants were Pharaoh and Moses," he said. "The outcome of that summit meeting has not come to an end. Pharaoh is not ready to capitulate. The Exodus began, but is far from having been completed. In fact, it was easier for the children of Israel to cross the Red Sea than for a Negro to cross certain university campuses."

The following year, King invited Heschel to join him in Selma for what would become a high point of the movement. Heschel described the march as an act of "service to God" and said he felt "as though my legs were praying." He wrote King, "The day we marched together out of Selma was a day of sanctification." A century after white Protestants in the North and South argued over whether Moses endorsed slavery, black Protestants and American Jews together formed what might be called a new Moses alliance to redefine power in the United States. And once again, Moses was on the winning side of a definitional change in American life.

"Hardly a day passed when somebody didn't make a reference to the Moses story," Andrew Young said. "It was our story. It was no longer a Jewish story. And Heschel, who was such a great man, understood that what we were doing was a theological event. There was no way we could stand up to the government of the United States on our own if we did not feel as though this was divinely motivated."

Susannah Heschel agrees. "My father came from a religious family," she told me. "If the movement had been about Jesus, it would

Abraham Joshua Heschel (far right) marches with (from left to right) Ralph Abernathy, Martin Luther King, Jr., and Maurice Eisendrath, in Selma, Alabama, March 24, 1965.

have been much harder for him to connect. The Exodus is much more unifying. Plus, it tapped into his sensitivities about racism. My father came out of Nazi Germany where Christians were throwing the Hebrew Bible out of the Christian Bible. 'No more Old Testament! It's too Jewish!' So just think of what it meant to him to hear these black Baptist preachers quoting Moses."

Heschel and King's friendship grew so strong that the rabbi invited King and his family to join the Heschels for a seder in 1968. The first night of Passover that year was on April 12. King was killed on April 4.

"I met Dr. King several times in my life, and he was always incredibly warm and wonderful," said Susannah, who was fifteen years old at the time. "The last time was just ten days before he was assassinated. There was a convention of Conservative rabbis in the Catskills honoring my father. Dr. King came to give the keynote, and when he came into the room there were a thousand rabbis, and they all stood up, linked arms, and sang, 'We Shall Overcome' in Hebrew."

I mentioned C. L. Franklin's 1950s speech about the Exodus and his idea that every generation raised up a Moses. "Was King that figure?"

"My father did feel that way," Susannah said. "He put it beautifully in his introduction of King that night in the Catskills. 'Where in America today do we hear a voice like the voice of the prophets of Israel? Martin Luther King is a sign that God has not forsaken the United States of America. God has sent him to us. His presence is the hope of America.'"

THE MASON TEMPLE is about a ten-minute drive from downtown Memphis, a few blocks from a bend of the Mississippi River that divides Tennessee and Arkansas. Not a Masonic temple, as I expected, the building got its name from Charles Mason, a local Pentecostal preacher who in 1897 founded the Church of God in Christ. Today the denomination boasts fifteen thousand pastors in fifty-six countries. Built in the 1940s, the blocky, concrete facility contains Bishop Mason's tomb and what the church claims was the largest black sanctuary in America at the time. With steel in low supply because of the war, the room was built with a tin roof and wooden folding seats that encircle the pulpit. The effect is even more church-in-the-round than the design of Plymouth Church in Brooklyn; most of the 3,732 seats are actually above the preacher, who stands near the lowest point of the room like a drum major at the fifty-yard line. The speaker preaches not from the top of a mountain but from the bottom of a bowl.

In early 1968, Mason Temple became ground zero for civil rights. On February 1, during a vicious rainstorm, Memphis's most famous resident, Elvis Presley, left Graceland for Baptist Hospital with his wife, Priscilla, who soon gave birth to their daughter, Lisa Marie. At the same hour, two black sanitation workers, seeking refuge from the weather, were crushed to death in the compactor of their garbage truck. Earlier, twenty-two black sewer workers had been sent home without pay while their white coworkers received their salaries. Two weeks later, eleven hundred black sanitation workers went on strike for better benefits. When the mayor balked at their demands, another of the rolling civil rights face-offs was under way. The difference now was that King was distracted by the backlash against his opposition to the war in Vietnam and his struggling Poor People's Campaign. On March 18, King visited Memphis and delivered a speech at the packed Mason Temple. Ten days later he led a march that descended into looting and death. In response, Tennessee imposed its first state of emergency since 1866, and King vowed to return in April to conduct a peaceful demonstration.

On Wednesday, April 3, King's Eastern Airlines flight from Atlanta to Memphis was delayed for more than an hour by a bomb scare. When King, Andrew Young, and their colleague Ralph Abernathy finally arrived in Memphis, police offered protection, but the tender was declined as King and company feared, correctly, that the white hierarchy was more interested in surveillance than security. King checked into room 306 at the black-owned Lorraine Motel, a frequent haven for musicians, preachers, and other traveling African Americans. A storm blew in, complete with tornado warnings and sheets of rain. A tornado actually hit Star City, Arkansas, at seven that evening, killing seven people. Fearing a low turnout, King decided to forgo the rally that night and asked Abernathy to speak on his behalf.

"Martin had been depressed and feverish," Young recalled. "But when we got there, the sanctuary was full and people were standing outside with umbrellas. We walked in and people started clapping. Ralph said, 'These people ain't clappin' for us. They think Martin's comin'." So we called and said, 'Martin, you've got to come.'" Young sent Abernathy to the pulpit and hopped into a car.

Abernathy spoke for nearly forty-five minutes, listing the accomplishments of King's life. King had not decided whether to become president of the United States, Abernathy joked, "but he is the one who tells the president what to do." Then King arrived and took a seat on the podium just as the winds and rain were reaching their peak. With no air-conditioning, the church had fans that would blow air out through the windows, but the fans were off and the tin shutters were slamming against the walls. "The shutters kept banging— *bam! bam!*," the Reverend Samuel "Billy" Kyles later explained to me. Kyles, a local preacher and a friend of King's, was seated on the podium along with Young and others. "Every time they would bang, Martin would flinch," Kyles continued. "He thought it was a shot. I called over the custodian and said, 'Turn on the fans and let the shutters blow out. The sound is really disturbing Dr. King.'"

Finally, at 9:30 P.M., King rose to speak. After a few jokes about Abernathy, he began with a bit of whimsy. "If I were standing at the beginning of time," he said, "and the Almighty said to me, 'Martin Luther King, which age would you live in?' I would take my mental flight by Egypt and would watch God's children in their magnificent trek from the dark dungeons of Egypt, across the Red Sea, through the wilderness, on toward the Promised Land. And in spite of its magnificence, I wouldn't stop there." He also wouldn't stop in the Roman Empire, the Renaissance, or at the time of the Emancipation Proclamation, he said. "Strangely enough, I would turn to the Almighty and say, 'If you allow me to live just a few years in the second half of the twentieth century, I will be happy.'"

King went on to celebrate the accomplishments of the Memphis movement and stressed the importance of maintaining unity. "Whenever the pharaoh wanted to prolong the period of slavery in Egypt, he had a favorite formula for doing it," he said. "He kept the slaves fighting among themselves. But whenever the slaves get together, something happens in Pharaoh's court, and he cannot hold the slaves in slavery." He discussed the parable of the Good Samaritan, in which a man is left to die beside the road from Jerusalem to Jericho. Several men pass him by, before a Samaritan stops to help. "That is the question before you tonight," King said. "If I do not stop to help the sanitation workers, what will happen to them?" Then he proceeded to his close.

In Deuteronomy 29 and 30, the 120-year-old Moses gathers the tribes together and gives a wrenching valediction. Informed by God that he will die short of the Promised Land, Moses steals one final moment to help shape the stiff-necked people he has guided for two generations, through a geography of miracles and a wilderness of doubt, to the lip of the land of milk and honey. "I led you through the wilderness for forty years," Moses says. "The clothes on your back did not wear out, nor did the sandals on your feet; you had no bread to eat and no wine or other liquor to drink." He was speaking not just to the people gathered before him on the mountain, Moses stressed, but to all their descendants throughout history. With everyone's emotions at their peak, Moses then rehearses the blessings God has bestowed on his chosen people. "You have seen all that the Lord did before your very eyes in the land of Egypt, to Pharaoh and to all his courtiers and to his whole country." He reiterates the people's obligations not to mingle with other nations or deities when they cross into Canaan. He renews their covenant with God. And finally Moses tells the Israelites that if they heed his advice and follow God's commandments, God will "grant you abounding prosperity in all of your undertakings."

Despite the overriding difference between the two talks—King didn't know his speech that night would be his last—King's emotion and structure bear striking similarities with Moses'. First, the thirty-nine-year-old preacher recounted the deeds God bestowed on his new chosen people. "I see God working in this period of the twentieth century in a way that men, in some strange way, are responding— something is happening in this world." He mentioned Johannesburg, Nairobi, and Accra, Ghana, as well as Atlanta, Jackson, and Memphis. Then he stressed the obligations the chosen people have not to mingle with other nations (in King's case, he called for a boycott of white-run companies that practiced discrimination, including those that made Sealtest milk and Coca-Cola—milk and honey!). He reminded his audience of the sacred covenant between freedom-loving people and God. And finally he reaffirmed that if black Americans made sacrifices and upheld their commitments, God would reward them with abundance and prosperity.

King's mood then turned darker. "Several years ago," he said, "I was in New York City autographing the first book that I had written." A woman came up to him and said, "Are you Martin Luther King?" then pulled a letter opener from her raincoat and plunged it into his chest. With the handle still protruding from his body, King was rushed to the hospital. "It was a dark Saturday afternoon," he continued, "and the X-rays revealed that the tip of the blade was on the edge of my aorta. And once that's punctured, you're drowned in your own blood." The *New York Times* reported the next day that "if I had merely sneezed, I would have died." Within days, he began to receive letters from all over the world. One was from a young girl.

> Dear Dr. King: I am a ninth-grade student at the White Plains High School. While it shouldn't matter, I would like to mention that I'm a white girl. I read in the paper of your misfortune and of your suffering. And I read that if you had sneezed, you would have died. And I'm simply writing you to say that I'm so happy that you didn't sneeze.

As the audience roared its applause, King turned his masterful trick. "And I want to say tonight that I, too, am happy that I didn't sneeze. Because if I had sneezed, I wouldn't have been around here for . . . ," and he went on to mention several highlights of the civil rights struggle.

King often spoke about death. As early as 1956, his mentor Bayard Rustin told him, "Dr. King, I have a feeling you had better prepare yourself for martyrdom, because I don't see how you can make the challenge that you are making here without a very real possibility of your being murdered." After John F. Kennedy was killed in 1963, King told his wife, "This is what is going to happen to me. I keep telling you, this is a sick society." And all through 1968, his aides commented that "he felt his time was up" or he appeared to be "a profoundly weary and wounded spirit." "You think I'm paranoid, don't you?" he asked Rustin. "Sometimes I do, Martin," his friend replied.

"One thing I learned from Martin," Andrew Young told me, "is that the price of leadership is death. We knew every time we left home it could be the end. Martin's home had been bombed. He had been arrested and thrown into a jail at a time when the jailers wanted him dead. Once in Atlanta, he had been thrown into the back of a paddy wagon in chains with a police dog and nobody else, then driven seven or eight hours to the state penitentiary, rolling back and forth. He said that was the most horrible night of his life.

"But he never wanted to talk about it," Young continued. "He'd just say, 'You don't know what it is to face death. You think you know, but I've been there, and it ain't easy. And you all need to get ready because your time will come.' And then he'd switch it and go all jovial. 'Because they'll be shootin' at me one of these days and one of you is gonna jump in front of the camera to get your picture taken and you're gonna take a bullet for me.' Whenever he'd get to thinking about death, he'd go real deep and melancholy, then he'd pull himself out of it by clowning."

In Memphis the night of April 3, King didn't pull himself out of it. Just past ten o'clock, as a tornado destroyed forty trailer homes north of Memphis, King reached the end of his sermon. He recounted the bomb scare that had delayed his plane that morning in Atlanta, and said that when he came to Memphis, some warned him that the death threats were so loud, something might happen "from some of our sick white brothers." "I don't know what will happen now," he said. "But it really doesn't matter with me now." He took a breath as the audience blurted, "Amen." Pulitzer Prize–winning historian Taylor Branch captures what happened next:

"Because I've been to the mountaintop," he declared in a trembling voice. Cheers and applause erupted. Some people jerked involuntarily to their feet, and others rose slowly like a choir. "And I don't mind," he said, trailing off beneath the second and third waves of response. "Like anybody I would like to live—a long life—longevity has its place." The whole building suddenly hushed, which let sounds of thunder and rain fall from the roof. "But I'm not concerned about that now," said King. "I just want to do God's will." There was a subdued call of "Yes!" in the crowd. "And he's allowed me to go up the mountain," King cried, building intensity. "And I've looked over. And I have s-e-e-e-e-n, the promised land." His voice searched a long peak over the word, "seen," then hesitated and landed with quick relief on "the promised land," as though discovering a friend. He stared out over the microphones with brimming eyes and the trace of a smile. "And I may not get there with you," he shouted, "but I want you to *know, tonight* ["Yes!"] that we as a people will get to the promised land!" He stared again over the claps and cries, while the preachers closed toward him from behind. "So I'm happy tonight!" rushed King. "I'm not worried about *any*thing! I'm not fearing *any* man! Mine eyes have seen the *glo*-ry of the coming of the Lord!" He broke off the quotation and stumbled sideways into a hug from Abernathy. The preachers helped him to a chair, some crying, and tumult washed through the Mason Temple.

When William Bradford landed with the Pilgrims on Cape Cod in December 1620, one of the first comparisons he made was to the final scene of the Five Books when Moses climbs to the top of Mount Nebo and peers longingly over the Jordan into the Promised Land he will not enter. When George Washington died in December 1799, one of the most quoted verses in his eulogies came from the same chapter of the Bible, in which the heralded leader leaves his young nation to carry on without him. When Abraham Lincoln was killed in April 1865, the scriptural passage that Henry Ward Beecher and many others cited to comfort a shocked and bewildered nation was also Deuteronomy 34. "This is the land of which I swore to

Abraham, Isaac, and Jacob," God says to Moses. "'I will give it to your offspring.' I have let you see it with your own eyes, but you shall not cross there."

On the eve of his death in April 1968, Martin Luther King, Jr., his name alone containing echoes of one of the great Mosaic figures of Christianity, Martin Luther, invoked the same passage of the Hebrew Bible to describe his own struggle. And as he had done since the opening of his national ministry in New York City a dozen years earlier, he once more used his talk to collapse time, linking the American South with ancient Egypt, the muddy flats of Memphis, Tennessee, with the sandy plains of Memphis, Egypt. He telescoped American history, connecting the Pilgrims' errand into the wilderness with the patriots' flight from the oppression of King George, weaving Lincoln's emancipation of the slaves into the march of the sanitation workers for greater rights. All these disparate moments became intermingled in the unity of divine cosmos, with King boldly placing himself at their lead, before he, too, is swept off the precipice to allow God's children to march forward, fatherless and full of fear.

I read King's final words to Andrew Young, then found myself speechless, unable to formulate a question. "It's almost unbelievable," I said.

"It is," Young said, "except that I had heard him make similar speeches on at least two other occasions. They were speeches when he was afraid, and when he thought death was near. But you could tell on this night, when he started talking about seeing the Promised Land, that he was thinking about his end."

"There's a great debate among people who love the Bible," I said, "as to whether Moses, after leading the Israelites across the Red Sea, putting up with their rebellions and their kvetching and complaining, climbing up and down Mount Sinai so many times with those tablets, then leading the people for thirty-eight more years while they get their act together, should have been allowed to enter the Promised Land. What do *you* think? Is it a tragedy?"

"You know, I never questioned it," this lifelong preacher said. "With Moses, I always thought it had something to do with his being a murderer. He had served, but it was time for new leadership. He was almost not worthy of going to the Promised Land.

"With Martin," he continued, "it was similar. I felt that he couldn't have led us into the Promised Land in the flesh, but he could in the spirit. And it was his spirit that empowered our movement from the time of his death on. When he was killed, I was really"—he thought for a second—"fussy. My grandmother used to get angry with God because he wouldn't take her home. She was ready to die and she bemoaned the fact that God was making her live on. I felt the same way about Martin. Death was the easy way out. Death would get him out of all this pressure and anxiety. And my attitude was, 'Dammit, you've gone off and left me.' I would much rather to have died with him, or instead of him, than to have to face the world without him."

He sat silent for a moment. "But we never had to face the world without him," he said. "His spirit has been more powerful in death than it was in life. And I suspect that's the way it was with Moses, too. When you come to the end of a God-ordained time, something new has to take over."

"So it was not a tragedy," I said.

"I don't think so. It was a triumph. That's where the Christian angle comes into the Moses narrative. We switch very quickly from the cross to the resurrection. And from the wilderness to the Promised Land."

"So let me ask you a question," I said. "It's a question that was debated about Martin Luther King his whole life." During the Montgomery boycott, I mentioned, *American Negro* called him "the Alabama Moses." *Jet* put him on its cover with the line "Alabama's Modern Moses." John Lewis called him a Moses; Ralph Abernathy agreed. "Was he a Moses?" I asked.

Young did not hesitate. "In many ways he was," he said. "He was Moses, Abraham, Isaac, and Jacob. He was humanity. But humanity in the hands of God. And that's what made the difference—that he put himself in God's hands. And that's what Moses did. One of the things that strengthened Martin's leadership is that he realized he didn't have to be perfect. God has always used frail human beings. And God was using him. There's a calypso song that says Moses was a murderer and God used him to lead his children out of Egypt. Not all prophets are judged by their moral perfection. They're judged by the poignancy of their proclamations. And Martin Luther King left a glorious proclamation."

THE LORRAINE MOTEL could not be a more dismal place. The poorly constructed motel with turquoise metal doors and flimsy white curtains deteriorated in the years after 1968 and was foreclosed in 1982. A local foundation purchased the bankrupt site and converted it to the National Civil Rights Museum. Lining the walkway to the front door are bricks from donors: Maya Angelou, Colin Powell, Rosa Parks, Yitzhak Rabin. A metal sculpture displays a quote from Genesis 37, the scene in which Joseph is thrown into a pit by his jealous brothers after he receives the coat of many colors from his father, Jacob. "They said one to another, 'Here comes that dreamer! Let us slay him and we shall see what becomes of his dreams!'"

When I first started writing about the Bible, I found it hard to grasp and accept the degree of shadow, oral history, and re-creation that went into creating the text. In particular the stories of the Five Books of Moses, which would have taken place hundreds of years before they were first written down, were passed down from generation to generation, inevitably going through changes, improvements, maybe even exaggerations. As happens with almost any story, heroes became more heroic, villains more villainous, miracles more miraculous. The process seems so alien today in a world of warts-and-all public figures and real-time paparazzi. There are no more heroes, right?

But walk a few paces in Martin Luther King's footsteps and you begin to see how even in a span of a few decades a similar process of sanctification is already happening to him. Even with all the people trying to harm him during his life—he had more than one FBI mole traveling with him in Memphis that week—a similar process of excavation, revision, and retelling is well under way. Stepping into the motel, I was struck by the power of narrative to turn this pedestrian place into a symbol of American loss. Just as Plymouth Harbor can become the Red Sea and the Ohio River the Jordan, the Lorraine Motel can be seen as Mount Nebo. And Martin Luther King can be transformed into an American prophet. Just when the Bible threatens to seem distant and archaic, I walk into a place like this and realize the impulse behind the writing of sacred scripture is still alive today.

Room 306 is on the second floor, overlooking a parking lot that in 1968 contained a swimming pool. The door opens onto a small, covered concrete walkway. Today the room has been preserved as a shrine, including a copy of the *Memphis Press-Scimitar* with the headline RACIAL PEACE SOUGHT BY TWO NEGRO PASTORS, a Bible, a black telephone, ruffled sheets, and an orange drink. The room has two beds, one for Abernathy, one for King. I found it jolting that a man who had won the Nobel Peace Prize and was one of the most recognizable Americans in the world was bunking two to a room in a two-story motel because he wasn't welcome in any other part of town.

At four o'clock on the afternoon of April 4, 1968, Andrew Young returned to the Lorraine after a bruising day in court defending the upcoming march. "Martin threw me down and started beating me with a pillow," he told me. "He was like a big kid. He was berating me because I hadn't reported to him. Finally I snatched a pillow and started swinging back. People started throwing pillows and piling on top on everybody, laughing and going on."

An hour later, Billy Kyles arrived. A veteran of recent marches, he was serving as King's unofficial host, and his wife had invited King and his colleagues for dinner. She had rallied the best cooks in their church to lay out a feast of roast beef, pork chops, turnip greens, candied sweet potatoes, and mounds of desserts. "King was really loose," Kyles told me. "I told him dinner was at five o'clock. But King had called the house and my wife told him dinner was really at six. So I went over to the room to get him, and he said, 'Oh, no. Dinner is not until six, and I'm in no hurry. Have a seat.' He was never in a hurry. That's why I told him five."

Samuel "Billy" Kyles was born in Shelby, Mississippi, in 1934. After a brief stint in Chicago, he moved to Memphis in 1959 to become the pastor of Monumental Baptist Church, a position he still holds. Tall, debonair, and gracious, with a graying mustache and wide smile, he had the serene demeanor of an apostle to history, and he reminded me of Nelson Mandela or Sidney Poitier, both of whom he's shown around the Lorraine Motel, as well as Desmond Tutu, Mikhail Gorbachev, and Lech Walesa, a total of eight Nobel laureates. He agreed to meet me at the spot of the killing to discuss King's final hour. Within several minutes, I could see that he didn't have the smoothed-over rage that Andrew Young still seemed to harbor. I asked him if he was angry during the peak years of the movement. "I learned very early," he said, "and Martin talked about it all the time, that hatred is more damaging to the hater than it is to the hated. My juices were flowing. I was more than disappointed. But I was not angry."

"Then what motivated you?" I asked.

"The knowledge, without being arrogant, that we were right. I don't think we thought what we were doing was going to change the world, but we believed it would change more than our neighborhood. And eventually it did change the world. Freedom-loving people all over the globe use Martin Luther King and the civil rights movement as the model."

King, Abernathy, and Kyles spent the five o'clock hour sitting together in room 306. "So the world will ask, 'What did three preachers do in a room for an hour?'" Kyles said. "I say, 'We talked preacher talk.' It was lighthearted. Ralph said, 'I don't know what kind of food we're gonna have tonight, 'cause Billy's wife is too pretty to cook.' Martin loved a good joke. He said a preacher who can't tell a good joke, don't even fool with him, he can't preach either. Then I picked out his tie, and about quarter to six we walked out on the balcony."

Reverend Kyles led me onto the narrow walkway that could have been on any roadside motel from the era. Across the parking lot and a narrow street was the back of South Main Street and a row of six- and seven-story buildings that contained a firehouse and Bessie Brewer's flophouse. It was so close you could throw a football to there from where I stood.

At four o'clock that afternoon an escaped convict had bought a pair of binoculars nearby and was now stationed with a .30-06 Remington Gamemaster in a bathroom window of the boarding house, where he had a clear view of room 306. Arriving on the balcony, King joked with Andrew Young and Jesse Jackson down below in the parking lot and asked the bandleader to play "Precious Lord, Take My Hand" at that night's meeting. "I turned to go down the stairs," Kyles told me. "I got about five steps and a sound rang out.

Kabpoooooooooow. At first I thought it was a car backfiring, but I turned and saw people ducking and then I knew it was a shot. I looked up where the shot came from. Then I looked back and Martin had been knocked from the railing onto the balcony. I rushed to his side. There was a tremendous hole in the side of his face. Blood was everywhere."

Kyles ran into the room to call the police, but the phone didn't work. The motel owner's wife, who was operating the switchboard, had heard the shot and run into the parking lot. When she saw King on the balcony, she suffered a cerebral hemorrhage; she died four days later. Running back onto the balcony, Kyles took a spread from one of the beds and covered King from the neck down. "He never spoke a word," Kyles said. "The ambulance finally came and I told them what hospital to take him to, Saint Joseph's. I did it instinctively because they were the least difficult to integrate." Kyles went silent.

"Did you have survivor's guilt?" I asked.

"I don't think I did," he said. "The killer just wanted one shot. He could have wiped out the whole team, but he wanted to kill King and that's what he did. But I did wonder, 'Why was I there?' We were friends and all that, but why was I there in that moment in history? Then at some point, God revealed to me why I was there. I was there to be a witness. Crucifixions have witnesses, and honest witnesses at that.

"Martin wasn't killed in some foolish, untoward way," he continued. "He wasn't shot leaving the scene of a crime. He wasn't murdered by a jealous lover. Here was a man who earned a Ph.D. degree, a Nobel Peace Prize, had oratorical skills off the charts, and of all the things he could have been, university president, senator, leader of megachurches around the country, he died on a balcony in Memphis, Tennessee, helping . . ." He paused. "Garbage workers. My God!

What a way to give meaning to your life. And what a message to send to your country."

He rested his hand on the balcony and gestured toward the city beyond. "And now we have a holiday in his honor," Kyles added. "And no matter what your politics may be, you've got to deal with his holiday, because there's no mail delivery, no banking. Only three individuals in American history have holidays named after them— George Washington, Abraham Lincoln, and in less than a hundred fifty years since slavery, Martin Luther King, Jr. And the amazing thing is, our foreparents could see the possibility. They believed that God would send them a leader."

"But why must the leaders die prematurely?" I asked. "Jesus. Moses. Lincoln. King. Why can't they get to the Promised Land?"

"It was not intended for them to get there. Moses did what he was supposed to do, and today we're still talking about him. The same with Jesus. With Martin, after all he did in his life, why wasn't he able to experience the Promised Land? Because the Promised Land would disappoint. If he had lived to be the age he would have been now, there would be no holiday, there would be no memorials. There would be no story. His transformation was to a better place. His story is bigger than his life. And in that way, he may be most like Moses of all."

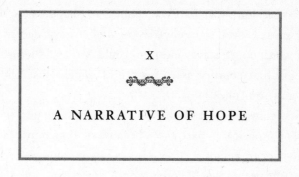

X

A NARRATIVE OF HOPE

THE DAYS LEADING up to Passover at my wife's childhood home outside Boston are filled with controlled chaos. My father-in-law rearranges furniture, brings out extra tables and chairs, and lugs home cases of kosher wine and tubs of chopped liver. My mother-in-law polishes goblets and horseradish bowls, stirs bathtubs of chicken soup, and brushes up on the school grades, hobbies, and musical instruments of the distant cousins and grandchildren-of-estranged-uncles who comprise the seventy or so guests. Bringing our two toddlers into this environment, with their assorted blankies, sippy cups, failed haircuts, and scratched lullaby CDs, only heightens the drama. "Why are these nights different?" the *hagadah* asks. In many ways, they're not.

This year, as we arrived on our annual pilgrimage, I was also thinking about the connections between Passover and the United States. Is Moses still relevant in America today? In an age when secularism, globalism, and pluralism threaten to undermine the Bible's influence, does the three-thousand-year-old story from the ancient Near East still have the ability to shape public debate? Having starred over the centuries in oral history, sacred canon, printed word, novel, stage, and film, could Moses be reinvented in the twenty-first century as a creature of shock jocks, the blogosphere, and YouTube?

At first glance, Moses might seem to be a missing person in contemporary America. In part, that's because of the country's rapidly changing face of religion. After a loosening of immigration laws in the 1960s, the percentage of foreign-born Americans more than doubled in the next four decades to 10 percent. The arrivals brought with them a host of faiths little known in the country, including Islam, Hinduism, Buddhism, and Sikhism, along with fresh waves of Pentecostal Christians and traditional Catholics. Three million Americans are Muslim today; twice that are said to be Buddhist. If the early-American centuries were Protestant and the last one Judeo-Christian, the new century will be even more hyphenated—at least among those who still cling to God. A tenth of Americans define themselves as atheist or agnostic.

As America's religious identity becomes more and more diffused, the Bible's role in the country's self-perception becomes increasingly imperiled. Almost all Americans say they believe in God, 93 percent of American homes have at least one Bible, and a third of the country believes the Bible is literally true. But few know more than its basic outlines. Half of Americans can't name the first book of the Bible, and only 20 percent can name a single prophet. Gallup calls the United States "a nation of biblical illiterates." But with Moses, something singular seems to have happened. The key themes of his story have continued to give shape and meaning to countless Americans who may know next to nothing about the root text in

Exodus, Leviticus, Numbers, and Deuteronomy (um, books two through five).

This trend is particularly true among outsiders. Betty Friedan in her leadership of the feminist movement was compared to Moses. Harvey Milk, the first openly gay city supervisor of San Francisco, was called the Moses of his people. In 1987, Richard "Cheech" Marin made a film, *Born in East L.A.*, likening Latino immigration to the Exodus. Microsoft founder Bill Gates's showdown with IBM was compared to Moses' showdown with the pharaoh; then Gates became the pharaoh, and Steve Jobs of Apple assumed the role of Moses.

The bulk of these comparisons were mere slogans, coined by clever headline writers or savvy marketers. But they resonated long after the Bible began to recede in the nation's memory, because they tapped into the larger American story: Oppression is merely temporary; mighty authoritarian figures can be toppled; and all people can be set free to achieve their promise. Even if the analogies bore little connection to the Bible, they invoked the memory of successive American liberations—from 1776 to the Civil War to civil rights. If outsiders want to legitimize their place in America, they have to make their cause fit the most American of templates—the Exodus.

In the presidency, the use of Mosaic language did not ebb with the decline of Scripture. In *The Making of the President, 1964*, Theodore White compared Lyndon Johnson's victory to the close of the Moses story. "It was as if Kennedy, a younger Moses, had led an elder Joshua to the height of Mount Nebo and there shown him the promised land which he himself would never enter but which Joshua would make his own." Not to be overshadowed, Johnson stood up at his inauguration and promptly claimed the Moses role for himself. "The American covenant called on us to help show the way for the liberation of man," he said. "And that today is our goal."

Three decades later, Bill Clinton, accepting the Democratic nomination in 1992, announced a "New Covenant, a solemn agreement between the people and their government—based not simply on what each of us can take but on what all of us must give to our nation." He added, "Our eyes have not yet seen, nor our ears heard, nor our minds imagined what we can build." Again, the uncredited reference comes from Moses' farewell speech on Nebo, the same passage quoted by Ronald Reagan at the Statue of Liberty, Martin Luther King at the Mason Temple, and John Winthrop on the *Arbella*. Moses was the original "bridge to the twenty-first century."

Republicans also claimed the legacy of Moses. Ronald Reagan was called the Moses of conservatism. At a reception following the inauguration of George W. Bush in 2001, a senator introduced the president as a leader who followed in the footsteps of Joshua. The president's pastor agreed, comparing Bush to "Moses who just crossed the river, leading his people to the mountain and from there to the Promised Land." He added, "I think you have brought healing and hope to the young, to the marginalized, to the dispossessed. And that's what Moses did. He was chosen by God, as you have been chosen by God." The rhetoric got so bloated that the *Independent* in London nicknamed the new president "George *M.* Bush (M for Moses)." Are comparisons to Moses a precondition of White House residency?

A FEW WEEKS before Passover, I got a call from my father. "The president of the United States mispronounced your name on national television last night," he reported. President George W. Bush, at the end of an interview with C-SPAN, had been asked what books he had been reading. "Well, I just finished a book called *Abraham* by a guy named Feiler," he said, pronouncing my name "Feeler" instead of "Filer." "And it's a really interesting book that studies the prophet Abraham from the Christian, Jewish, and Muslim perspective." The president went on to give a generous description of the book and express hope that Abraham could promote reconciliation. Not long afterward, I received a telephone call: Could I appear at the White House ten days later to meet the president?

I hadn't exactly been a supporter of President Bush, but the opportunity to engage him one-on-one in the White House seemed like a once-in-a-lifetime opportunity. So I pressed my suit, shined my shoes, and, with my wife and parents in tow, made the overnight trek to 1600 Pennsylvania Avenue. And when I woke that morning to find that my collar was lacking a stay, I took a Q-tip, circumcised it with a nail clipper, and inserted it into my collar. That's right: I wore a Q-tip into the Oval Office.

We arrived at the Northwest Appointment Gate at 8:45 A.M. An extremely charming aide led us past "Pebble Beach," where the networks keep their outdoor cameras, through the front door of the West Wing, into what she described as a "holding room." It turned out to be the Cabinet Room. The familiar table filled most of the space, and through the windows you could see the Rose Garden. A Charles Willson Peale portrait of George Washington hung on one wall, with the first president posed as Napoléon; opposite was a marble bust of Washington looking like Caesar. There was a painting of the signing of the Declaration of Independence, a portrait of Eisenhower, and, oddly, I thought, the bust of a non-president, Benjamin Franklin. Each leather chair at the table had a brass plate on the back bearing the title of the person who sat there, including THE PRESIDENT.

At about 9:50, we were moved into a dark foyer, then through the open door into the Oval Office. My first impression was how light the room was, and how heavy the air. Part of this is an architectural trick. I renovated an apartment a few years ago, and my architect talked about the power of making small anterooms darker, so that the large room you enter has even more impact. That's exactly what happens with the Oval Office. You first pass through a warren of windowless rooms, then burst into the Oval Office, which has huge windows, an illuminated ceiling, and stage lighting. Reagan communications guru Mike Deaver had relit the room, and the effect on your irises, if nothing else, is intense. Russian president Vladimir Putin, upon entering, is said to have uttered, "Oh, my God."

The other source of intensity, of course, is the person entering the room. You bring a lot of emotion with you—the anxiety, the nervous twisting of hands, the sense of history. And I wasn't coming to make a major decision, or negotiate a bill, or apply for a Supreme Court judgeship. I can only imagine the emotion some visitors feel.

President Bush was standing on the light-colored rug designed by his wife in front of the desk used by FDR and JFK. Wearing a blue suit, a red tie, and cowboy boots, he was very shouldery and formal. He welcomed us to the Oval Office. Friends who had met him led me to expect joking, maybe even towel snapping. Instead, the first words out of his mouth were serious: "You're entering the Oval Office at an important time in our history," he said. "This is where we make history, and our actions will be judged by history." He went on to defend his strategy in Iraq. Afterward we shook hands, and the president repeated some nice words about my work. Then I decided to inquire about his faith. I asked if he had a Bible in the Oval Office.

"Of course I have a Bible here," he said, and pointed to the table behind his desk, where a green leather-bound Bible sat in front of his family photographs. It was closer to his chair than the telephone. "But I read it only in the private residence," he said.

"Are there any specific verses that speak to you?"

"I'm strengthened by people who pray for me," he said, "not by specific verses. You have to be the president of all the people. This is not a Christian country. The strength of our country is that we can all worship freely—not like the Islamic extremists who say we must believe in their God. A sinner like me, I don't presume to tell other people they must believe in God. I'm not that vain."

What followed was a twenty-minute conversation about church, state, and the role of religion in the presidency. Bush stressed that a president's faith should be private and Americans should not vote for a candidate just because he wears his faith on his sleeve. He said he had been criticized for mentioning in a Republican debate in 2000 that his favorite philosopher was Christ. "What was I supposed to say, Hobbes or Locke?" he quipped.

He spoke to my wife for a few minutes, and the time was approaching to take photographs. I told the president that I had spent the last year or so looking at the role of Moses in American history, that Moses had played a role with many presidents, from George Washington on. Could President Bush think of any moments where Moses had inspired him?

The president thought for a second. "Only one," he said. At his second inaugural as governor of Texas, Pastor Mark Craig gave a sermon saying that America was starved for honest leaders. "He told the story of Moses, asked by God to lead his people to a land of milk and honey," Bush recalled. "Moses had a lot of reasons to resist, and his reaction was, 'Sorry, God, I'm busy. I've got a family. I've got a life. Who am I that I should go to Pharaoh and bring the sons of Israel out of Egypt? The people won't believe me. I'm not a very good speaker.' Pastor Craig noted that it's not always convenient for leaders to step forward. 'Even Moses had doubts.'"

That night, the president said, his mother, Barbara, approached him. "He's speaking about you," she said. The occasion was a turning point in his decision to run for president.

When George Washington refused to be sworn in as president until a Bible was summoned from the Masonic lodge, he created an indelible partnership between the pinnacle of American power and the embodiment of Israelite religion. Forty-two presidents later, though many things about the presidency have changed, that partnership has not. One reason may be the kinship of history. Every room I entered in the White House featured a depiction of George Washington. The past is omnipresent here, as is the future. Nearly every sentence out of President Bush's mouth related to how someone before him had conducted himself, or someone later would judge his actions. He was steeped in the weight of time. Given that, it's no wonder that many presidents in moments of crisis have turned to the Bible. How many documents have withstood the crush of so much time?

But beyond that, the idea that one biblical story has inspired such radically different leaders as George Washington and Abraham Lincoln, Lyndon Johnson and Ronald Reagan, George W. Bush and Barack Obama, suggests that the story has transcended time and political party to become a leitmotif of the American presidency. One reason may be the importance of leadership to Moses' life. As political scientist Aaron Wildavsky wrote in *Moses as Political Leader*, the Five Books of Moses are a "primer on leadership." Moses can teach so much, Wildavsky suggests, because "far from being beyond us, [he] was full of human faults, from passivity to impatience to idolatry." He doubts his own abilities, faces rebellions from his people, and still manages to persuade them to follow him through the wilderness even as he fails to achieve his dream. "Difficulty and disappointment punctuate Moses' entire career," Wildavsky observed. "At his most successful, Moses teaches us that we can do without him."

Moses embodies both passion and frustration, success and failure, and that may be why he still haunts the halls of 1600 Pennsylvania Avenue. I certainly saw a mixture of determination and resignation in the eyes of President Bush that morning, and a quick catalogue of the presidents linked with Moses suggests a similar balance of vision achieved and promise deferred. Moses is an emblem of the American presidency precisely because he captures both the grandeur of leading a free people and the anguish of being alone at the top of the mountain.

IN WASHINGTON, MOSES doesn't just live in the White House. His statue stands in the Library of Congress. His tablets are embedded in the floor of the National Archives. And his face appears in the House chamber, along with that of Hammurabi, Maimonides, and Napoléon, in a tribute to twenty-three figures who inspired American law. Eleven of the bas-reliefs face left, and eleven face right; they all look toward Moses, who hangs in the middle, the only one shown full-figured.

Perhaps the most surprising Mosaic representations in the capital are the *six* in the nation's highest court. Moses is practically the mascot of the U.S. Supreme Court. He appears at the center of the east pediment, flanked by Solon of Athens and Confucius of China in a tribute to the legal traditions of other civilizations. He appears in the gallery of statues that leads into the court, as well as the south frieze in the chamber. The Ten Commandments are displayed on the bronze gates leading into the courtroom as well as on the interior panels of the chamber doors.

Are these depictions an anachronism, or do they still speak in America today?

To answer that question I spoke to two of the most vocal combat-

East pediment of the Supreme Court of the United States, with Moses seated in the center, holding the tablets of the law. *(Courtesy of The Supreme Court of the United States)*

ants in church-state cases before the Supreme Court—Rabbi David Saperstein of Religious Action Center of Reform Judaism and Jay Sekulow of Pat Robertson's American Center for Law and Justice. Saperstein, who descends from a long line of rabbis, has been called the "quintessential religious lobbyist." Sekulow, who was born a Jew but converted to Christianity, has been deemed "the Almighty's Attorney-at-Law." Both men presented briefs in the two Ten Commandments cases that appeared before the Court in 2005. The first reviewed whether a granite Ten Commandments on the grounds of the Texas Capitol violated the establishment clause of the First

Amendment; the second examined whether government-sponsored displays of the Ten Commandments in Kentucky courtrooms violated the same clause.

Saperstein was against displaying the commandments because he sees them as "unambiguously religious." Unlike "God Bless America" or "In God We Trust," both of which are part of the "background sounds of American life," the Decalogue promotes specific religious traditions. Sekulow argued that displaying the Commandments does not endorse one faith but honors their "extraordinary influence" on American law. The Ten Commandments are like other expressions of America's cultural heritage, including Thanksgiving and "one nation under God" in the Pledge of Allegiance.

In the Texas case, the Court agreed with Sekulow, ruling that the commandments were donated by a civic group and did have the secular purpose of reducing juvenile delinquency, while in Kentucky, the Court found the displays had no such purpose and had to be removed. In yet another cultural civil war, Moses had somehow found a way to survive. When he is aligned with America's secular tradition, he can stand on public ground. When he assumes the role of religious prophet, he must remain on private property.

"There are two different narratives in America," David Saperstein explained. "The Enlightenment and the religious. 'I think therefore I am' versus 'In the beginning was God.' And there was no day that Western civilization went to the polls and said, 'That's it for the God-oriented world. We're going with the rationalist world.' We're an amalgam of all these things."

"So where is the balance of power today?"

"I think it's a dead heat. I think the American people believe in the Ten Commandments and don't like the idea that the government can say, 'Don't post them in some place.' But I think the American people don't like the idea of government imposing religious messages and values." In 1776, I mentioned, America was clearly a biblical nation. The same could be said of 1865, and probably even 1932. "Is America a biblical nation today?"

"Ninety-six percent of Americans say they believe in God," Rabbi Saperstein said. "Eighty-five percent say that religious values are important in their lives. People cherish the Bible, but I think there is a comfort level with functionally separating government and religion. So it is a biblical nation in terms of amorphous values that people trace back to the Bible, but the idea that government should somehow impose the Bible on others is becoming increasingly troublesome for Americans."

Jay Sekulow agreed. "I think we're a religious nation," he said. "I think our institutions presuppose the existence of a supreme being. But are we a biblical nation? I think that's a harder question right now, because I think we've moved away from involving the Bible in government. The Bible is still present in America, but it's muted."

"So is America weaker because of that muting?"

"I think if we lose our religious underpinnings, we lose our compass. And not just because of abortion and same-sex marriage. That includes decency, how we view the poor, helping those in need. The biblical overtones in all those are significant, and if we lose that, we lose something about our culture."

One irony of this decline in biblical influence is that it forces combatants like Saperstein and Sekulow into a shared allegiance. They may disagree about the degree of religion's involvement in contemporary American life, but they absolutely agree that the Bible forms one of the main threads of the country's DNA. And I couldn't help wondering if that alliance might provide an opening to crack the cultural gridlock the country faces. As I had found, one biblical story has served as a touchstone for all Americans. Could understanding the role of Moses in American history illuminate the changing role of faith in our national life? Could Moses restore some of the civility that both left and right say is missing?

Could all those marble Moseses scattered around the nation's capital remind us of our shared heritage of freedom and law?

"I think so," said Jay Sekulow. "Christians, by nature, accept the biblical story of Moses with no hesitation. It's a political story. Jesus, on the other hand, was above politics. His was a kingdom not of this world. Plus, if you look at the way Moses approached issues and leadership, there's a great example there. Moses never presumed he had the complete allegiance of the people. He operated under the assumption that you had to maintain people's allegiance."

David Saperstein said: "I believe he can, because every generation is a new generation. So every generation is reinspired by the narrative. Every generation feels that if we march down the right path, we can really make it to the Promised Land. The difference now is that our generation faces threats so lethal to our planet that they can truly alter human history. This is the generation that has to make it to the Promised Land. This generation truly needs a Moses."

BEYOND HIS ROLE in politics, Moses also plays a part in what may be the country's larger conversation: the path to personal fulfillment. During our visit to Boston, I slipped out one morning to meet one of the most famous Jews in the city (after Kevin Youkilis, the Red Sox first baseman, and Bob Kraft, the owner of the New England Patriots). Harold Kushner was a little-known suburban rabbi in 1981 when he wrote a book inspired by the loss of his first child, Aaron, from a rare genetic disease that produces premature aging. *When Bad*

Things Happen to Good People became one of the most influential books of popular theology in American history, selling more than four million copies and making the soft-spoken Brooklyn native America's rabbi-in-chief.

Kushner went on to write numerous pastoral books, and one of them, *Overcoming Life's Disappointments*, published in 2006, uses the story of Moses to explore how individuals can cope with personal crisis. "What was the wisdom of Moses that enabled him to carry on day after day, year after year, as leader of a people who exasperated him more often than they appreciated him?" Kushner asked. "It was a recognition of the frailty of the human character, the occasional unreliability of even the best of people, and the sometimes unexpected goodness of even the worst of them."

Moses has long been a pivotal figure in the mixing of psychology and religion, beginning with Sigmund Freud. The founder of psychotherapy had a lifelong fascination with Moses, and in his final book, *Moses and Monotheism*, published in 1939, he portrays the leader of the Israelites as the father figure of Western thought. Freud contended that Moses was a renegade Egyptian priest, who led a rebellious group of monotheists into the desert. The former slaves could not handle the burdens of a new faith and murdered Moses, then repressed their crime. The memory of the murder returned over time in the form of respect for morality, ethics, and other "intellectual" ways of relating to God. This interest in ideas over idolatry and sensuality became the centerpiece of Western civilization.

In 1946, Joshua Liebman, another Boston rabbi, published one of the first pop-psychology mega-sellers, *Peace of Mind*, which argued that spiritual health was related to psychological maturity. Of Americans' obsession with material success, he wrote, "We are still like the Children of Israel dancing around the golden calf. Psychology today can aid religion in giving many people insights into the reason for this neurotic idolatry." In the 1990s, Promise Keepers, the evangelical men's movement, trumpeted Moses as the ultimate role model, a "man's man [who] was God's man." "For Moses, the call was to lead a nation," wrote one of the group's leaders, "whereas your call and mine will likely be less visible. But make no mistake, we *are* leaders!" Even the 1998 animated film *Prince of Egypt* presents Moses as a confident youth showered with love and his rival, Rameses, as starved for fatherly attention. "All he cares about is your approval," Moses tells the pharaoh about Rameses.

Is this what Moses has become in America—a self-help guru?

"In many ways, yes," Rabbi Kushner said. "There is still a population of immigrants for whom America represents leaving Egypt and coming to a better life. And there are minorities—blacks, Asians, Hispanics—who are teaching us what it means to be American today. But there is a phenomenon going on in this country. For the first time there's a generation of Americans growing up who cannot look forward confidently to being more successful than their parents. The American promise always was: You can outdo your parents. But we have a generation of parents—my generation—who are so well educated and so successful they leave very little room for their children to outstrip them. And I think that's a psychological need, especially for males. So what a lot of people are doing is redefining success, saying things like, 'Okay, I'm not going to make as much money as my father made, but I'm going to have my priorities straight. I'm not going to be so busy I can't watch my kids at a dance recital.' I think they're redefining the Promised Land. And I think Moses becomes the one who shows the way."

"How?"

"He sets an example. As you know, the biblical name for Egypt means 'the confining place.' So both in geographical terms and individual terms, Moses resonates with the idea of leaving the confinement of Egypt and heading out into the desert. You've left the confinement of parents, upbringing, hometown, expectations. You may even have made it across the desert. But you're not going to find the Promised Land you envisioned when you started out. How do you define fulfillment? Come up with your own sense of promised land. That's what Moses calls people to do.

"I had occasion just a few weeks ago to speak to a woman who's recently gone through a divorce," Rabbi Kushner continued. "She was very uncomfortable about facing Passover for the first time without the husband that she had shared the occasion with for years. I said, 'See it as a Passover story—that you're leaving a belittling, confining situation. It's scary to go out into the desert, but the desert is something you have to get through to find the reward at the other end.' There's something universal, and something specifically American, about that."

"There's a risk in what you're saying," I mentioned. "The risk is that you become so involved with your own personal drama that you forget that caring for others is a central part of the story."

"Perhaps, but look at what Moses does when he realizes that everyone else is going to the Promised Land and he isn't," Rabbi Kushner said. "He doesn't go off and sulk. He doesn't go somewhere for counseling. He gathers the people together on Mount Nebo and prepares them for what they will face in the future. In the Jewish tradition, we speak of him as Moses *Rabeinu*—Moses, Our Teacher— not Moses, Our Political Leader; not Moses, Who Freed the Slaves. Moses, Our Teacher. He dedicates himself to getting the people to embrace the ideas that they have to live by when he's no longer around to remind them.

"The example I gave before," he said. "The no-longer-young man who says, 'Okay, I'll never earn the amount of money my father earned.' Where does he find his fulfillment? In being a better father. In being a better husband. That's not narcissism. That's not saying, 'I'm going to spend my sixteen hours of wakefulness figuring out how I can make myself a success.' That is defining success as caring for other people."

"How much of Moses' message on Mount Nebo is 'Take care of your own house?'" I asked, "and how much is 'Take care of your neighbor's house, too?'"

"Ninety percent is take care of the house of your neighbor— maybe even more than ninety. The whole idea is that this is a communal enterprise. It is the biblical ethos that says, 'You can't make it through this world alone. You can only make it in community.'"

"So when I sit down with my daughters at future seders, what should I tell them is the story's central lesson?"

"That in every generation, there are forces, individual and collective, that try to inhibit our human fulfillment. And in every generation, God acts as the impulse to strike out for freedom, even though the path to freedom is not always easy. But in the end, the burden is on each of us to finish the journey. When we were slaves, God had to break our chains. We couldn't do it for ourselves. In fact it took an outsider like Moses to be a catalyst, as it took an outsider like Martin Luther King, Jr., to lead the civil rights movement. But once we're no longer slaves, we can't say to God, 'Fix this for us.' Now we have the opportunity and obligation to fix it for ourselves."

I'VE BEEN TO a lot of seders in my life. When I was growing up, my parents used a popular *hagadah* with contemporary watercolors, abundant songs, and readings from Anne Frank, Abraham Joshua Heschel, and others. Published in 1974, the book was unabashedly liberal; it says of the plagues, "Our triumph is diminished by the slaughter of the foe." In Jerusalem one year, I attended a more traditional seder where they read every prayer and followed every dictate and the evening didn't end until 2 A.M. That night answered a question I'd had since childhood: In Jerusalem they also end the service by saying, "Next year in Jerusalem."

The start of Passover brings the two nights a year when my father-in-law, Alan, an attorney and elder sage around Boston, is in charge of a portion of his home, which is otherwise dominated by women. In keeping with contemporary Jewish custom (and in violation of international copyright laws) he has gone through numerous *hagadah*s and pieced together his own service. The word *seder* means "order," and the Passover service follows a strict order of rituals recreating the Israelites' exodus from Egypt. These include drinking four glasses of wine, which recall the four acts of redemption God performs for the Israelites; dunking greens, which represent the lowly Israelites, into salt water, which symbolizes their tears; and breaking matzoh, bread baked without leavening because the Israelites were hurrying to flee Egypt. Other observances include tasting bitter herbs, representing the harshness of slavery; eating *haroset,* a mixture of apples, nuts, cinnamon, and wine, symbolizing the mortar used to build the pharaoh's cities; and opening the door for Elijah, the prophet who is believed to herald the Messiah.

At the heart of the seder is a deeper message: History is not prerecorded. It is something we write ourselves. As Jonathan Sacks, the chief rabbi of Britain, put it: "We are not condemned endlessly to repeat the tragedies of the past. Not everywhere is an Egypt; not all politics are the exploitation of the many by the few; life is something other and more gracious than the pursuit of power." The seder, which Sacks calls the "oldest surviving ritual in the Western world," calls on participants to do more than retell the story of the Exodus; they are to relive it themselves: "In every generation, a person should look upon himself as if he personally had come out of Egypt." Passover is not a commemoration, it's a call to action. Participants are summoned to become cocreators of a better world.

In America, Passover has long maintained a sacred time for Jews, in part because of its deep parallels with American history. In 1997 Rabbi David Geffen, an Atlanta native whose grandfather was asked in 1935 to guarantee that the secret formula for Coca-Cola was kosher (he insisted they remove glycerin made from beef tallow), compiled a survey of Passover traditions in the United States. As early as 1889, on the centennial of George Washington's inauguration, anyone who bought ten pounds of matzoh got a free picture of the first president. The chief rabbi of New York composed a special prayer for Washington that year to be read in all American synagogues, many of which decorated their buildings with red, white, and blue bunting.

American wars, with their language of defending freedom, have provided many poignant settings for seders. During the Civil War, the Union Army actually provided matzoh to some regiments. Joseph Joel, a soldier from Cleveland, hosted a seder—which included lamb and a scavenged bitter herb—for twenty comrades in West Virginia in 1862. "The ceremonies were passing off very nicely," he recalled, until the time came to eat the mysterious "weed." "Each ate his portion, when horrors! The herb was very bitter and fiery like cayenne pepper, and excited our thirst to such a degree that we forgot the law authorizing us to drink only four cups and the consequence was that we drank up all the cider. Those that drank more freely became excited and one thought he was Moses, another Aaron and one had the audacity to call himself a pharaoh."

"In every generation one should regard oneself as though he had come out of Egypt." The large letter "bet" contains the word "bad" and images of ancient Egypt at top and Nazi concentration camps at bottom. Drawing by Yosef Dov Sheinson from *A Survivors' Haggadah*. (*Courtesy of The Jewish Publication Society*)

In 1946, the Third United States Army hosted two "Survivors' Seders" in Munich for four hundred people liberated from Nazi concentration camps. The front cover of their special *hagadah* declared, "We were slaves to Hitler in Germany," and the introductory essay called Eisenhower "Moses the Liberator." "They spoke of Pharaoh and the Egyptian bondage," the text observed. "They spoke of slave labor and torture cities of Pithom and Rameses. . . . [But] Pharaoh and Egypt gave way to Hitler and Germany. Pithom and Rameses faded beneath fresh memories of Buchenwald and Dachau."

During the civil rights movement, many American Jews paid tribute to blacks in their seders. In 1961, President and Mrs. Kennedy attended the seder of secretary of labor Arthur Goldberg and his wife, Dorothy, whose Passover meals for Washington's elite were famous. The margin notes in Dorothy's *hagadah* reminded her to mention that "one of the best descriptions of the exodus is the great Negro spiritual 'Go Down, Moses,'" a clear paean to the marches going on across the South. By the 1970s, presidential seder attending had become more challenging. President Jimmy Carter and his wife attended a seder at the home of advisor Stuart Eizenstat. When the time came for Eizenstat to open the front door for Elijah, a Secret Service agent jumped up and stopped the two-thousand-year-old ritual, declaring it a security risk. Back and forth the two sides went, Eizenstat recalled, until "I was able to persuade him to permit me to open our rear door—the only time Elijah has been relegated to the back door in my home." In 2009, Barack Obama hosted the first-ever seder in the White House, a milestone merging of African-American culture, Jewish ritual, and the American story.

From seder wineglasses in the 1920s that were molded like Lady Liberty to honor immigration to "matzohs of unity" for Soviet Jews during the Cold War to prayers against genocide in Darfur in 2008, Passover has always been a time for American Jews to renew the bond between America's struggles to fulfill its own ideals of liberty and the Israelites' flight of freedom. The holiday has thrived in settings like war zones and Washington precisely because it is so universal to the American experience. The Passover story is America's story.

At the start of my journey, I knew I would find the themes of Moses' life in key moments in America's past. But I did not anticipate the depth, breadth, and intensity of America's attachment to the Exodus. I hadn't known that the Pilgrims were so steeped in Mosaic language or that Americans took the words of Moses on a cracked state bell and turned it into an international symbol of liberty. I hadn't known that Jefferson, Franklin, and Adams proposed Moses for America's seal, or that Washington was eulogized as the American Moses. I hadn't realized how deeply Moses motivated the slaves or how richly he echoed at Gettysburg. I was surprised how directly he shaped the Statue of Liberty and how vividly he colored popular culture, from Cecil B. DeMille to Superman. And I was inspired that nearly every defining American leader—from Washington to Lincoln to Reagan—invoked the Moses story in times of crisis. From Christopher Columbus to Martin Luther King, from the age of Gutenberg to the era of Google, Moses helped shape the American dream. He is our true founding father. His face belongs on Mount Rushmore.

At the beginning, I hadn't even thought to compare the influence of Moses in America with that of Jesus. The United States at its founding was essentially 100 percent Christian and is 80 percent Christian today. Of course, Jesus was influential in American life. But I found a real difference in their public roles. As important as Jesus was to the faith and private lives of Americans, he seemed to have had far less influence than Moses during the great transformations of American history. The themes of Jesus' life—love, charity, the alleviation of poverty, forgiveness, spreading the good news of salvation, developing the kingdom of God—certainly echo throughout American history, but they would not make many lists of the defining characteristics of Americans. By contrast, the themes of Moses' life—social mobility, reluctance to lead, standing up to authority, forming a persecuted people into a nation of laws, dreaming of reaching a promised land, coping with the disappointment of falling short—would be at home on any short list of America's defining traits.

In the early 2000s, two books tracing the history of Jesus in the United States were published: *Jesus in America* by Richard W. Fox and *American Jesus* by Stephen Prothero. Both authors, distinguished scholars, trace Americans' changing attitudes toward Jesus and show how his presence evolved, from his near absence during the Revolution to a more approachable, feminized savior in the nineteenth century, to a manly, aggressive redeemer in the early twentieth century, to a friendly superstar in the celebrity culture of the twenty-first century. "In a country divided by race, ethnicity, gender, class, and religion, Jesus functions as a common cultural coin," wrote Prothero of Boston University. "Though by most accounts he never set foot in the United States, he has commanded more attention and mobilized more resources than George Washington, Abraham Lincoln, and the Reverend Martin Luther King, Jr., combined."

My conclusions about Moses are somewhat different. Not only did Americans' attitude toward him evolve, not only did he provide a common cultural language, and not only did he command attention and mobilize resources, Moses actually helped shape American history and values, helped define the American dream, and helped create America. Moses was more important to the Puritans, more meaningful in the Revolution, more impactful during the Civil War, and more inspiring to the immigrant rights, civil rights, and women's rights movements of the last century than Jesus. Beyond that, Moses had more influence on American history than any other figure from the Bible or antiquity. Also, while certain intellectuals might have had a greater impact on particular periods of American life, no single thinker has had more sustained influence on American history over a longer period than Moses—and that includes Plato, Aristotle, Locke, Hobbes, Montesquieu, Marx, Darwin, Freud, and Einstein.

In addition, my own view of America was completely transformed by my travels. Like many people, I carried around in my head certain narrative frameworks through which I view the main story lines of American history. These involved the interplay between North and South, black and white, East and West, immigrant and native, urban and rural, rich and poor, left and right, and so on. Now I have a completely new frame—not only one I didn't know before but one I'd never even heard before. The Exodus. Discovering how much the biblical narrative of the Israelites has colored the vision and informed the values of twenty generations of Americans and their leaders was like discovering a new front door to a house I'd lived in all my life. You can't understand American history, I now believe, without understanding Moses. He is a looking glass into our soul.

But why?

The answer comes down to three themes. The first is the courage to escape oppression and seek the Promised Land. As the Protestant theologian Walter Brueggemann has written, Moses' influence on Western thought stems from his role as the prophet who sought to evoke in Israel a commitment to improve the world. The prophet's vocation, Brueggemann wrote, is "to keep alive the ministry of imagination, to keep on conjuring and proposing alternative futures to the single one the king wants to urge as the only thinkable one."

That is Moses' gift and his legacy: He proposes an alternative reality to the one we face at any given moment. He suggests that there is something better than the mundane, the enslaved, the second-best, the compromised. He encourages people to be restless, and revolutionary. Brueggemann noted that a prophet does not ask if the dream can be implemented. As countless American visionaries have insisted, imagination must come before implementation. Perhaps Americans' chief debt to Moses is his message that we should never settle for the status quo, and always aspire to what Thoreau termed the "true America." In the words of W. E. B. Du Bois, "Not America, but what America might be—the Real America." As Langston Hughes put it:

> America never was America to me,
> And yet I swear this oath—
> America will be!

Moses is the patron saint of "America will be."

The second Mosaic theme is the tension between freedom and law. The earliest biographies of Moses, written in the first century C.E., downplay the prophet's role as liberator and celebrate his vision as a lawgiver. Moses could have indulged his own freedom, Josephus said, and used it to his advantage. Instead, he extolled virtues—"justice, fortitude, temperance, and the universality of law"—that have become the foundation of civil society. The Pilgrims understood this balance long before the founders. While still on board the *Mayflower*, they "used their own liberty" to sign the Mayflower Compact, vowing to "covenant and combine ourselves together into a civil body politic." *Liberty* and *order*. *Freedom* and *covenant*. The words have reverberated through American history. From the Revolution to the Civil War to the civil rights movement, the great liberation struggles in the United States have involved over-turning unjust laws to advance freedom, then sidestepping anarchy by quickly imposing new laws. Sometimes the new order impeded liberty, as happened with slavery and Jim Crow, but still the pattern persevered. And once more it paralleled—and in many cases was inspired by—the story of Moses, where *liberty* from Egypt was followed by the *order* of Sinai, where the *freedom* of Exodus was balanced by the *covenant* of the commandments. As Michael Walzer summed up the challenge facing the Israelites, the "crucial struggle" begins in the wilderness but continues in the Promised Land: "to create a free people and to live up to the terms of the covenant." Few descriptions better encapsulate American history, even though this one was written about the Bible.

The final theme is the building of a society that welcomes the outsider and uplifts the downtrodden. The Moses story is infused with compassion. It opens with the pharaoh ruthlessly oppressing the Israelites with harsh labor, then issuing the order to kill all Israelite boys. The Israelites groan under the bondage and cry out, which produces the turning point in the Bible: God responds to their anguish. "Their cry for help from the bondage rose up to God," says Exodus 2. "God heard their meaning . . . and remembered his covenant." As God tells Moses in the next scene, "I have marked well the plight of my people in Egypt and have heeded their outcry . . . I am mindful of their suffering." But the story goes on to say that it is not enough for God alone to be mindful of suffering. If humans are made in God's image, they, too, must heed the outcry of those in pain. "You shall not oppress a stranger," God tells his people in Exodus 23, "for you know the feelings of the stranger, having yourselves been strangers in the land of Egypt."

The moral core of Exodus is built on remembering the oppression the Israelites suffered, then recalling the liberation God delivered as a result. As African American historian Eddie Glaude wrote, "The brutality of bondage and the euphoria of freedom are kept in 'living memory' to remind people whence they came, to serve as conceptual tools for problem-solving, and to combat injustice." *Thirty-six times* the Five Books of Moses urge the Israelites to love the stranger, and the Israelites' experience with oppression becomes the foundation for a host of Mosaic laws that mandate that God's people care for the poor, tend the sick, comfort the grieving, and welcome the hurting into their arms. The Israelites' lament at the start of Exodus, Walter Brueggemann wrote, is the "primal scream that permits the beginning of history," for there is no history when someone cries and can't be heard.

To be sure, the Exodus story and the notion of being God's chosen people have been used over the years as fodder for American exceptionalism, which contributed to the country's mistreatment of everyone from slaves to Native Americans to immigrants to gays. Anyone who thinks the Bible is exclusively a source for good in American life must confront the legacy of slaveholders quoting Moses. Also, the idea that Americans were somehow tapped like the ancient Israelites to spread freedom around the world played a role in some of America's foreign-policy missteps over the years. Still, time and again, the greater pull of Exodus has been toward liberating those under duress. From John Winthrop to Harriet Beecher Stowe, from Lady Liberty to "I have a dream," the arc of America has tilted toward the outsider. The Exodus has been so oft quoted in American rhetoric precisely because it fixed the country's moral heart in the body of those on the perimeter of society.

And many of these key traits—especially the idea that the strength of a society comes from its ability to protect its entire population and provide everyone with a path out of pain into promise—have only become *more* true in contemporary America. In an age when more Americans leave their families and head out into the world alone, when more people are literate, itinerant, mobile, when greater numbers of people are touched by the isolation of divorce or the dislocation of financial strain, when some gripe that the concentration of power in Wall Street and Corporate America Street leave many Americans groaning under the yoke of modern pharaohs, when others complain that illegal immigrants and alternative lifestyles threaten the country's moral foundation, the themes of Moses seem as relevant as ever. We are as much a nation of strangers today as at any time in our history, and more in need of the unifying call Moses offers to free the suffering, build a nurturing community, and befriend the stranger.

And sure enough, those cries are beginning to be heard. In nearly every interview I conducted, I asked, "Where are the Moseses of today?" Depending on the news, the political orientation, or the mood of the person I was speaking with, I heard every answer imaginable—preacher, politician, artist, activist, entrepreneur. Perhaps the most poignant answer came from Jonathan Sarna, the historian of American Judaism. "I think America still believes in the Moses story," he said. "I think it's ingrained into our soul. Americans don't want to be selfish, or hateful. We want to do better. We want to be a community. And I think we know a lot about this figure. He will come out of nowhere, like Moses. He'll remind us of the virtues we have forgotten, like Moses. He'll save us, like Moses. But then he'll fall short, like Moses, so in the end, we'll still need another Moses to come after him."

"DEBBIE'S TASTY BRISKET" was the highlight of the seder meal, and the potatoes, as always, reminded me of my mother's. I even enjoyed a slice of Auntie Barbara's Jell-O mold, and it occurred to me that it wouldn't take much midrashic wizardry to link it to the Exodus. *The red food coloring reminds us of the blood of oppression, and the chunks of canned pineapple of the straw bricks.* Passover is like Thanksgiving in one regard: Most families have a favorite dish that would make traditionalists blanch.

After the meal, at my father-in-law's urging, I asked everyone a question: "What does freedom mean to you?" Alan went first. In the 1980s, the Rottenbergs hosted an exchange student from China. "Every night, when I came home from work," Alan said, "Danhai would stand behind me waiting for me to finish dinner so he could ask me questions. One day I had a little argument with my son. Well, maybe it was a big argument." Everyone laughed. "And my son talked back to me. Danhai was visibly upset. 'I've never seen a son talk back to a father before,' he said. 'Children in China don't do that.' Today, reading the *hagadah,* one of the comments I noticed is that freedom is the right to ask questions. For me, freedom is the ability to question authority."

Around the table we went. Kyle, a sixteen-year-old, said, "When I think of freedom, I think of being able to do *whatever* you want, including murder somebody and not get in trouble. But then I realize there are laws that restrict you from doing that, which contradicts the fact that people say it's a free country."

Uncle Murray said: "I think freedom is difficult for us to discuss because the United States is still such a polarized society. The fact that the United States is still separated by economic disparity is something we need to work on."

Freedom to challenge authority. The tension between freedom and law. The obligation to extend freedom to the stranger.

Finally, my mother-in-law, Debbie, spoke. "When you first asked the question, I was thinking that for me, freedom is the ability to go to sleep at night with the peace of mind that you and your family will be safe." A native of small-town Rhode Island and a graduate of Mount Holyoke College, Debbie has devoted her life to her husband, her three children, and now her grandchildren. Though at first she was skeptical that a globe-traveling writer was right for her (even more globe-traveling) daughter, Debbie has warmed to me considerably. My wife says we're a lot alike.

Debbie continued: "But then I was relating the question to Passover, and there's a line in the seder that says, 'Our ancestors were slaves but today we are free.' There's something about Passover that makes us want to remember that freedom is fragile, and that makes me want to treasure it even more."

For the first time all night, silence settled over the table.

My daughters had reached the end of their night, and I took them upstairs to bed, leaving my wife to enjoy her family. After our bedtime routine, I sat in the darkness for a few minutes to ensure that one of them didn't try out her new skill: vaulting out of the crib. Downstairs, the seder was reaching its conclusion.

I realized my own views of Moses had undergone a change. I was surprised at the start of my journey to discover how much Moses is downplayed in the Five Books. Fewer than 10 percent of chapters focus on his life, and the Bible does not describe his physical features, gives no clues about his dress, and provides only the briefest glimpse of his inner life. The *hagadah* gives him even less attention: *It mentions Moses only once.* The book Jews have read for centuries to celebrate the Israelites' exodus from slavery barely acknowledges the man God chose to lead that liberation. Scholars have debated this absence for generations, and the best explanation I've heard is that rabbis did not want to risk elevating Moses so much that he threatened God. Whatever the reason, between the Bible and the *hagadah,* Moses emerges as a kind of invisible hero, subservient to his savior, disrespected by his followers, marginalized between the chosen people and their all-powerful God.

Ancient storytellers minimized Moses for the same reasons so many Americans have been attracted to him—and why he's so relevant today. He's not divine. He's human. If anything, his identity issues seem very contemporary. He's a man without a home. Despite growing up in the pharaoh's house, he's not exactly Egyptian; despite marrying a Midian woman and living in the desert, he never becomes a Midianite; despite leading his people for forty years, he never enters the Promised Land and thus never becomes a true Israelite. Also, he's torn among families. Orphaned by his birth mother, he later abandons his adopted mother and then leaves the mother of his son to free a people he hardly knows. And though he's known for winning showdowns with the pharaoh, with his followers, and with God, he is plagued by self-pity and self-doubt.

The tension between these personal struggles and Moses' public feats is one of the things that most draws me to him. Moses is the ultimate outsider. You can feel the pain in his struggles even though the Bible does not articulate them. The man of strength brims with internal weakness. Yet he takes any feelings of alienation and converts them into a commitment to community. He transforms his weakness into a strength. Faced with pivotal choices, Moses is repeatedly governed by a concern for others. Given the choice, he chooses the public good. And his farewell message to his people encourages them to do the same. *Choose life*. He may not always display ideal character—he kills, he purges, he pouts. His struggles may be far grander than those of today. But I still see him as a powerful benchmark of self-sacrifice and community service.

And a stirring example for my children.

The years I worked on this book overlapped with the first years of my daughters' lives, and because of that a moment in the Moses story took on special meaning. The moment comes in Exodus 12:26, on the eve of the tenth plague, just before Moses tells the Israelites how to conduct the first seder. Moses says, "And when your children ask you, 'What do you mean by this rite?' you shall say . . ." A similar exchange occurs twice more. "And when, in time to come, your child asks you, saying, 'What does this mean?' you shall say . . ." I began to wonder how I would answer that question. What will I tell my children about the meaning of Moses?

First, the power of story. Exodus opens with a memorable statement: "A new king arose over Egypt who did not know Joseph." The story begins with forgetting. The pharaoh does not remember how a son of Israel saved Egypt from famine. The rest of the Five Books of Moses becomes an antidote to this state of forgetfulness. God hears the groaning of Israel and "remembers his covenant" (Exod. 2:24). Moses leads the Israelites from Egypt and urges them to "remember this day" (Exod. 13:3). The Israelites are ordered to "remember the Sabbath day" (Exod. 20:8) and to observe Passover as a "day of remembrance" (Exod. 12:14). Moses' goal is to build a counter-Egypt. He must construct a society that offers an alternative to ignorance and unknowingness. He must devise a community that remembers.

Moses' success in this regard may be his most underappreciated accomplishment: The Five Books of Moses are a memory device. They are a telling, designed to create a tradition of retelling, intended to mold a nation of retellers. In slavery, the Israelites made bricks; in freedom, they make stories. As Jonathan Sacks put it, "By telling the Israelites to become a nation of educators, Moses turned a group of slaves into a people of eternity." So my first message to my daughters: Remember. Keep the story, as Moses says in Deuteronomy 30, "in your mouth and in your heart."

Second, the story is a narrative of hope. "This year we are slaves, but next year . . ." History is not set in stone. It is not an immovable pyramid. It can be remade. The pyramid can be flipped. When you despair, when you hurt, when you fear—and especially when you encounter those feelings in others—remember the slaves who first groaned under bondage. In America, the Pilgrims, the founders, the enslaved, and the segregated, all read the Israelites' story and believed that they, too, might be free. You should read the Israelites' story, too, and remember this lesson: There is a moral dimension to the universe. Right can prevail over might; justice can triumph over evil. As Michael Walzer wrote, "Anger and hope, not resignation, are the appropriate responses to the Egyptian house of bondage." You should read the story of Moses and remember to flip a few pyramids yourselves along the way. And as long as it's not your parents (remember that fifth commandment!), you should question authority. Overturn injustice. Befriend the stranger, for you, yourselves, were once strangers in a land with no hope.

Which leads to my third message: Act. One reason Moses has inspired so many Americans over the centuries is that he evangelizes action; he justifies risk. He gives ordinary people the courage to live with uncertainty. As I found in my own travels in the Sinai desert over the years, no matter how full of hope the Israelites were when they departed Egypt, they were still leaving the most civilized place on earth for the most barren, based only on the word of a God they'd never actually seen and a leader they barely knew. Moses is the enemy of caution, which is one reason he has inspired so many visionaries—Christopher Columbus, William Bradford, Benjamin Franklin, Harriet Tubman, Abraham Lincoln, Martin Luther King. And these people were not born to greatness. They became great by tapping into the anger and hope within themselves. The moral of their lives, like that of Moses, is that each of us must become our own agitator, our own entrepreneur, our own freedom fighter. Our own Moses.

We must take these steps ourselves because Moses cannot do it for us. If we are to achieve the Promised Land, we must do it without him. In 1879, the English novelist George Eliot wrote a poem called "The Death of Moses." The climactic image is adapted from the last chapter of Deuteronomy, which says, "Never again did there arise in Israel a prophet like Moses—whom the Lord singled out, face to face." In Eliot's version, "face to face" means something more than a meeting: ". . . Upon the death-dewed lips/A kiss descended, pure, unspeakable." In the end, God summons Moses' body to heaven but leaves behind his soul.

The Bible suggests a similar ending in Deuteronomy 34 when it says that Moses' successor "was filled with the spirit of wisdom" because Moses had laid his hands on him. Moses' farewell gesture is also an act of love: He teaches. He may not achieve the Promised Land, but he transfers his wisdom to those who shall. The man becomes a book. Born on the lip of the Nile, he dies on the brink of the Jordan. The boy who was given life by being floated on the water becomes the prophet who yields to death at water's edge. And in doing so, he leaves the crossing to each of us, who must hear his words and heed his story. Left with only his telling and his wisdom, we must split the sea ourselves now. We must run our own errand into the wilderness.

I will tell my daughters that this is the meaning of the Moses story and why it has reverberated through the American story. America, it has been said, is a synonym for human possibility. I dream for you, girls, the privilege of that possibility. Imagine your own Promised Land, perform your own liberation, plunge into the waters, persevere through the dryness, and don't be surprised—or saddened—if you're stopped just short of your dream. Because the ultimate lesson of Moses' life is that the dream does not die with the dreamer, the journey does not end on the mountaintop, and the true destination in a narrative of hope is not this year at all.

But next.

Giving Thanks

I would like to thank the dozens of people who appear by name in this book, many of whom welcomed me into their homes, workplaces, or houses of worship and answered my sometimes probing, sometimes personal questions with wisdom, wit, and good cheer. Their insights and intimate recollections provide the heart of this story and I am grateful for their time and generosity. Many other people provided assistance, counsel, or ideas along the way, and I am pleased to offer a small expression of my appreciation. A partial list includes: Peggy Baker, Arnold Belzer, Darren Boch, Gabor Boritt, Walter Brueggemann, Eric Campbell, Joanne and Sidney Cohen, Jane Cowley, Frances Delmar, John Duncan, Paula Fisher, Roger Freet, Wes Gardenswartz, Bruce Gill, Andrew Heinze, Joe Hough, Wayne Kempton, Andrea Kornbluh, David Kraemer, Sandy Lloyd, David McClain, Michael Miller, Carol Muldawer, James Nevius, Michelle Pecararo, Letty Pogrebin, Steven Jay Perlman, Richard

Shenk, Phil Sheridan, Barry Shrage, Donald Smith, Gordon Smith, and David Tribble.

David Black is my agent, friend, and partner. I can't imagine my life without him. Brian Murray and Michael Morrison have created a home for me at HarperCollins that extends far beyond work. First Lisa Gallagher, then Liate Stehlik, were strong and creative advocates for this project. Henry Ferris lived inside this book with me for its duration and edited every draft with passion, precision, and care. I am extremely appreciative of his judgment and wisdom. Sharyn Rosenblum is an unparalleled professional and one of the treats of my life. Thanks also to Lynn Grady, Mary Schuck, Debbie Stier, Holden Richards, Peter Hubbard, Shawn Nicholls, and all my colleagues at William Morrow. And a huzzah to Antonella Iannarino, Dave Larabell, and the gang at Black Inc.

The multitalented Greg Takoudes helped track down many of the original sources quoted in this book, along with the photographs, prints, and drawings that are assembled here. I am grateful for Carlton Sedgeley, Helen Churko, and all the masters at Royce Carlton. Thanks to Steve Waldman and all my friends at beliefnet.com. I am honored to work closely with Craig Jacobson and Alan Berger. Special appreciation to Roger Triemstra.

I have a long-standing, long-suffering community of fellow writers and friends who embolden and inspire me, even as I get distracted for long periods of time. My love to Sunny Bates, Laura Benjamin, Justin Castillo, Avner Goren, Bob Hormats, Corby Kummer, Karen Lehrman, Evan Oppenheimer, Will Philipp, Joshua Ramo, Lauren Schneider, Chip Seelig, David Shenk, Jeff Shumlin, Max Stier, Teresa Tritch, Joe Weisberg, and Bob Wunsch, along with their spouses and kids. Karen Essex read an early draft of this book and offered support and edits in just the right measure. Jane Lear read the completed manuscript and navigated my many humiliations with her typical acumen and grace.

Beth Middleworth brought her inimitable eye at just the right hour. The incomparable Ben Sherwood has been kind enough to lend me his ferocious mind and unflagging friendship in endless abundance.

I sit around a Thanksgiving table of unimaginable blessing every year. My parents, Jane and Ed Feiler, believe in me when few others do and lift me up when few others can. My sister, Cari Feiler Bender, is a town crier for Philadelphia and helped me gain access to places few ever get to see. I offer an embrace to devoted readers present and future—Rodd, Max, and Hallie Bender. My brother, Andrew, seems never to have forgotten any history he learned and is ever willing to pause his own life to read an extra draft of mine, apply his forceful logic to my ill-formed pages, and open his heart to making my life richer.

I have been double-blessed to enter a family where Passover is the table of choice. I treasure the camaraderie and love of Elissa and Dan Rottenberg, Rebecca and Mattis Goldman. I know of no two people who devote their lives so selflessly to the comfort and well-being of those around them as Debbie and Alan Rottenberg. I simply would not have had the space or time to undertake this project without their unending support. I am honored to dedicate this book to them.

Their daughter Linda provided the foundation of our family and the moral focus of this endeavor, all while extending her own peerless vision to the far reaches of her own Endeavor community around the globe. As I wavered in my search or stared anxiously with nighttime doubts, she rested the only hand that comforts and re-sent me on my way. And when over a period of many months I sent out pages flailing for clarity and meaning, she gave up yet another evening and found in my confusion thoughts I didn't know I had.

For nearly twenty years, I have been blessed to write books on a schedule of my own choosing. Oh, well! I wrote this book in an office that shares a wall with my daughters' bedroom; on a timetable that adjusted variously for overnight feedings, abandoned naps, four-lung tantrums, and the occasional erased page; and in an atmosphere of wonder and joy, giggles and awe that reminded me on a daily basis of the true fortune of freedom and family. It is a gift far greater than I have ever known to imagine this story sitting quietly for years to come until they are ready to retrace its steps and understand how much I made it for them.

The Books of Moses

The bulk of this book is drawn from my own travels, interviews, and reading (or, in the case of films, viewing) of primary sources. But at every step, I have been educated, entertained, and uplifted by the extraordinary work of scholars who understand these issues far more than I and whose work shaped and deepened my own ideas.

First, a few notes. Except when otherwise mentioned, or when quoting a historical figure citing a different translation of the Bible, I have tried to quote passages from *The Torah: A Modern Commentary,* edited by W. Gunther Plaut and published by the Union of American Hebrew Congregations. Quotations from the remainder of the Hebrew Bible are taken from *Tanakh: A New Translation of the Holy Scriptures According to the Traditional Hebrew Text,* published by the Jewish Publication Society. Quotations from the New Testament are taken from *The Holy Bible: New Revised Standard Version,* published by Oxford University Press. In keeping with long-standing academic custom and a recent trend in popular writing,

I have used the nonsectarian terms B.C.E. ("before the common era") and C.E. ("of the common era") in lieu of the terms B.C. and A.D.

A number of scholars discuss the broad themes of this book and how they apply to specific periods in American history. I found myself referring to their work repeatedly. These books include Sydney E. Ahlstrom's *A Religious History of the American People*, Sacvan Bercovitch's *The Rites of Assent*, Brian Britt's *Rewriting Moses*, Conrad Cherry's *God's New Israel*, Eddie S. Glaude, Jr.'s *Exodus!*, Nathan O. Hatch and Mark A. Noll's *The Bible in America*, Martin E. Marty's *Pilgrims in Their Own Land*, Mark A. Noll's *America's God* and *A History of Christianity in the United States and Canada*, Jonathan Sacks's *The Chief Rabbi's Haggadah*, Michael Walzer's *Exodus and Revolution*, and Melanie J. Wright's *Moses in America*.

Pilgrims

My account of the Pilgrims' departure from Europe, arrival in the New World, and landing on Clark's Island draws on William Bradford's *Of Plymouth Plantation* and Edward Winslow's *Mourt's Relation* and *Good Newes from New England*, as well as Cotton Mather's *The Life of William Bradford, Esq., Governor of Plymouth Colony*. Nathaniel Philbrick's *Mayflower* presents a captivating, hour-by-hour retelling of these events.

The history of Moses in Jewish, Christian, and Muslim thought is discussed in *Images of Moses* by Daniel Jeremy Silver and *Moses* by Mordecai and Miriam Roshwald. For a more detailed discussion of the history, science, and archaeology behind the Moses story, see my extensive, on-the-ground reporting across Egypt, Israel, and Jordan in *Walking the Bible*.

The quotations from Columbus come from *The Four Voyages of Columbus*, edited by Cecil Jane; they also appear in Charles Brock's *Mosaics of the American Dream*. The statistics about Bible production during the Reformation are found in *The Reformation* by Diarmaid MacCulloch. My historical discussion of the Bible in Europe also draws on *Martin Luther as Prophet, Teacher, and Hero* by Robert Kolb, and *Bible and Sword* by Barbara W. Tuchman.

The influence of Moses on Puritan thought in the New World is detailed in *The Puritan Heritage* by Joseph Gaer and Ben Siegel, as well as *God's Sacred Tongue* and *Hebrew and the Bible in America* by Shalom Goldman, and *The Puritan Dilemma* by Edmund S. Morgan. I was also helped by Perry Miller's *The New England Mind* and *The Life of the Mind in America*.

Revolution

George Whitefield and the Great Awakening are admirably depicted in Frank Lambert's *Inventing the "Great Awakening"* and *"Pedlar in Divinity,"* as well as Harry S. Stout's *The Divine Dramatist.* Charlene Miers has written a detailed history of the Pennsylvania State House called *Independence Hall in American Memory.* For my discussion of the Liberty Bell, Jacob Duché, and Philadelphia in 1776, I also benefited from *Ring in the Jubilee* by Charles Michael Boland, *Christ Church, Philadelphia* by Deborah Mathias Gough, *American Gospel* by Jon Meachem, *The Meaning of Independence* by Edmund S. Morgan, and *Starting America: The Story of Independence Hall* by Edward M. Riley. Samuel Sherwood's *The Church's Flight into the Wilderness,* along with many sermons of the era, are available at the Digital Commons of the University of Nebraska at Lincoln. Many of the primary documents associated with the history of the seal can be viewed at John MacArthur's www.greatseal.com.

George Washington

Freemasonry is explored in impressive detail in Steven C. Bullock's *Revolutionary Brotherhood* and Paul Naudon's *The Secret History of Freemasonry.*

I also benefited from *The Radicalism of the American Revolution* and *The Creation of the American Republic* by Gordon S. Wood; *The First American* by H. W. Brands and *Benjamin Franklin* by Walter Isaacson; *His Excellency* by Joseph J. Ellis, *Washington* by James Thomas Flexner, and *Washington's God* by Michael Novak and Jana Novak.

Details about George Washington's Bible come from Paul Gutjahr's *An American Bible.* The sermons of Nicholas Street and Samuel Langdon appear in Conrad Cherry's *God's New Israel.* Samuel Cooper's sermon appears in *We the People,* edited by James F. Gauss. Franklin's essay appears in *The Works of Dr. Benjamin Franklin,* edited by Henry Steuber, published in 1834.

The analysis of the use of biblical quotations during the Revolutionary period comes from Donald Lutz, "The Relative Influence of European Writers on Late Eighteenth-Century American Political Thought" (*The American Political Science Review,* vol. 78, 1984), and Martin E. Marty, "Religion and the Constitution" (*The Christian Century,* March 23–30, 1994).

The lyrics sung to Washington during his crossing to New York come from *Sweet Freedom's Song* by Robert James Branham and Stephen Hartnett. The Papers of George Washington at the Alderman Library at the University of Virginia contain many of the documents and sermons surrounding Washington's death and funeral. Philander D. Chase, the editor in chief, has written a detailed account of the events, which is published at http://gwpapers.virginia.edu. Robert Hay's study of the sermons is "George Washington: American Moses" (*American Quarterly,* vol. 21, no. 4, Winter 1969).

Underground Railroad

Fergus M. Bordewich has written an extraordinary overview of the Underground Railroad, *Bound for Canaan.* Ripley, Ohio's role in the movement is impressively detailed in Ann Hagedorn's *Beyond the River,* which also contains an extensive discussion of the name of the slave girl who crossed the Ohio River. I have followed the consensus that she was called Eliza. John Rankin's letters are gathered in *Letters on American Slavery*; John P. Parker's memories are recorded in *His Promised Land*.

The role of religion in general, and the Exodus in particular, in slave communities is explored in Albert J. Raboteau's *Slave Religion* and Eugene D. Genovese's *Roll, Jordan, Roll*. My discussion of the use of quilts in the Underground Railroad draws on *Hidden in Plain View* by Jacqueline L. Tobin and Raymond G. Dobard. The life of Harriet Tubman is painstakingly re-created from limited sources in two recent biographies, *Harriet Tubman* by Catherine Clinton and *Bound for the Promised Land* by Kate Clifford Larson.

Civil War

My discussion of the exegetical battle over Moses in antebellum America is deeply indebted to Mark A. Noll's *The Civil War as a Theological Crisis*, which also contains many of the statistics I cite covering the influence of the Second Great Awakening on American life. Jonathan Blanchard and Nathan L. Rice's Cincinnati debate has been recently republished as *A Debate on Slavery*. My account of the life and writing of Harriet Beecher Stowe draws on Joan D. Hedrick's *Harriet Beecher Stowe*. The quotation from journalist D. B. Corley comparing Uncle Tom to Moses comes from *A Visit to Uncle Tom's Cabin*, published in 1893.

The religious views of Abraham Lincoln are artfully mined in *The Almost Chosen People* by William J. Wolf and Allen Guelzo's *Abraham Lincoln*. I benefited tremendously from the essays gathered in *Religion and the American Civil War*, edited by Randall M. Miller, Harry S. Stout, and Charles Reagan Wilson, as well as Stout's *Upon the Altar of the Nation*.

Lyman Beecher's sermon, "A Plea for the West," as well as the sermons by Benjamin Palmer and Henry Ward Beecher on the eve of the Civil

War, appear in Conrad Cherry, *God's New Israel*. Gabor Boritt's *The Gettysburg Gospel* and Garry Wills's *Lincoln at Gettysburg* dissect the events and reaction to Lincoln's famous oration. My version of Henry Ward Beecher's journey to Charleston is informed by Debbie Applegate's *The Most Famous Man in America* as well as by research at Plymouth Church of the Pilgrims in Brooklyn Heights.

Emory University's "The Martyred President" gathers fifty-seven sermons given on the assassination of Abraham Lincoln at http://beck.library.emory.edu/lincoln. I also consulted Waldo W. Braden's *Building the Myth*, as well as *Sermons Preached in Boston on the Death of Abraham Lincoln* and *Our Martyr President, Abraham Lincoln: Voices from the Pulpit of New York and Brooklyn,* which contains Beecher's eulogy. Charles Stewart's analysis of the sermons appears in "A Rhetorical Study of the Reaction of the Protestant Pulpit in the North to Lincoln's Assassination," an unpublished 1963 dissertation.

Statue of Liberty

The history of the Statue of Liberty is explored in Marvin Trachtenberg's *The Statue of Liberty*, as well as in Barry Moreno's *The Statue of Liberty Encyclopedia* and Hertha Pauli and E. B. Ashton's *I Lift My Lamp*. I also benefited from Albert Boime's *Hollow Icons* and *The Changing Face of the Statue of Liberty: A Historical Resource Study for the National Park Service,* compiled in 2005 by John Bodnar, Laura Burt, Jennifer Stinson, and Barbara Truesdell and stored at the library on Ellis Island. Esther Schor has written a wonderful biography, *Emma Lazarus*.

My discussion of the Jews in America draws from *Jews and the American Soul* by Andrew R. Heinze, *The Jews in America* by Arthur Hertzberg, *Religion and State in the American Jewish Experience* by Jonathan D. Sarna and David G. Dalin, as well as Sarna's *American Judaism* and "The Cult of

Synthesis in American Jewish Culture" (*Jewish Social Studies*, vol. 5, nos. 1–2, Fall 1998/Winter 1999). The cartoon of Moses dressed as Uncle Sam and splitting the Atlantic Ocean, called "The Modern Moses," was drawn by Frederick Burr Opper and Joseph Keppler and appeared, along with an unsigned editorial, in *Puck,* December 1881.

The Ten Commandments

I have gathered details about *The Ten Commandments* from *The Autobiography of Cecil B. DeMille* and *Cecil B. DeMille* by Charles Higham. Katherine Orrison's two books were extremely helpful, *Written in Stone* and *Lionheart in Hollywood.* The connection between the final shot of the film and the Statue of Liberty was first made by Michael Wood in *America in the Movies.* The box-office statistics come from www.boxofficemojo.com.

A number of scholars have explored the link between *The Ten Commandments* and the culture of the 1950s. These include Alan Nadel, "God's Law and the Wide Screen: *The Ten Commandments* as Cold War 'Epic'" (*PMLA*, vol. 108, no. 3, 1993); Melani McAlister, "'Benevolent Supremacy': Biblical Epic Films, Suez, and the Cultural Politics of U.S. Power," published in her *Epic Encounters;* Ilana Pardes, "Moses Goes Down to Hollywood: Miracles and Special Effects" (*Semeia* 74, 1996); and G. Andrew Tooze, "Moses and the Reel Exodus" (*Journal of Religion and Film,* vol. 7, no. 1, April 2003). Additional information comes from Neal Gabler, *An Empire of Their Own.* The 20th Century-Fox DVD of *Brigham Young* contains an extremely helpful commentary by James d'Arc.

My survey of Mosaic comparisons in twentieth-century letters was shaped by *Moses in Red* by Lincoln Steffens, as well as *The Autobiography of Lincoln Steffens* and *Lincoln Steffens* by Justin Kaplan. I also quoted from *The Man Nobody Knows* and *The Book Nobody Knows* by Bruce Barton and benefited from Richard M. Fried's biography of Barton, *The Man Everybody*

Knew. Other evocations of Moses came from *The Social Message of the Modern Pulpit* by Charles Reynolds Brown and *Moses, Persuader of Men*, issued by the Metropolitan Casualty Insurance Company.

Civil Rights Movement

Anyone who writes about Martin Luther King, Jr., is indebted to Taylor Branch's magisterial series, *Parting the Waters, Pillar of Fire*, and *At Canaan's Edge*. The extended quotation describing the final moments of King's mountaintop speech comes from page 758 of *At Canaan's Edge*. I found three other books extremely helpful: *Voice of Deliverance* by Keith D. Miller, which contains the similar passages in King's and Phillips Brooks's sermons on Egyptians and evil; *To the Mountaintop* by Stewart Burns; and *Prophetic Politics* by David S. Gutterman. I also drew from *An Easy Burden* by Andrew Young and *Singing in a Strange Land* by Nick Salvatore.

The quotation from Zora Neale Hurston is taken from the introduction to her novel *Moses, Man on the Mountain*. My portrait of the relationship between King and Abraham Joshua Heschel was informed by Susannah Heschel's essay "Theological Affinities in the Writings of Abraham Joshua Heschel and Martin Luther King, Jr." in *Black Zion*, edited by Yvonne Chireau and Nathaniel Deutsch. Charlton Heston's quotation about why he was chosen to speak at the March on Washington appears in Emilie Raymond's *From My Cold Dead Hands*.

Passover

Two books explore the fascinating history of Freud's *Moses and Monotheism*—*Freud and the Legacy of Moses* by Richard J. Bernstein and *Freud's Moses* by Yosef Hayim Yerushalmi. My discussion of the political influence of Moses benefited from *Moses as Political Leader* by Aaron Wildavsky. David Geffen's delightful compilation of American Passover stories is *American Heritage Haggadah*. The Jewish Publication Society has recently republished an edition of *A Survivors' Haggadah*, written, designed, and illustrated by Yosef Dov Sheinson.

My conclusion also draws from *The Jewish Century* by Yuri Slezkine and *The Prophetic Imagination* by Walter Brueggemann. The Henry David Thoreau quote comes from *Walden;* the W. E. B. Du Bois quote from *The Crisis,* November 1918; the Langston Hughes quote from "Let America Be America Again." The evocative phrase that America is a "synonym for human possibility" is from Bercovitch, *The Rites of Assent.*

Final Word

I am grateful to the many people who provided the images that appear in this book. Reproductions of some of those images, as well as additional material I've collected during my research that does not appear in the final book, can be viewed at www.brucefeiler.com. The site also contains discussion materials, a homemade film about Moses and my family, a film of Martin Luther King, Jr., giving his Mountaintop speech in Memphis, video clips of Moses in film (including DeMille's speech at the opening of *The Ten Commandments,* as well as Moses splitting the Red Sea), and a way to e-mail me directly. I welcome comments, queries, and reports from discussion groups, as well as stories about how Moses continues to inspire fresh generations to renew the story of freedom.

Select Bibliography

Ackerman, Bruce. *We the People: Foundations*. Cambridge, MA: Harvard University Press, 1991.

Ahlstrom, Sydney E. *A Religious History of the American People*. New Haven: Yale University Press, 1972.

Antin, Mary. *The Promised Land*. Boston: Houghton Mifflin, 1912.

——. *They Who Knock at Our Gates: A Complete Gospel of Immigration*. Boston: Houghton Mifflin, 1914.

Applegate, Debbie. *The Most Famous Man in America: The Biography of Henry Ward Beecher*. New York: Doubleday, 2006.

Bailyn, Bernard. *The Ideological Origins of the American Revolution*. Cambridge, MA: Harvard University Press, 1967.

Barton, Bruce. *The Man Nobody Knows* and *The Book Nobody Knows*. Indianapolis: Bobbs-Merrill Company, 1956.

Bellah, Robert Neelly. "Civil Religion in America." *Journal of the American Academy of Arts and Sciences* 96 (Winter 1967).

Bercovitch, Sacvan. *The Rites of Assent: Transformations in the Symbolic Construction of America*. New York: Routledge, 1993.

Berkin, Carol. *A Brilliant Solution: Inventing the American Constitution*. Orlando: Harcourt, 2002.

Bernstein, Richard J. *Freud and the Legacy of Moses*. Cambridge: Cambridge University Press, 1998.

Bialik, Hayim Nahman, and Yehoshua Hana Ravnitzky, eds. *The Book of Legends: Sefer Ha-Aggadah*. New York: Schocken Books, 1992.

Blanchard, Jonathan, and Nathan L. Rice. *A Debate on Slavery*. Dahlonega, GA: Confederate Reprint Company, 2003.

Boime, Albert. *Hollow Icons: The Politics of Sculpture in Nineteenth-Century France*. Kent, OH: Kent State University Press, 1987.

Boland, Charles Michael. *Ring in the Jubilee: The Epic of America's Liberty Bell*. Riverside, CT: Chatham Press, 1973.

Bordewich, Fergus M. *Bound for Canaan: The Epic Story of the Underground Railroad, America's First Civil Rights Movement*. New York: Amistad, 2005.

Borritt, Gabor. *The Gettysburg Gospel: The Lincoln Speech That Nobody Knows*. New York: Simon & Schuster, 2006.

Braden, Waldo W., ed. *Building the Myth: Selected Speeches Memorializing Abraham Lincoln*. Urbana: University of Illinois Press, 1990.

Bradford, William. *Of Plymouth Plantation: 1620–1647*. New York: Modern Library, 1981.

Branch, Taylor. *At Canaan's Edge: America in the King Years, 1965–68*. New York: Simon & Schuster, 2006.

———. *Parting the Waters: America in the King Years, 1954–63*. New York: Simon & Schuster, 1988.

———. *Pillar of Fire: America in the King Years, 1963–65*. New York: Simon & Schuster, 1998.

Brands, H. W. *The First American: The Life and Times of Benjamin Franklin*. New York: Random House, 2000.

———. *What America Owes the World: The Struggle for the Soul of Foreign Policy*. Cambridge: Cambridge University Press, 1998.

Branham, Robert James, and Stephen J. Hartnett. *Sweet Freedom's Song*. Oxford: Oxford University Press, 2002.

Britt, Brian. *Rewriting Moses: The Narrative Eclipse of the Text*. London: T&T Clark International, 2004.

Brock, Charles. *Mosaics of the American Dream: America as New Israel—A Metaphor for Today*. Wheatley: Bayou Press, 1994.

Brown, Charles Reynolds. *The Social Message of the Modern Pulpit*. New York: Charles Scribner's Sons, 1906.

Brueggemann, Walter. *The Prophetic Imagination*. Philadelphia: Fortress Press, 1978.

Bunyan, John. *The Pilgrim's Progress*. London: Simpkin, Marshall, and Co., 1856.

Burns, James MacGregor. *The Vineyard of Democracy*. New York: Alfred A. Knopf, 1982.

———. *The Workshop of Democracy*. New York: Alfred A. Knopf, 1985.

Burns, Stewart. *To the Mountaintop: Martin Luther King, Jr.'s Mission to Save America, 1955–1968*. San Francisco: HarperSanFrancisco, 2004.

Cashin, Edward J. *Beloved Bethesda: A History of George Whitefield's Home for Boys, 1740–2000*. Macon, GA: Mercer University Press, 2001.

Cashman, Sean Dennis. *America in the Gilded Age: From the Death of Lincoln to the Rise of Theodore Roosevelt.* New York: New York University Press, 1984.

Chabon, Michael. *The Amazing Adventures of Kavalier & Clay.* New York: Picador, 2000.

Cherry, Conrad, ed. *God's New Israel: Religious Interpretations of American Destiny.* Chapel Hill: University of North Carolina Press, 1998.

Childs, Brevard S. *The Book of Exodus.* Louisville: Westminster Press, 1974.

Clinton, Catherine. *Harriet Tubman: The Road to Freedom.* New York: Little, Brown and Company, 2004.

Cohen, Joel. *Moses: A Memoir.* New York: Paulist Press, 2003.

Cohen, Norman J. *Moses and the Journey to Leadership: Timeless Lessons of Effective Management from the Bible and Today's Leaders.* Woodstock, VT: Jewish Lights Publishing, 2007.

Coulter, E. Merton. *Georgia: A Short History.* Chapel Hill: University of North Carolina Press, 1947.

Cronon, William. *Changes in the Land: Indians, Colonists, and the Ecology of New England.* New York: Farrar, Straus and Giroux, 1983.

Darden, Robert. *People Get Ready! A New History of Black Gospel Music.* New York: Continuum, 2004.

Davis, Kenneth. *America's Hidden History: Untold Tales of the First Pilgrims, Fighting Women, and Forgotten Founders Who Shaped a Nation.* New York: Collins, 2008.

DeMille, Cecil B. *The Autobiography of Cecil B. DeMille.* Edited by Donald Hayne. Englewood Cliffs, NJ: Prentice-Hall, 1959.

Dilenschneider, Robert L. *Moses: C.E.O.* Beverly Hills: New Millennium Press, 2000.

The Declaration of Independence and the Constitution of the United States. New York: Bantam, 1998.

Doherty, William T. "The Impact of Business on Protestantism, 1900–29." *The Business History Review* 28, no. 2 (June 1954), 141–153.

Douglass, Frederick. *Narrative of the Life of Frederick Douglass, An American Slave.* New Haven: Yale University Press, 2001.

Dumenil, Lynn. *The Modern Temper: American Culture and Society in the 1920's.* New York: Hill and Wang, 1995.

Eck, Diana L. *A New Religious America: How a "Christian Country" Has Become the World's Most Religiously Diverse Nation.* San Francisco: HarperSanFrancisco, 2001.

Eig, Jonathan. *Opening Day: The Story of Jackie Robinson's First Season.* New York: Simon & Schuster, 2007.

Ellis, Edward Robb. *The Epic of New York City: A Narrative History.* New York: Carroll & Graf Publishers, 1966.

Ellis, Joseph J. *Founding Brothers: The Revolutionary Generation.* New York: Alfred A. Knopf, 2001.

———. *His Excellency: George Washington.* New York: Vintage Books, 2004.

Feiler, Bruce. *Abraham: A Journey to the Heart of Three Faiths.* New York: William Morrow, 2002.

————. *Walking the Bible: A Journey by Land Through the Five Books of Moses*. New York: William Morrow, 2001.

Fleg, Edmund. *The Life of Moses*. Pasadena, CA: Hope Publishing House, 1995.

Flexner, James Thomas. *Washington: The Indispensable Man*. New York: Plume, 1969.

Foner, Eric. *The Story of American Freedom*. New York: W. W. Norton & Company, 1998.

Fox, Richard Wightman. *Jesus in America: A History*. San Francisco: HarperSanFrancisco, 2004.

Frankel, Estelle. *Sacred Therapy: Jewish Spiritual Teachings on Emotional Healing and Inner Wholeness*. Boston: Shambhala, 2005.

Freud, Sigmund. *Moses and Monotheism*. New York: Vintage Books, 1939.

Fried, Richard M. *The Man Everybody Knew: Bruce Barton and the Making of Modern America*. Chicago: Ivan R. Dee, 2005.

Gabler, Neal. *An Empire of Their Own: How the Jews Invented Hollywood*. New York: Crown Publishers, 1988.

Gaer, Joseph, and Ben Siegel. *The Puritan Heritage: America's Roots in the Bible*. New York: New American Library of World Literature, 1964.

Gaustand, Edwin, and Leigh Schmidt. *The Religious History of America: The Heart of the American Story from Colonial Times to Today*. San Francisco: HarperSanFrancisco, 2002.

Geffen, David, ed. *American Heritage Haggadah: The Passover Freedom Experience*. Jerusalem: Geffen Publishing House, 1992.

Genovese, Eugene D. *Roll, Jordan, Roll: The World the Slaves Made*. New York: Vintage Books, 1972.

Ginzberg, Louis. *Legends of the Bible*. Philadelphia: Jewish Publication Society of America, 1909.

————. *The Legends of the Jews*. Volume 3: *Moses in the Wilderness*. Baltimore: Johns Hopkins University Press, 1911.

Glaude, Eddie S., Jr. *Exodus! Religion, Race, and Nation in Early Nineteenth-Century Black America*. Chicago: University of Chicago Press, 2000.

Goldman, Shalom. *God's Sacred Tongue: Hebrew and the American Imagination*. Chapel Hill: University of North Carolina Press, 2004.

————. *Hebrew and the Bible in America: The First Two Centuries*. Hanover: Brandeis University Press, 1993.

Gomes, Peter J. *The Good Book: Reading the Bible with Mind and Heart*. San Francisco: HarperOne, 2002.

————. *The Scandalous Gospel of Jesus: What's So Good About the Good News*. San Francisco: HarperOne, 2007.

Gough, Deborah Mathias. *Christ Church, Philadelphia: The Nation's Church in a Changing City*. Philadelphia: University of Pennsylvania Press, 1995.

Gregory of Nyssa. *The Life of Moses*. San Francisco: HarperSanFrancisco, 1978.

Grose, Peter. *Israel in the Mind of America*. New York: Schocken Books, 1983.

Guelzo, Allen C. *Abraham Lincoln: Redeemer President.* Grand Rapids, MI: William B. Eerdmans Publishing Company, 1999.

————. *Lincoln and Douglas: The Debates That Defined America.* New York: Simon & Schuster, 2008.

————. *Lincoln's Emancipation Proclamation: The End of Slavery in America.* New York: Simon & Schuster, 2004.

Gutjahr, Paul C. *An American Bible: A History of the Good Book in the United States, 1777–1880.* Stanford: Stanford University Press, 1999.

Gutterman, David S. *Prophetic Politics: Christian Social Movements and American Democracy.* Ithaca: Cornell University Press, 2005.

Hagedorn, Ann. *Beyond the River: The Untold Story of the Heroes of the Underground Railroad.* New York: Simon & Schuster, 2002.

Hatch, Nathan O., and Mark A. Noll, eds. *The Bible in America: Essays in Cultural History.* New York: Oxford University Press, 1982.

Hay, Robert. "George Washington: American Moses." *American Quarterly* 21, no. 4 (Winter 1969).

Heath, Dwight B., ed. *Mourt's Relation: A Journal of the Pilgrims at Plymouth.* Bedford, MA: Applewood Books, 1963.

Hedrick, Joan D. *Harriet Beecher Stowe: A Life.* New York: Oxford University Press, 1994.

Heinze, Andrew R. *Jews and the American Soul: Human Nature in the 20th Century.* Princeton: Princeton University Press, 2004.

Hertzberg, Arthur. *The Jews in America: Four Centuries of Uneasy Encounter.* New York: Touchstone, 1989.

Higham, Charles. *Cecil B. DeMille.* New York: DaCapo, 1973.

Hofstadter, Richard. *The American Political Tradition and the Men Who Made It.* New York: Vintage Books, 1973.

Holifield, E. Brooks. *Theology in America: Christian Thought from the Age of the Puritans to the Civil War.* New Haven: Yale University Press, 2003.

The Holy Bible: Containing the Old and New Testaments with the Apocryphal/Deuterocanonical Books: New Revised Standard Version. New York: Oxford University Press, 1989.

Hovey, Kenneth Alan. "The Theology of History in *Of Plymouth Plantation* and Its Predecessors." *Early American Literature* 10 (1975): 47–66.

Humes, Edward. *Monkey Girl: Evolution, Education, Religion, and the Battle for the American Soul.* New York: Ecco, 2007.

Hurston, Zora Neale. *Moses, Man of the Mountain.* New York: HarperPerennial, 1939.

Jane, Cecil, ed. *The Four Voyages of Columbus.* New York: Dover Publications, 1988.

Johnson, Paul E., ed. *African-American Christianity: Essays in History.* Berkeley: University of California Press, 1994.

Joselit, Jenna Weissman. *The Wonders of America: Reinventing Jewish Culture, 1880–1950.* New York: Henry Holt and Company, 1994.

Josephus, Flavius. *The Works of Josephus.* Peabody, MA: Hendrickson Publishers, 1987.

Kaplan, Justin. *Lincoln Steffens: A Biography*. New York: A Touchstone Book, 1974.

Keels, Christine, and Bernard Keels. *Exodus: The Journey to Freedom*. New York: United Methodist Church, 2003.

Kimball, David. *The Story of the Liberty Bell*. Fort Washington, PA: Eastern National, 1989.

Kirsch, Jonathan. *Moses: A Life*. New York: Ballantine Books, 1998.

Kolb, Robert. *Martin Luther as Prophet, Teacher, and Hero: Images of the Reformer, 1520–1620*. Grand Rapids, MI: Baker Books, 1999.

Kushner, Harold S. *Overcoming Life's Disappointments*. New York: Alfred A. Knopf, 2006.

———. *When Bad Things Happen to Good People*. New York: Anchor, 2004.

Lambert, Frank. *Inventing the "Great Awakening."* Princeton: Princeton University Press, 1999.

———. *"Pedlar in Divinity": George Whitefield and the Transatlantic Revivals, 1737–1770*. Princeton: Princeton University Press, 1994.

Larson, Kate Clifford. *Bound for the Promised Land: Harriet Tubman, Portrait of an American Hero*. New York: Ballantine Books, 2004.

Levenson, Jon D. *The Hebrew Bible, the Old Testament, and Historical Criticism*. Louisville, KY: Westminster/John Knox Press, 1993.

———. *Sinai & Zion: An Entry into the Jewish Bible*. San Francisco: HarperSanFrancisco, 1985.

Liebman, Joshua Loth. *Peace of Mind*. New York: Simon & Schuster, 1946.

Lutz, Donald. "The Relative Influence of European Writers on Late Eighteenth-Century American Political Thought." *American Political Science Review* 78 (1984).

Lyon, Peter. *Success Story: The Life and Times of S. S. McClure*. New York: Charles Scribner's Sons, 1963.

MacCulloch, Diarmaid. *The Reformation: A History*. New York: Penguin Books, 2003.

Maier, Pauline. *American Scripture: Making the Declaration of Independence*. New York: Vintage Books, 1997.

Marks, Gary L. *Pilgrims Then and Now*. Philadelphia: The Genealogical Society of Pennsylvania, 1990.

Marom, Daniel. "Who Is the 'Mother of Exiles'?: Jewish Aspects of Emma Lazarus's 'The New Colossus.'" *Prooftexts* 20 (2000).

Marsden, George M. *Fundamentalism and American Culture*. Oxford: Oxford University Press, 2006.

Marty, Martin E. *Pilgrims in Their Own Land: 500 Years of Religion in America*. New York: Penguin Books, 1958.

———. *Politics, Religion, and the Common Good: Advancing a Distinctly American Conversation About Religion's Role in Our Shared Life*. San Francisco: Jossey-Bass Publishers, 2000.

———. "Religion and the Constitution." *The Christian Century*, March 23–30, 1994.

Matthiessen, F. O. *American Renaissance: Art and Expression in the Age of Emerson and Whitman*. London: Oxford University Press, 1941.

McAlister, Melani. *Epic Encounters: Culture, Media, and U.S. Interests in the Middle East Since 1945*. Berkeley: University of California Press, 2005.

McCullough, David. *John Adams*. New York: Simon & Schuster, 2001.

————. *1776*. New York: Simon & Schuster, 2005.

McPherson, James M. *Hallowed Ground: A Walk at Gettysburg*. New York: Crown Publishers, 2003.

Meachem, Jon. *American Gospel: God, the Founding Fathers, and the Making of a Nation*. New York: Random House, 2006.

Mead, Sidney E. *The Lively Experiment: The Shaping of Christianity in America*. New York: Harper & Row, 1963.

Meier, Levi. *Moses—The Prince, the Prophet: His Life, Legend & Message for Our Lives*. Woodstock, VT: Jewish Lights Publishing, 1998.

Menand, Louis. *The Metaphysical Club: A Story of Ideas in America*. New York: Farrar, Straus and Giroux, 2001.

Meyer, Isidore S. *The Hebrew Exercises of Governor William Bradford*. Plymouth, MA: Pilgrim Society, 1973.

Miers, Charlene. *Independence Hall in American Memory*. Philadelphia: University of Pennsylvania Press, 2002.

Miller, Keith D. *Voice of Deliverance: The Language of Martin Luther King, Jr., and Its Sources*. Athens, GA: University of Georgia Press, 1992.

Miller, Nathan. *New World Coming: The 1920s and the Making of Modern America*. New York: DaCapo Press, 2003.

Miller, Perry. *The American Puritan: Their Prose and Poetry*. New York: Columbia University Press, 1956.

————. *Errand into the Wilderness*. New York: Harper & Row, 1956.

————. *The Life of the Mind in America, from the Revolution to the Civil War*. New York: Harcourt, Brace: World, 1965.

————. *The New England Mind: The Seventeenth Century*. Cambridge, MA: Harvard University Press, 1939.

Miller, Randall M., Harry S. Stout, and Charles Reagan Wilson, eds. *Religion and the American Civil War*. New York: Oxford University Press, 1998.

Miller, Robert Moats. *Harry Emerson Fosdick: Preacher, Pastor, Prophet*. New York: Oxford University Press, 1985.

Mitchell, Joshua. *Not by Reason Alone: Religion, History, and Identity in Early Modern Political Thought*. Chicago: University of Chicago Press, 1993.

Moreno, Barry. *The Statue of Liberty Encyclopedia*. New York: Simon & Schuster, 2000.

Morgan, Edmund S. *American Slavery, American Freedom: The Ordeal of Colonial Virginia*. New York: W. W. Norton & Co., 1975.

————. *The Birth of the Republic: 1763–89*. Chicago: University of Chicago Press, 1956.

————. *The Meaning of Independence: John Adams, George Washington, and Thomas Jefferson*. Charlottesville: University of Virginia Press, 1976.

————. *The Puritan Dilemma: The Story of John Winthrop.* New York: Pearson, 2006.

Mulder, John M. *Woodrow Wilson: The Years of Preparation.* Princeton: Princeton University Press, 1978.

Myers, Marvin, ed. *The Mind of the Founder: Sources of the Political Thought of James Madison.* Hanover, NH: Brandeis University Press, 1973.

Nadel, Alan. "God's Law and the Wide Screen: *The Ten Commandments* as Cold War 'Epic.'" *PMLA* 108, no. 3 (1993).

Naudon, Paul. *The Secret History of Freemasonry: Its Origins and Connection to the Knights Templar.* Rochester, VT: Inner Traditions, 1991.

Needleman, Jacob. *The American Soul: Rediscovering the Wisdom of the Founders.* New York: Jeremy P. Tarcher/Putnam, 2002.

Noerdlinger, Henry S. *Moses and Egypt: The Documentation to the Motion Picture "The Ten Commandments."* Los Angeles: University of Southern California Press, 1956.

Noll, Mark A. *America's God: From Jonathan Edwards to Abraham Lincoln.* Oxford: Oxford University Press, 2002.

————. *The Civil War as a Theological Crisis.* Chapel Hill: University of North Carolina Press, 2006.

————. *A History of Christianity in the United States and Canada.* Grand Rapids, MI: William B. Eerdmans Publishing Company, 1992.

Novak, Michael, and Jana Novak. *Washington's God: Religion, Liberty, and the Father of Our Country.* New York: Basic Books, 2006.

Oren, Michael B. *Power, Faith, and Fantasy: American in the Middle East, 1776 to the Present.* New York: W. W. Norton & Company, 2007.

Orrison, Katherine. *Lionheart in Hollywood: The Autobiography of Henry Wilcoxin.* Lanham, MD: Scarecrow Press, 1991.

————. *Written in Stone: Making Cecil B. DeMille's Epic "The Ten Commandments."* Lanham, MD: Vestal Press, 1999.

Pardes, Ilana. *The Biography of Ancient Israel: National Narratives in the Bible.* Berkeley: University of California Press, 2000.

————. "Moses Goes Down to Hollywood: Miracles and Special Effects." *Semeia* 74 (1996).

Parker, John P. *His Promised Land.* New York: W. W. Norton & Company, 1996.

Pauli, Hertha, and E. B. Ashton. *I Lift My Lamp: The Way of a Symbol.* New York: Appleton-Century-Crofts, Inc., 1948.

Philbrick, Nathaniel. *Mayflower: A Story of Courage, Community, and War.* New York: Viking, 2006.

Pixley, George V. *On Exodus: A Liberation Perspective.* Maryknoll, NY: Orbis Books, 1983.

Plaut, W. Gunther, ed. *The Torah: A Modern Commentary.* New York: Union of American Hebrew Congregations, 1981.

Polzin, Robert. *Moses and the Deuteronomist: A Literary Study of the Deuteronomic History, Part One.* Bloomington: Indiana University Press, 1980.

Ponder, Catherine. *The Millionaire Moses: His Prosperity Secrets for You!* Camarillo, CA: DeVorss Publications, 1977.

Pory, John, Emmanuel Altham, and Isaack De Rasieres. *Three Visitors to Early Plymouth.* Bedford, MA: Applewood Books, 1997.

Prothero, Stephen. *American Jesus: How the Son of God Became a National Icon.* New York: Farrar, Straus and Giroux, 2003.

———. *Religious Literacy: What Every American Needs to Know—And Doesn't.* San Francisco: HarperSanFrancisco, 2007.

Raboteau, Albert J. *Slave Religion: The "Invisible Institution" in the Antebellum South.* Oxford: Oxford University Press, 1978.

Rakove, Jack N. *Original Meanings: Politics and Ideas in the Making of the Constitution.* New York: Vintage Books, 1996.

Rankin, John. *Letters on American Slavery.* Newburyport: Charles Whipple, 1836.

Rappoport, Angelo S. *Ancient Israel.* Volume One. London: Gresham Publishing Company, 1995.

Reynolds, David S. *Walt Whitman's America: A Cultural Biography.* New York: Vintage Books, 1995.

Riley, Edward M. *Starting America: The Story of Independence Hall.* Gettysburg, PA: Eastern National Park & Monument Association, 1954.

Ritchie, Andrew. *The Soldier, the Battle, and the Victory: Being a Brief Account of the Work of Rev. John Rankin.* Cincinnati: Western Tract and Book Society, 1868.

Roshwald, Mordecai, and Miriam Roshwald. *Moses: Leader, Prophet, Man.* New York: Thomas Yoseloff, 1969.

Rubin, Saul Jacob. *Third to None: The Saga of Savannah Jewry, 1733–1983.* Savannah: Congregation Mickve Israel, 1983.

Sacks, Jonathan. *The Chief Rabbi's Haggadah.* New York: HarperCollins, 2003.

Sandmel, Samuel. *Alone Atop the Mountain: A Novel About Moses and the Exodus.* Garden City, NY: Doubleday & Company, 1973.

Sarna, Jonathan D. *American Judaism: A History.* New Haven: Yale University Press, 2004.

———. "The Cult of Synthesis in American Jewish Culture." *Jewish Social Studies* 5, nos. 1–2 (Fall 1989/Winter 1999).

Sarna, Jonathan D., and David G. Dalin. *Religion and State in the American Jewish Experience.* Notre Dame, IN: University of Notre Dame Press, 1997.

Schlessinger, Laura, and Stewart Vogel. *The Ten Commandments: The Significance of God's Laws in Everyday Life.* New York: HarperPerennial, 1998.

Schor, Esther. *Emma Lazarus.* New York: Nextbook, 2006.

Silver, Daniel Jeremy. *Images of Moses.* New York: Basic Books, 1982.

Slezkine, Yuri. *The Jewish Century.* Princeton: Princeton University Press, 2004.

Slotkin, Richard. *Regeneration Through Violence: The Mythology of the American Frontier, 1600–1860.* New York: HarperPerennial, 1973.

Sniderman, Paul M. *A Question of Loyalty.* Berkeley: University of California Press, 1981.

Sollors, Werner. *Beyond Ethnicity: Consent and Descent in American Culture.* New York: Oxford University Press, 1986.

Southgate, Joan E., and Fran Stewart. *In Their Path: A Grandmother's 519-Mile Underground Railroad Walk.* Solon, OH: Eagle Creek Press, 2004.

Steffens, Lincoln. *The Autobiography of Lincoln Steffens.* Volume II: *Muckraking/Revolution/Seeing America at Last.* San Diego: A Harvest/HBJ Book, 1931.

———. *Moses in Red.* Philadelphia: Dorrance and Company Publishers, 1926.

Stephanson, Anders. *Manifest Destiny: American Expansion and the Empire of Right.* New York: Hill and Wang, 1995.

Stout, Harry S. *The Divine Dramatist: George Whitefield and the Rise of Modern Evangelicalism.* Grand Rapids, MI: William B. Eerdmans Publishing Company, 1991.

———. *Upon the Altar of the Nation: A Moral History of the Civil War.* New York: Viking, 2006.

Stowe, Harriet Beecher. *A Key to Uncle Tom's Cabin.* Carlisle, MA: Applewood Books, 1998.

———. *Uncle Tom's Cabin: Or, Life Among the Lowly.* New York: Penguin Books, 1981.

Tanakh: A New Translation of the Holy Scriptures. Philadelphia: Jewish Publication Society, 1985.

Tobin, Jacqueline L., and Raymond G. Dobard. *Hidden in Plain View: A Secret Story of Quilts and the Underground Railroad.* New York: Anchor Books, 1999.

Tooze, G. Andrew. "Moses and the Reel Exodus." *Journal of Religion and Film* 7, no. 1 (April 2003).

Trachtenberg, Marvin. *The Statue of Liberty.* New York: Penguin Books, 1986.

Tuchman, Barbara W. *Bible and Sword: England and Palestine from the Bronze Age to Balfour.* New York: Ballantine Books, 1956.

Waldman, Steven. *Founding Faith: Providence, Politics, and the Birth of Religious Freedom in America.* New York: Random House, 2008.

Walzer, Michael. *Exodus and Revolution.* New York: Basic Books, 1985.

Walworth, Walter. *Woodrow Wilson.* Baltimore: Penguin Books, 1958.

Weinstein, Simcha. *Up, Up, and Oy Vey!: How Jewish History, Culture, and Values Shaped the Comic Book Superhero.* Baltimore: Leviathan Press, 2006.

West, Cornel. *Prophetic Fragments: Illuminations of the Crisis in American Religion and Culture.* Grand Rapids, MI: William B. Eerdmans Publishing Company, 1993.

Wiesel, Elie. *Messengers of God: Biblical Portraits and Legends.* New York: Summit Books, 1976.

Wildavsky, Aaron. *Moses as Political Leader.* Jerusalem: Shalem Press, 2005.

Williams, Juan, and Quinton Dixie. *This Far by Faith: Stories from the African American Religious Experience.* New York: Amistad, 2003.

Wills, Garry. *Lincoln at Gettysburg: The Words That Remade America.* New York: A Touchstone Book, 1992.

Winslow, Edward. *Good Newes from New England: A True Relation of Things Very Remarkable at the Plantation of Plimoth in New England.* Bedford, MA: Applewood Books, 1996.

Wisse, Ruth. "The Hebrew Imperative." *Commentary,* June 1990.

Wolf, William J. *The Almost Chosen People.* Garden City, NY: Doubleday & Company, 1959.

Wood, Gordon S. *The American Revolution: A History.* New York: Modern Library, 2002.

———. *The Creation of the American Republic, 1776–1787.* Chapel Hill: University of North Carolina Press, 1969.

———. *The Radicalism of the American Revolution.* New York: Vintage Books, 1991.

Wood, Michael. *America in the Movies: "Santa Maria, It Had Slipped My Mind."* New York: Columbia University Press, 1975.

Wright, Melanie J. *Moses in America: The Cultural Uses of Biblical Narrative.* Oxford: Oxford University Press, 2003.

Yerushalmi, Yosef Hayim. *Freud's Moses: Judaism Terminable and Interminable.* New Haven: Yale University Press, 1991.

Young, Andrew. *An Easy Burden: The Civil Rights Movement and the Transformation of America.* New York: HarperCollins Publishers, 1996.

———. *A Way Out of No Way: The Spiritual Memoirs of Andrew Young.* Nashville: Thomas Nelson Publishers, 1994.

Index

Note: Page numbers in italics refer to illustrations.

and covenant, 27, 97, 98, 186, 300

elevation of, 21, 23

farewell speech to the Israelites, 8–9, 12, 25–26, 93, 204, 206, 262–63, 278, 290, 308

Five Books of (Pentateuch), 13, 70, 91, 93, 173, 266, 269–70, 282, 301, 306

freedom and law, 27, 97, 186–87, 299–300

and the golden calf, 17

grave of, 152

and leadership, 15, 91, 94, 152, 253, 268, 277–78, 282–83, 287, 289, 296

Michelangelo's statue of, 184, 185

and Mormonism, 220

at Mount Sinai, 16–17, 27, 60, 96, 97, 185–86, 196, 267, 300

murder committed by, 14

and personal fulfillment, 287–91

and pharaoh, 15–16

and Pilgrims, 12, 22, 29–33, 151, 296, 299

in popular culture, 210, 212–14, 225, 288, 289, 296

and the Promised Land, 17–18, 31, 33, 266, 268

as prophet, 20–21, 29, 191, 225

radical ideals attributed to, 22, 157

Red Sea divided by, 16, 98, 267

relevance today, 275–77, 283–87, 289–91, 302, 306–9

and revolution, 96

story of, 13–18, 20, 27, 91, 107, 184, 187, 205–7, 221, 234, 282, 297, 306–7

and Ten Commandments, 17, 22, 27, 87, 96, 155, 185, 300

uplifting the downtrodden, 300–301

as voodoo figure, 246–47

Moses and the Exodus from Egypt (film), 213

Mount Sinai, 16–17, 27, 60, 94, 96, 97, 185–86, 191, 196, 267, 300

Muir, Rev. James, 101

NAACP, 256

Napoléon Bonaparte, 104

Napoléon III, emperor of France, 180

National Civil Rights Museum, Memphis, 269

Ndungane, Archbishop Njongonkulu, 71–72

New Israel, America as, 24, 89

New Republic, 235

New York City:
    Cathedral Church of Saint John the Divine in, 241, *242,* 243, 245, 251
    Federal Hall in, 77, *78,* 81–82
    as nation's capital, 77
    population of, 77
    September 11 attacks on, 73, 81–82, 85, 192
    and Washington's inauguration, 73, 76, 78, 82–83

New York Harbor, 176–77

Ninety-five Theses (Luther), 22

Noerdlinger, Henry, 216, 219, 239

Noll, Mark, 38
    The Civil War as a Theological Crisis, 153, 154, 157

Norris, Isaac, 40, 42, 43, 44, 45

North Star, navigation by, 134

Novak, Michael, 79

About the author

About the book

Insights,
Interviews
& More . . .

Read on

Meet Bruce Feiler

© Andrew Feiler

BRUCE FEILER is one of America's most popular voices on faith, family, and finding meaning in everyday life. He is the bestselling author of eleven books, including *Walking the Bible*, *Abraham*, and *America's Prophet*, and one of only a handful of writers to have four consecutive *New York Times* nonfiction bestsellers in the past decade. He also writes the "Family Matters" column for the *Sunday New York Times* and is the writer/presenter of the PBS miniseries *Walking the Bible*. His latest book, *The Council of Dads*, tells the uplifting story of how friendship and community can help one survive life's greatest challenges.

Bruce Feiler's early books involve immersing himself in different cultures and bringing other worlds vividly to life. These include *Learning to Bow*, an account of the year he spent teaching in rural Japan; *Looking for Class*, about life inside Oxford and Cambridge; and *Under the Big Top*, which depicts the year he spent performing as a clown in the Clyde Beatty–Cole Bros. Circus.

His recent work has made him one of

the country's most respected authorities on religion, politics, and the emotional issues of our time. *Walking the Bible* describes his perilous ten-thousand-mile journey retracing the Five Books of Moses through the desert. The book was hailed as an "instant classic" by the *Washington Post* and "thoughtful, informed, and perceptive" by the *New York Times*. It spent more than a year and a half on the *New York Times* bestseller list, has been translated into fifteen languages, and is the subject of a children's book and a photography book.

Abraham recounts his personal search for the shared ancestor of Jews, Christians, and Muslims. "Exquisitely written," wrote the *Boston Globe*, "100 percent engaging." The book was featured on the cover of *Time* magazine, became a runaway *New York Times* bestseller, and inspired thousands of grassroots interfaith discussions.

Where God Was Born describes his yearlong trek retracing the Bible through Israel, Iraq, and Iran. "Bruce Feiler is a real-life Indiana Jones," wrote the *Atlanta Journal-Constitution*. *America's Prophet* recounts his unprecedented journey through American history—from the Pilgrims to the founding fathers, the Civil War to the civil rights movement—exploring how the Exodus is America's greatest story and Moses is our true founding father. Both were *New York Times* bestsellers.

In 2006, PBS aired the miniseries *Walking the Bible*, which received record ratings and was viewed by 20 million ▶

66 Feiler's recent work has made him one of the country's most respected authorities on religion, politics, and the emotional issues of our time. 99

people in its first month. "Beguiling," wrote the *Wall Street Journal*. "Mr. Feiler is an engaging and informed guide."

Bruce Feiler has written for numerous publications, including *The New Yorker*, the *New York Times Magazine*, and *Gourmet*, where he won three James Beard Awards. He is also a frequent contributor to National Public Radio, CNN, and Fox News. He has been the subject of a Jay Leno joke and a *Jeopardy!* question, and his face appears on a postage stamp in the Grenadines.

His latest book, *The Council of Dads*, describes how he responded to a diagnosis of cancer by asking six men from all passages of his life to be present through the passages of his young daughters' lives. "I believe my daughters will have plenty of opportunities in their lives," he wrote these men. "They'll have loving families. They'll have each other. But they may not have me. They may not have their dad. Will you help be their dad?"

A native of Savannah, Georgia, Bruce Feiler lives in New York with wife, Linda Rottenberg, and their twin daughters. For more information, please visit www.brucefeiler.com. ❧

❝ Feiler has been the subject of a Jay Leno joke and a *Jeopardy!* question, and his face appears on a postage stamp in the Grenadines. ❞

How Moses Shaped America

Reprinted from Time *magazine, October 12, 2009.*

"WE ARE IN THE PRESENCE of a lot of Moseses," Barack Obama said on March 4, 2007, three weeks after announcing his candidacy for President. He was speaking in Selma, Alabama, surrounded by civil rights pioneers. Obama cast his run for the White House as a fulfillment of the Moses tradition of leading people out of bondage into freedom. "I thank the Moses generation, but we've got to remember that Joshua still had a job to do. As great as Moses was . . . he didn't cross over the river to see the Promised Land."

Eight months into his presidency, Obama might want to give Moses a second look. On issues from health care to Afghanistan, the President faces doubts and rebellions, from an entrenched pharaonic establishment on one hand and restless, stiff-necked followers on the other. There's good reason, then, for Obama to heed the leadership lessons of history's greatest leader. Like presidential predecessors from Washington to Reagan, Obama can use the Moses story to help guide Americans in troubled times. From the Pilgrims to the founding fathers, the Civil War to the civil rights movement, Americans have turned to Moses in periods of crisis because his narrative offers a road map of peril and promise. ▶

Plight of the Pilgrims

The Moses story opens in the thirteenth century B.C.E. with the Israelites enslaved in Egypt. After the pharaoh orders the slaughter of all Israelite male babies, Moses is floated down the Nile, picked up by the pharaoh's daughter, and raised in the palace. An adult Moses murders an Egyptian for beating "one of his kinsmen," then flees to the desert, where, later, a voice in a burning bush recruits him to free the Israelites. This moment represents Moses's first leadership test: Will he cling to his unburdened life or attempt to free a people enslaved for centuries?

The plight of the Israelites resonated with the earliest American settlers. For centuries, the Catholic Church had banned the direct reading of Scripture. But the Protestant Reformation, combined with the printing press, brought vernacular Bibles to everyday readers. What Protestants discovered was a narrative that reminded them of their sense of subjugation by the Church and appealed to their dreams of a Utopian New World. The Pilgrims stressed this aspect of Moses. When the band of Protestant breakaways left England in 1620, they described themselves as the chosen people fleeing their pharaoh, King James. On the Atlantic, they proclaimed their journey to be as vital as "Moses and the Israelites when they went out of Egypt." And when they got to Cape Cod, they thanked God for letting them pass through their fiery Red Sea.

66 Protestants discovered . . . a narrative that reminded them of their sense of subjugation by the Church and appealed to their dreams of a Utopian New World. 99

6

By the time of the Revolution, the theme of beleaguered people standing up to a superpower had become the go-to narrative of American identity. The two bestselling books of 1776 featured Moses. Thomas Paine, in *Common Sense*, called King George the "hardened, sullen tempered pharaoh." Samuel Sherwood, in *The Church's Flight into the Wilderness*, said God would deliver the colonies from Egyptian bondage. The Moses image was so pervasive that on July 4, after signing the Declaration of Independence, the Congress asked Thomas Jefferson, Benjamin Franklin, and John Adams to propose a seal for the United States. Their recommendation: Moses, leading the Israelites through the Red Sea as the water overwhelms the pharaoh. In their eyes, Moses was America's true Founding Father.

But escaping bondage proved to be only half the story. After the Israelites arrive in the desert, they face a period of lawlessness, which prompts the Ten Commandments. Only by rallying around the new order can the people become a nation. Freedom depends on law.

Americans faced a similar moment of chaos after the Revolution. One Connecticut preacher noted that Moses took forty years to quell the Israelites' grumbling: Now "we are acting the same stupid part." And so just as a reluctant Moses led the Israelites out of Egypt, then handed down the Ten ▶

> " By the time of the Revolution, the theme of beleaguered people standing up to a superpower had become the go-to narrative of American identity. "

Commandments, a reluctant George Washington led the colonists to victory, then presided over the drafting of the Constitution. The parallel was not lost. Two-thirds of the eulogies at Washington's death compared the "leader and father of the American nation" to the "first conductor of the Jewish nation."

Let My People Go

While Moses was a unifying presence during the founding era, a generation later he got dragged into the issue that most divided the country. The Israelites' escape from slavery was the dominant motif of slave spirituals, including "Turn Back Pharaoh's Army," "I Am Bound for the Promised Land," and the most famous, "Go Down, Moses," which was called the national anthem of slaves: "When Israel was in Egypt Land, / Let my people go; / Oppressed so hard they could not stand, / Let my people go."

Spirituals sent coded messages. As Frederick Douglass wrote, when he and his comrades sang, "O Canaan, sweet Canaan, / I am bound for the land of Canaan," overseers believed they were worshipping the white god. But to them, it meant they were about to escape on the Underground Railroad. The movement's famous conductor Harriet Tubman was called the Moses of her people.

And yet even as abolitionists used the Exodus to attack slavery, Southerners used it to defend the institution. The

66 Two-thirds of the eulogies at Washington's death compared the 'leader and father of the American nation' to the 'first conductor of the Jewish nation.' 99

War Between the States became the War Between the Moseses. Slaveholders cited a bevy of biblical passages—Abraham acquires slaves; Moses invites slaves to the first Passover; Jesus does nothing to free slaves—to claim the Bible endorsed slavery. The book that joined Americans together was torn asunder by slavery.

It took America's most Bible-quoting President to reunite the country. Called a pharaoh by his opponents, Abraham Lincoln freed the slaves after a "vow before God"; he invoked the Exodus at Gettysburg. When he died, Lincoln, like Washington before him, was compared to Moses. "There is no historic figure more noble than that of the Jewish lawgiver," Henry Ward Beecher eulogized. "There is scarcely another event in history more touching than his death." Until now. "Again a great leader of the people has passed through toil, sorrow, battle, and war, and come near to the promised land of peace, into which he might not pass over."

Lincoln's assassination initiated an even more long-lasting tribute to Moses, the Statue of Liberty, given to America by the French to honor the slain President. The sculptor, Frédéric Bartholdi, chose the goddess of liberty as his model, but he enhanced her with two icons from Moses: the nimbus of light around her head and the tablet in her arms, both from the moment Moses descends Mount Sinai with the Ten Commandments. The message: Freedom comes with law. ▶

> " The sculptor, Frédéric Bartholdi, chose the goddess of liberty as his model [for the Statue of Liberty], but he enhanced her with two icons from Moses. "

Moses and Superman

With the rise of secularism and the declining influence of the Bible in the twentieth century, Moses might have melted away as a role model. But something curious happened. He was so identified as a hero of the American Dream that he superseded scripture and entered the realm of popular culture, from novels to television.

Superman was modeled partly on Moses. The comic book hero's creators, two bookish Jews from Cleveland named Jerry Siegel and Joe Shuster, drew their character's backstory from the superhero of the Torah. Just as baby Moses is floated down the Nile in a basket to escape annihilation, baby Superman is launched into space in a rocket ship to avoid extinction. Just as Moses is raised in an alien world before being summoned to liberate Israel, Superman is raised in an alien environment before being called to assist humanity.

But it was Cecil B. DeMille who turned Moses into a symbol of American power in the Cold War. The 1956 epic *The Ten Commandments*, which in its inflation-adjusted total ranks as the fifth highest grossing movie of all time, opened with DeMille appearing onscreen. "The theme of this picture is whether men ought to be ruled by God's law or whether they are to be ruled by the whims of a dictator," he said. "The same battle continues throughout the world today." To drive home his point, DeMille cast mostly Americans as Israelites and

> 66 Just as baby Moses is floated down the Nile in a basket to escape annihilation, baby Superman is launched into space in a rocket ship to avoid extinction. 99

Europeans as Egyptians. And in the film's final shot, Charlton Heston adopts the pose of the Statue of Liberty and quotes the line from the third book of Moses—Leviticus—inscribed on the Liberty Bell: "Proclaim liberty throughout all the land unto all the inhabitants thereof."

To modern Americans, Moses's heartbreak, in many ways, ensures his ongoing appeal. Though a champion of freedom, he was also a prophet of disappointment. After leading the Israelites for forty years, Moses is denied entry to the promised land for disobeying God. No one understood this aspect of the Moses story better than Martin Luther King Jr. In his first national speech, in 1956, he likened the U.S. Supreme Court to Moses for splitting the Red Sea of segregation. On the night before his death twelve years later, King predicted he would not fulfill his dream. "I've been to the mountaintop," he declared. "And I've looked over. And I've seen the promised land. And I may not get there with you, but I want you to know tonight that we as a people will get to the promised land." Both Moses and King are reminders that even the greatest leaders fall short.

So what lessons can the current occupant of the White House learn from a figure that nearly every one of his predecessors has invoked?

First, sell the milk and honey. Obama is the first president to hold a Passover seder in the White House, but he seems to be forgetting the main point of the service: The story of Moses is, above all, ▶

> 66 To modern Americans, Moses's heartbreak, in many ways, ensures his ongoing appeal. Though a champion of freedom, he was also a prophet of disappointment. 99

a story. It's a narrative of hope. Details are fine for negotiating policy, but it's the vision of milk and honey that gets people to plunge into the Red Sea.

Second, remember the Nile. As he wrestles with a variety of issues, the President should recall that from the moment God hears his people moaning under slavery, the entire moral focus of the Moses story is to build a society that nurtures everyone. Thirty-six times, the Torah urges the Israelites to befriend the stranger, for they were strangers in Egypt.

Third, the one on Sinai takes the heat. The Bible outlines at least a dozen rebellions in which the people attempt to overthrow Moses. At one point, God offers to destroy the people, but Moses brokers a compromise. The strongest leaders face the harshest criticism and hold fast against their naysayers.

Finally, you may not enter the promised land. Forced to die across the Jordan on Mount Nebo, Moses confronts his final choice: Will he fight or prepare the Israelites for the future? He chooses the latter. "I have put before you this day life and prosperity, death and adversity," he says. "Choose life."

These words capture what may be the most trying lesson of leadership: You may fail, but your legacy is to prepare your followers to succeed without you. So plunge into the waters, persevere through the dryness, and don't be surprised if you don't reach your goal. For the true destination is not this year at all, but next. ◑

> **You may fail, but your legacy is to prepare your followers to succeed without you.**

12

A Conversation with Bruce Feiler

Many of your books, such as Abraham *and* Where God Was Born, *deal with stories from the Bible and are set in the Middle East.* America's Prophet *explores the Bible as it impacted the United States. What sparked your interest in writing about America?*

After a decade of traveling across the Middle East, my wife gave birth to identical twin daughters. "You're done traveling through war zones!" she declared. Around this time, I began to notice something. On a trip to Plymouth, I took a tour of the *Mayflower II*. A reenactor was reading from the Bible. "The Book of Exodus," he explained. "Our leader read it to us when we were crossing our Red Sea." Hmmm, Moses in the story of Thanksgiving. On a visit to my sister in Philadelphia, we went to see the Liberty Bell, which has a quote from Moses on its face. Hmmm, Moses in the middle of July 4. I began to find it everywhere: Columbus, Benjamin Franklin, Harriet Tubman all using the Moses story. Washington, Lincoln, FDR. The sheer number of uses was staggering and, for me, completely unknown. I realized you can't understand American history without understanding Moses. And I should tell this story.

You say at the end of the book that many of Moses's "identity issues seem very ▶

> ❝ I realized you can't understand American history without understanding Moses. And I should tell this story. ❞

contemporary." How do you see the story of Moses playing out in America today?

Any number of people may step forward and claim to be the Moses for this generation. But that's not where I see the echo today. We have been living through troubled times of late. Americans have been asking, Who are we? What are our values? What is our place in the world? And in every troubled time in American history—from the cliffs of Plymouth to the camps of Valley Forge, from the fields of the Civil War to the streets of the civil rights movement—people have turned to the Moses story for inspiration and hope. So when I see the spirit of resilience and rebirth in families hit hard during this time, I hear the echo of the Exodus. We may be in pain now, but there is promise ahead. It's the American Dream, of course, and its roots go back to the Sinai.

As in much of your work, America's Prophet *begins with a personal anecdote—your family at Thanksgiving—and ends with a beautiful prayer for your daughters. How does writing about your family contribute to your writing about history?*

Bookstores tend to divide books into categories—history, personal narrative, inspiration. But our own bookshelves rarely make these distinctions. And our dinner-table, car-ride, and long-walk conversations never do. I grew up in

66 When I see the spirit of resilience and rebirth in families hit hard during this time, I hear the echo of the Exodus. We may be in pain now, but there is promise ahead. 99

Savannah, Georgia; married a woman from Boston, Massachusetts; and live in Brooklyn now. All of these places are rich with history but also rich with family memories for me. So I live my life in a way that constantly mingles history with daily life, and where towering figures from the past are constantly appearing to me as I play with my daughters. I walk my girls to school past a courthouse that has an image of Moses on its side. I feel more alive because of these unexpected connections, and I try to capture these in my writing.

As you make clear in this book, the story of Moses is a story of deliverance and transcendence over adversity. You write that Moses "gives ordinary people the courage to live with uncertainty." Your most recent book, The Council of Dads, *is the uplifting story of how you responded to a cancer diagnosis by reaching out to your closest friends. Did you draw on the story of Moses during your struggle?*

After working on *America's Prophet* for three years, I draw on Moses for everything I can! Seriously, the answer is yes. Several weeks after completing this book, I learned that I had a seven-inch osteosarcoma in my left femur. I instantly thought of my daughters and what their lives might be like without me. Would they wonder who I was? Would they yearn for my voice? Three days later I awoke with an idea ▶

> 66 I live my life in a way that constantly mingles history with daily life, and where towering figures from the past are constantly appearing to me as I play with my daughters. 99

A Conversation with Bruce Feiler *(continued)*

of how to give them my voice. I would
reach out to six men from all parts of
my life and ask them to form a "Council
of Dads." My book is a celebration of
friendship and how those around you
can help sustain you in trying times.
What I learned time and again is exactly
what the Moses story conveys. You can
be in a dark, oppressed place; you can
imagine a brighter, more promised place;
but the only way to get there is with the
help of community.

New Chapter:
The Bush Burned
with Fire

THE TWENTY-TWO SQUARES that fill downtown Savannah today read like the invitation list for a game of "If You Could Have Dinner with One Person from the Eighteenth Century, Who Would It Be?" The squares—miniature parks introduced as part of a bold city plan when the colony was founded in 1733—are named after Washington, Franklin, Madison, and Lafayette, among others. Yet had you been playing the dinner guest game on the morning of, say, July 4, 1776, most people would likely have chosen what was then the most celebrated name on the list, a name that is virtually unrecognized today.

On a humid summer morning, I drove past Whitefield Square, the southeasternmost park, with a white wooden gazebo, and headed nine miles southwest to Whitefield Avenue. A few minutes later, I passed through the red brick arch of Bethesda Home for Boys, an orphanage founded in 1740 by the Reverend George Whitefield, the evangelical preacher and populist gadfly who is universally regarded as the first American known from New Hampshire to Georgia. A century after William Bradford, George Whitefield was another fiery outsider who tried to liberate believers from the yoke of the Church of England. He was also among the first figures to tap into ▶

the antiauthoritarian feelings that were bubbling up in the colonies, link them with the theme of exodus in the Bible, and help legitimize the idea that Americans might need a similar revolution. His actions raised tantalizing questions: Could the Israelites' story inspire a real confrontation with England? If so, would a preacher be the one to spark it?

Put another way: Was George Whitefield America's newest Moses?

The entrance drive to Bethesda's six-hundred-fifty-acre campus is covered by a canopy of two dozen live oaks sagging under Savannah's signature Spanish moss. A horse was nibbling on hay. Although I grew up just a few miles from here, I had never been on Bethesda's campus. I came today to meet the minister who serves as executive director to discuss Whitefield's role as a liberator and his lifelong affinity with the Hebrew prophet. And right away I was in for a surprise. Inside the main building hangs a piece of stained glass featuring the burning bush. It's surrounded with a quotation from Exodus 3: "The bush was burned by fire, yet not consumed."

Bethesda's mascot is the burning bush.

"It was Whitefield's favorite image," explained David Tribble, an ordained Baptist minister who felt called to work with children. "Our athletic teams are called the Blazers. The school newspaper is called *The Blaze*. Our football helmets have a big B on the side with flickering flames coming out of it. Our whole philosophy is about teaching kids they may have been burned in their lives, but they don't necessarily have to be consumed by it." He gestured toward the door. "Would you like to see the original in the chapel?"

And with that he led me outside.

The heart of the Bethesda campus is a circular pasture surrounded by Georgian-style, gray brick buildings used as dormitories and classrooms. Serving just under a hundred residents and half as many day students, the campus has a barn, woods, and wetlands, and is situated on the banks of what's now called Moon River, after the beloved lyrics written by Savannah native and Bethesda neighbor Johnny Mercer. "The most delightful place on earth," Whitefield called it in the late 1730s.

The religious revivals that blossomed in the 1730s, known as the Great Awakening, introduced a new form of worship, one that influenced all denominations and became the foundation of a new American way of God. A new style of preacher offered believers—many estranged from existing institutions—the opportunity to read the Bible themselves, hear the good news of salvation in a language that was inviting, and experience a "new birth." These revivalists ushered in a more democratic, popular style of Christianity that linked American striving with the larger story of freedom in the Bible.

Time and again, revivalists relied on the language of Exodus to cast their efforts as encouraging individuals to stand up to oppressive forces. As Whitefield wrote of existing churches, "Let us break their slavish bands, and cast their chains away." Together, these leaders created the first intercolonial movement, stretching from Plymouth to Savannah. This breadth is what made the Great Awakening great, and also what gave it political importance, as the crusade promoted a shared unity among the disparate thirteen colonies.

George Whitefield was a native of Gloucester, England. He wrote a gospel-like account of his early life in which he observed that he was born, "like my dear Saviour," in an inn. In his case, the inn belonged to his parents, so his nativity was not quite as providential. A flair for mimicry drove him into the theater in school, where his teachers soon wrote plays for him, often thrusting the effeminate boy into girls' clothes. Though playing women was considered the mark of a good actor, it still traumatized him. "The remembrance of this has often covered me in confusion of face," he wrote.

As the seventh child of innkeepers, Whitefield was exposed to an endless parade of pols, prostitutes, and day laborers, not unlike *The Canterbury Tales*. He thrived on the passions of these outsiders. "I soon made great proficiency in the school of the devil," he wrote. But one day, Whitefield had a vision that God wanted something grander for him. In a dream, he saw himself on Mount Sinai with God calling out to him. He must pursue college and enter the ministry. George Whitefield's destiny was set: He ▸

would be Moses leading the downtrodden and former sinners like himself into the Promised Land.

Admitted to Oxford, Whitefield joined with fellow students John and Charles Wesley for a series of religious meetings of what were dubbed the "Bible Moths." Unhappy with the debauchery of campus life, they formed the "methodist" movement, based on a strict "method" involving close reading of Scripture, proscribed hourly ethical conduct, and a direct appeal to commoners neglected by the Church of England. Like Reformers before them, the Methodists wanted to return to a purer form of religion. Also like those Reformers, they took inspiration from the figure in the Bible who is most known for standing up to worldly power.

Whitefield argued that Moses was a Methodist. He cited the example of how Moses was tending the flock of his father-in-law when he was called to Mount Sinai and encountered God in the burning bush. Moses could have demurred, pleading "I am merely a keeper of sheep," but he didn't. "This shows how persons ought to methodize their time," Whitefield preached, saying Methodists would never shirk their responsibilities. "Moses was a Methodist, and a very fine one," Whitefield said. "He kept his flock, but that did not hinder his going to [Sinai]." Whitefield's sermon fit into the tradition mined by Cotton Mather, William Bradford, and John Winthrop of drawing out one dimension of the Moses story—in this case, self-control and ethical behavior—to align a bold new movement with the greatest new movement in the Hebrew Bible, the creation of the Israelite nation. To justify your leadership with examples from Moses was to give it legitimacy.

John Wesley ventured to Savannah first, in 1736, three years after the colony of Georgia had been founded by James Oglethorpe as a buffer between the English in the Carolinas and the Spanish in Florida. Wesley urged Whitefield to follow, and the newly ordained minister landed on Tybee Island on May 8, 1738. Like Columbus and Bradford before him, Whitefield compared his crossing to the crossing of the Red Sea. "We have not seen the waters stand purposely on a heap," he wrote. "Neither have we been pursued by pharaoh; but we have been led through sea as through the wilderness." Based on a suggestion from Wesley, Whitefield arrived with the intention of founding an orphanage, but he quickly gleaned that the mix of poor farmers, Lutherans, and other dissenters in the area would be open to his message of New Birth. He vowed to come back the following year with a radical plan: He would take his outsider gospel across the colonies in open, public rallies, and he would use these revivals to raise funds for Bethesda.

In an age when newspapers were just gaining popularity, Whitefield understood the need to publicize his upcoming crusade. He returned to London and began preaching his antiestablishment message. The growing crowds he attracted drew the ire of the Anglican bishop of London, who accused him of being an extremist. Whitefield's deft reaction was to have the critique published, as well as his response, in which he accused the bishop of infidelity. Anglican clergy were "indolent, earthly-minded, [and] pleasure-seeking," he added. The resulting media firestorm played right into his hands. By the time Whitefield returned to the colonies in 1739, Anglican leaders in New York, Philadelphia, and Charleston had barred him from their churches.

The move backfired. Whitefield reveled in the role of martyr and took his message to the streets. In the coming decade, Whitefield would make more than half a dozen trips up and down the eastern seaboard, speaking in parks, squares, and empty fields to the largest public gatherings North America had ever seen. By brilliantly promoting and merchandising his appearances, Whitefield created the first self-sustaining mega-ministry in American history and raised the largest philanthropic sums yet known.

For the colonists, galled by the growing nuisances of English authority, the appeal was partly his message and partly his technique. At a time when most preachers still read their sermons, Whitefield used theatrical techniques to animate his off-the-cuff presentations. Even his crossed eyes, the result of measles, were viewed less as an oddity and more as a mark of special dispensation. Fans praised him as a prophet, "another Moses." "He must be a Stranger in Israel," a group of ministers wrote, "who has not heard of the uncommon religious Appearances in several Parts of this Land."

For Bethesda's David Tribble, Whitefield belongs alongside ▶

Washington on a short list of great patriots. "I put George
Whitefield in the same place where I put a lot of the early
founders," Tribble said. "He had such passion for what he did.
He put his life at stake. And the risks were enormous. I think
of him riding on horseback from Savannah to Newburyport,
Massachusetts—in a car, it took me two days—and he did it
not once, but multiple times.

"For sure, a lot of people didn't have confidence in him,"
Tribble continued. "He was thought to be an early vaudevillian,
or a huckster. Some wondered whether their offerings were really
going to Bethesda—though none of these charges were ever
proven. And he's not going to impress you as a husband.
Bethesda needed a mistress, so he got married. But in terms
of pure devotion, I wish I could have his dedication. Given
his asthmatic condition and congestive heart failure, he literally
preached until he died. There's estimation that he preached over
fifteen thousand sermons—three, four times a day. You can't help
but be moved by how he moved people."

I asked him why he thought Whitefield's message resonated so
deeply in America.

"When I read his sermons, rebirth was a very personal
experience, and it could be expressed in individual ways, which
obviously rankled authorities. Like a number of early evangelists,
Whitefield most wanted to touch people that existing churches
ignored. I think this is why Moses was so important to him. He
genuinely felt attracted to outsiders. He said, 'We need a new
exodus of people the institutional church has rejected.' And if
you look at his life, he worked the way Moses did. He roamed
the wilderness. He went to places *nobody else would go to*. He
even engaged the Cherokee! He befriended the stranger in part
because he was a stranger himself—and what's more Mosaic
than that."

The Bethesda chapel was built in 1925. It's small and tidy with
a red brick arched doorway in front and milk-white trim. The
upright pews inside seem appropriate for issuing stern rebukes.
The only distraction from the austere setting is a beautiful arched
stained glass window designed by Henry Lee Willet, whose father

made the chapel windows at West Point and whose son did the same for the National Cathedral.

At the bottom of the window are two foxes, after Jesus' line in Matthew 8: "Foxes have holes, and birds of the air have nests; but the Son of Man has nowhere to lay his head." Above that is another line from Matthew—"Suffer little children to come unto me for such is the Kingdom of Heaven"—and a depiction of bumblebees and butterflies. The uppermost image is the burning bush. It has blue branches, several sprouts of green leaves, and red flames leaping out of the top. "Our tradition suggests the bush was passed down from Whitefield," Rev. Tribble said. "He preached a famous sermon in which he said that the bush represents the church. God didn't chose a cedar, or some glorious tree; he chose a humble shrub. But while it may be modest on the surface, it is glorious within."

"That raises a question I've been thinking about," I said. "Whitefield seems to mix his metaphors between the New Testament and the Hebrew Bible. The burning bush represents the church, even though Jesus wasn't born until twelve centuries after Moses. A sinner crosses the Red Sea, but instead of arriving in the wilderness, he lands in the body of Christ. Is Whitefield more interested in Moses or Jesus?"

"My sense is that Whitefield saw Jesus as the new Moses. Moses didn't go looking for God, but once he encountered him in the burning bush, he had a New Birth. Jesus also calls people to their own personal burning bush moment. It's as if Jesus and Moses work together to draw people closer to God."

"So when you bring your students in here," I said, "what lessons do you draw?"

"In Whitefield's sermon about the burning bush," David Tribble said, "he pointed out that in the story, God calls out, 'Moses, Moses, my people shall burn in this bush to the end of time, but be not afraid, I will succor them.' The lesson is that God gives comfort to the outcast and heals the sick. He offers the little children a place to lay their head. And I tell my teachers all the time that, like the burning bush, God reaches out at unexpected times, through inglorious vehicles. And sometimes a teacher will come to me and say, 'I had it. I had a burning bush moment—'" ▶

"A *burning bush* moment?" I said.

"What happens in that moment is that a student begins to see
that life can be transformed. You can go through a lot of fire and
rubble and not be consumed by it. You can move on with your
education. You can move on with your love for God. And together
they will take you to a place that is very different from where we
found you."

"And it works?"

"Every time."

"Because on the other side of the burning bush is . . . ?"

"New life."

Franklin Square is the northwestern most of Savannah's squares,
the farthest from Whitefield Square. Recently renovated, it has
red brick walkways, several live oaks, and a monument to Haitian
volunteers who fought during the War of Independence.

Benjamin Franklin never came to Savannah, but he did have
a curious fascination—and friendship—with George Whitefield.
The Philadelphia printer first saw Whitefield preach in front of six
thousand people in 1739. He was awestruck. Whitefield's delivery,
Franklin wrote, "was so improved by frequent repetitions that
every accent, every emphasis, every modulation of voice, was
so perfectly well turned and well placed that, without being
interested in the subject, one could not help being pleased
with the discourse." Later, the famously dyspeptic Franklin
recorded how at one sermon he vowed to resist the charismatic
preacher's plea for a contribution:

> I had in my pocket a handful of copper money, three or
> four silver dollars, and five pistoles in gold. As he proceeded
> I began to soften, and concluded to give the coppers.
> Another stroke of his oratory made me ashamed of
> that, and determined me to give the silver; and he
> finished so admirably, that I emptied my pocket
> wholly into the collector's dish, gold and all.

Recognizing a good investment, Franklin began publishing
Whitefield's journals and sermons, helping to make Franklin

rich and Whitefield popular. Between 1739 and 1741, more than half the books Franklin printed were by Whitefield. Their financial arrangement ensured that Franklin's coverage of the controversial evangelist was frequent and favorable. Whitefield appeared in forty-five weekly issues of the *Pennsylvania Gazette*, eight times on the front page.

Franklin and Whitefield also developed an intimate friendship that lasted three decades. Despite the bon vivant's vocal antipathy to organized religion, he confessed to his companion a deep-seated religious consciousness and a belief in a personal God. After sixty years of favors from Providence, Franklin wrote, "Can I doubt that he loves me?" Whitefield stayed in Franklin's home; Franklin contributed to Bethesda. But as their friendship deepened, the two pioneers shared a growing dissatisfaction with life in the colonies, which Franklin described as "sunk in vice, and wickedness." The tone of their letters is reminiscent of Bradford's latter years. The dream of a better America was once more in decline. The Promised Land would not be achieved in America.

Then in an extraordinary, often overlooked letter dated July 2, 1756, a dispirited, fifty-year-old Franklin wrote Whitefield that he was looking for an epigram for his life, a "bright Point" that would serve as climax to his civil work. "Being now in the last Act, I begin to cast about for something fit to end with." His proposal: that Whitefield and Franklin together cross the Appalachians and found a new colony in the wilderness of the West. "You mention your frequent Wish that you were a Chaplain to an American Army," Franklin wrote:

> I sometimes wish, that you and I were jointly employ'd by the Crown to settle a Colony on the Ohio. I imagine we could do it effectually, and without putting the Nation to much experience. . . . What a glorious Thing it would be, to settle in that fine Country a large Strong Body of Religious and Industrious People!

Whitefield's response has been lost, but the letter is testament to a regenerating of the biblical cycle of struggle, success, adversity, and disappointment, followed by a renewed dream of success. ▶

The Bush Burned with Fire *(continued)*

Here Franklin proposes that he and Whitefield be joint Moseses leading a new exodus of chosen people into yet another Promised Land.

Franklin's scheme never materialized, of course, and his final act found that "something fit to end with." But Franklin seemed to understand that for America to succeed, Enlightenment gurus like himself needed spiritual gurus like Whitefield. Franklin appreciated that Whitefield was shaking up the British establishment and understood the implications the Awakening held for politics. The religious revivals of the 1730s and '40s were a vital precursor to the Revolution. At a time when newspapers were few and books were expensive, the pulpit was still the dominant source of information. As one of Whitefield's biographers put it, "Ordinary people knew their Whitefield and Edwards better than they knew their Locke and Montesquieu."

Whitefield's chief contribution to America was to introduce a language of dissent that emboldened people to challenge conventional truths. His *new birth* could easily be reimagined as a *new country*. His cry to stand up to the Church of England could easily be converted into standing up to the Crown itself. Whitefield perceived among the colonists, even before most realized it themselves, a desire for a unifying bond and a shared political allegiance that came from being repressed by a distant authority. And what happened first in churches happened next in government. The Revolutionary period, preacher Horace Bushnell said, was marked by "Protestantism in religion producing republicanism in government."

Whitefield didn't live to see the Revolution. The man who saw himself called by God on Mount Sinai died like his hero, short of God's kingdom on earth, in Newburyport, Massachusetts, in 1769. "His Integrity, Disinterestedness, and indefatigable Zeal," Franklin wrote, "I have never seen equalled, and I shall never see exceeded." But his status as an American patriot was secure. On September 16, 1775, five months after Lexington and Concord, a group of Continental Army volunteers gathered at the First Presbyterian Church in Newburyport, about to embark for Canada under the command of Benedict Arnold. After hearing an extemporaneous sermon, the soldiers proceeded to the crypt underneath the altar and pried open the coffin of George Whitefield. The men snipped off pieces of Whitefield's collar and wristbands and bore them into battle.

Just as Joseph, before dying in Egypt, makes his sons vow to carry his bones with them on their Exodus out of slavery, so George Whitefield would accompany his own adopted heirs on their impending march out of tyranny. Just as Moses dies shy of the Promised Land but leaves his followers with the wisdom to carry on without him, so the man who saw himself as God's new liberator died short of his destination but left his followers with the spiritual roadmap to secure their own independence. ∾

Have You Read?
More by Bruce Feiler

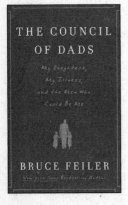

THE COUNCIL OF DADS

When Bruce Feiler was diagnosed with cancer in 2008, he instantly worried what his daughters' lives would be like with him not around: "Would they wonder who I was? Would they wonder what I thought? Would they lack for my approval, my discipline, my voice?" *The Council of Dads* is the inspiring story of what happened after he decided how to give his daughters that voice. Bruce reached out to six men from all the passages in his life and asked them to be present in his daughters' lives. And he would call this group "The Council of Dads." This is a touching, funny, and ultimately deeply moving book on how to live life, how the human spirit can respond to adversity, and how to deepen and cherish the friendships that enrich our lives.

"*The Council of Dads* . . . reminds us of which values we value most, and helps us make sure we transmit them." —*Time*

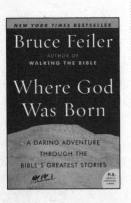

WHERE GOD WAS BORN

Continuing the gripping journey he began with *Walking the Bible*, Bruce Feiler travels ten thousand miles through the heart of the Middle East— from the Garden of Eden to the rivers of Babylon—uncovering the little-known origins of Western religion. Combining the excitement of an adventure story and the insight of spiritual exploration, *Where God Was Born* offers a rare, universal vision of God that can inspire different faiths into a shared dialogue for hope.

"Breathtaking. . . . Goes from cover to cover, from one eye-opening story to the next, without letup."   —*Boston Globe*

ABRAHAM

Both immediate and timeless, *Abraham* tells the powerful story of one man's search for the shared ancestor of Judaism, Christianity, and Islam. Traveling through war zones, braving violence at religious sites, and seeking out faith leaders, Bruce Feiler uncovers the defining yet divisive role that Abraham plays for half the world's believers. Provocative and uplifting, *Abraham* offers a thoughtful and inspiring vision of unity that redefines what we think about our neighbors, our future, and ourselves.

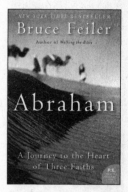

"An exquisitely written journey."
                          —*Boston Globe*

WALKING THE BIBLE

Feeling disconnected from the religious community he had known as a child, Bruce Feiler set out on a perilous ten-thousand-mile journey across the Middle East to discover the roots of the Bible. Traveling through three continents, five countries, and four war zones, Feiler is the first person ever to complete such an adventure in an attempt to answer the

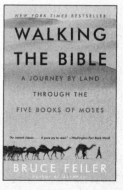

question: Is the Bible just an abstraction, some book gathering dust, or is it a living, breathing entity with relevance to contemporary life? From Turkey to Israel, the Sinai to the heart of Egypt, Feiler explores how geography affects the larger narrative of the Bible and ultimately realizes how much these places—and his experience—have affected his faith.

"Ranks among the great spiritual autobiographies."
                    —*Washington Post Book World*

WALKING THE BIBLE:
A PHOTOGRAPHIC JOURNEY

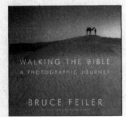

Featuring Bruce Feiler's own photography as well as his selections from professional collections, *Walking the Bible: A Photographic Journey* brings together breathtaking vistas, intimate portraits, and fascinating panoramas, providing firsthand access to the inscrutable land where three of the world's great religions were born—and finally puts a face on the stories that have long inspired the human spirit.

"Beautifully depicts the dramatic land that gave birth to three of the world's great religions."   —*USA Today*

DREAMING OUT LOUD

Country music has exploded across the United States and undergone a sweeping revolution, transforming the once ridiculed world of Nashville into an unlikely focal point of American pop culture. In writing this fascinating book, Feiler was granted unprecedented access to the private moments of the revolution. Here is the acclaimed report: a chronicle of the genre's biggest stars as they changed the face of American music. With intimate portraits of Garth Brooks, Wynonna Judd, and Wade Hayes, Feiler has written the defining book on the new Nashville.

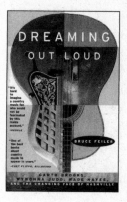

"Penetrating and insightful."
— Elvis Mitchell, *New York Times*

UNDER THE BIG TOP

It's every child's dream: to run away and join the circus. Feiler did just that, joining the Clyde Beatty–Cole Bros. Circus as a clown for one year. This is the story of that crazy, chaotic, heartbreaking ride, a book that will remind you of how dreams can go horribly wrong—and then miraculously come true.

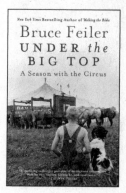

"A stunning collective portrait."
— *The New Yorker*

31

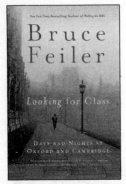

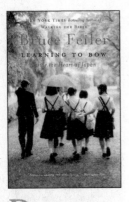

Don't miss the next book by your favorite author. Sign up now for AuthorTracker by visiting www.AuthorTracker.com.

Have You Read? *(continued)*

LOOKING FOR CLASS

An irresistible, entertaining peek into the privileged realm of Wordsworth and Wodehouse, Chelsea Clinton and Hugh Grant, *Looking for Class* offers a hilarious account of Feiler's year at Britain's most exclusive universities, Oxford and Cambridge—the garden parties and formal balls, the high-minded debates and drinking Olympics—and gives us a eye-opening view of the often romanticized but rarely seen British upper class.

"A trenchant, witty, and engaging critique of the English establishment."
—*San Francisco Chronicle*

LEARNING TO BOW

Feiler's first book, *Learning to Bow*, is one of the funniest, liveliest, and most insightful books ever written about the clash of cultures between America and Japan. With warmth and candor, Feiler recounts the year he spent as a teacher in a small rural Japanese town. Beginning with a ritual outdoor bath and culminating in an all-night trek to the top of Mount Fuji, Feiler teaches his students about American culture, while they teach him everything from how to properly address an envelope to how to date a Japanese girl.

"Incisive, often hilarious, and presents a rounded portrait of the modern Japanese."
—*USA Today*

12-19